RUN
FOR
GOD.

DEVOTIONS

Finding God in a Runners Space

Volume One

CROSS
BOOKS

VISIT RUN FOR GOD ONLINE AT www.RunforGod.com

ISBN: 9781462744824 (Hard Cover)
ISBN: 9781462744831 (Soft Cover)
Library of Congress Control Number: 2014916619
Printed in the United States of America by Crossbooks Publishing, a division of Lifeway.

If you require medical, fitness, or nutritional advice, you must contact your own health care professional. You should seek the advice of a doctor before starting any exercise routine.

This book may contain information relating to various medical conditions and their treatment and an exercise/nutrition protocol. Such information is provided for informational purposes only and is not meant to be a substitute for the advice of a physician or health care professional. You should not use this information for diagnosing or treating a health problem or injury.

To make informed health care decisions, you should always consult your physician for your personal medical needs. Neither Run for God nor its agents, affiliates, partners, or licensors are providing these materials to you for the purpose of giving you medical advice.

For any questions about your health and well-being, please consult your physician.

table of contents

before you get started

The Thing about a Shirt

THIS PAST WEEKEND I WAS IN
Richmond, Virginia, for the youth
and junior elite draft-legal triathlon.
Some of our young athletes were
competing, and it was an all-around
great trip. Something happened
this weekend that happens quite
often to our entire Run for God
family. A gentleman went out of his way
to comment on our shirts, specifically, the
kids' Run for God Triathlon Suits. He said
that his son had recently come to know the
Lord, and when he saw one of our athletes
on the course wearing their **Run for God**

gear, it inspired him. The other part of our Tri team was competing at another
venue, and while getting a race summary from that venue; I heard similar stories
of people commenting on the Run for God tent and shirts. On the eight-hour drive
home, I pulled up my Facebook and began reading how Ben Reed, an instructor in
Westerville, Ohio, had volunteered his class to work the packet pick-up at a local
race where 14,500 runners were present. Guess what, they were all wearing their
Run for God shirts, and to hear the impact they had on those runners was awesome.

I wear a **Run for God** shirt 95% of the time, and I get many comments from many
people. The vast majority of comments are great, inspiring, and the type that let
me know that the Lord has reached down and touched someone's day, even if it's
just a small touch. Others are witty and sometimes rude, like the guy who asked

me "What's God running for—President?" I'm convinced that even those people are touched in some way.

Can a t-shirt make a difference? I say yes, but I say that with a strong word of caution. People today seem to be more aware than ever of how others handle and portray themselves. A **Run for God** shirt, or any spiritual shirt for that matter, on the shoulders of someone who is out in the world living for Christ and reflecting Jesus can be a very powerful thing. It says a lot about who you are and whom you follow. It lets others know what you stand for without you ever having to open your mouth. But you must be walking with Christ and reflecting His light for that shirt to have any power.

I have a friend that had a quote printed on the back of his **Run for God** shirt: "Preach the Gospel, and if necessary, use words." That statement is so true! We can talk all we want about how we live for God and even have a closet full of spiritual shirts, but if our actions do not back up what we are representing, then we are only hurting the cause and our words have no validity.

"Now then, we are ambassadors for Christ, as though God were pleading through us: we implore you on Christ's behalf, be reconciled to God. For He made Him who knew no sin to be sin for us, that we might become the righteousness of God in Him" *(2 Corinthians 5:20–21).*

Get your shirt at **www.RunforGod.com**

"Preach the Gospel, and if necessary, use words."

getting started

WE HOPE YOU'LL ENJOY READING RUN FOR GOD—DEVOTIONS as much as we enjoyed putting it together. Devotions came together as a result of the outpouring of letters and e-mails that come into the Run for God camp each week. These stories of ordinary people doing extraordinary things and Run for God's role in their lives prompted us to find a way to preserve these memories. From a desire to both preserve and share these stories, *Devotions* was born.

This Bible study is not your ordinary study. No, it's a study that is made up of stories from people just like you and me, real stories from real people. These thoughts and experiences are brought to you from pastors, deacons, Sunday school teachers, new Christians, old Christians, and even Christians who had lost their way for a time. So if you're looking for a study that is authored by a renowned theologian, this isn't it. But if you're looking for a study that shows what God can do through someone just like you and me, then you've definitely come to the right place.

So how do you use this book? I'm glad you asked. *Devotions* is designed to be a weekly one-year study in which you tackle a task each weekday and recap on the weekends. Let me just lay out a typical week for you.

Monday	*Read the main story.*
Tuesday	*Look up and study the scriptures provided.*
Wednesday	*Write down, recite, and commit to memory the verses of the week.*
Thursday	*Ponder and write down your response to the questions of the week.*
Friday	*Read "Running Observations by Dean." You're going to love this guy!*
Weekend	*Recap and journal your thoughts from the previous week in your Sticky Notes.*

You may be wondering if this study could be used in small groups? You bet! While we have **5K**, **10K**, and **Half Marathon Challenges** that are designed for small group settings, you may be part of a running club full of seasoned runners or a **Run for God** class that has graduated from all the *Challenges*. Whichever the case may be, grab some friends, agree on a time to get together each week, share the study, and hold each other accountable for your training. Feel free to use the training schedules located in the back of the book as a workout guide.

I think you now have all the tools to get started. From all of us here at **Run for God**, we hope you enjoy this study. Should you need anything or if you have a story you'd like to share, feel free to reach out to us at **www.RunforGod.com**.

Keep pointing people to Jesus!
Mitchell Hollis

who is dean?

DEAN THOMPSON IS A GREAT FRIEND OF THE RUN FOR GOD MINISTRY and a really fast runner. While we were planning this *Devotions* project, we wanted the input of someone who was both a veteran to the sport of running and very open about his relationship with Christ. It didn't take very long to decide he was the man for the job.

Our challenge to Dean was very simple. Take the most common topics that you discuss with runners and non-runners alike, and tell us about them in your own words. I think that you will find Dean's thoughts inspiring, informational, and even funny at times. Needless to say, we think Dean is a pretty cool guy.

Here's a little more about Dean as told by his wife Debbie.

"Running is the only thing I'm good at." I've heard Dean say these words many times, but they simply are not true.

Born in Perth Amboy, New Jersey, Dean's family moved to Miami, Florida, when he was five years old. This is where his running career began.

He and his family lived in one of the large mobile home parks in Miami. In fact, the park was so large that the Thompson's home sat on Lot # Z15. When Dean's mother drove to the park's post office to pick up their mail, Dean wouldn't ride in the car. He would run in front of the car all the way to the post office and back home again. With every trip to the post office, Dean's competitiveness would kick in, pushing him to run faster than he did in his last "race against mom's car."

He played baseball while attending Flamingo Elementary and Redland Elementary schools in Florida and continued to play after his family moved to Riverdale, Georgia, when he was 10 years old. He always led his team in stolen bases. "I was offended if anyone got close to my total," he said. "When someone got close, I'd just steal more bases." He was a true runner, even on the baseball field.

While in the ninth grade, he tried out for the track team, running a 5:31 mile in his first-ever timed mile and securing a place on the team. He ran the 880, the mile, and the mile relay, finishing second in the county for the mile, losing by one-hundredth of a second. In his sophomore year, he began running with the cross-country team. Leading his first JV 5K race, a volunteer pointed him in the wrong direction. He soon recognized this, turned around, and still finished in second place. He continued to run through his junior and senior years and was named to the 2nd All-Southeastern Cross Country Team. He won a state championship in cross-country and two state championships in track. After high school, he attended Georgia Tech on an athletic scholarship, running both cross-country and track.

Dean continued to run after college, but it wasn't until he turned forty that he began to get serious again. He has run the Boston Marathon two times and the Myrtle Beach Marathon three times, winning the race in 2013. He runs numerous local races in the North Georgia and Chattanooga areas. He is also a member of the Chattanooga Track Club Masters team that competes nationally.

While his passion for running is obvious, so is his love for our Lord. I see this passion as he encourages other runners, including myself, to do their best in a race. He is always eager to talk with people about running as well as their walk with Christ. Recognizing that our love for each other is strengthened by our love for our Lord, we are very active in our church and community.

So when Dean says that running is the only thing he's good at, I have to politely disagree. He is also a good husband, father, athlete, and encourager, giving God the glory while pressing on toward the goal for the prize of the upward call of God in Christ Jesus *(Philippians 3:14)*.

1
Week

the joy of the race

ON MY MORNING RUN THIS MORNING, God was speaking to me. You see, it was almost a month ago that two major events happened in my life within hours of each other. My mom passed away, and I finished my first full marathon. This morning, God was reminding me of the lesson that He hit me with in the middle of the marathon. Hours before the start of the race, I received the phone call that my mom had gone home to be with the Lord. Needless to say the first half of the race I had my game face on and was determined to get to the finish line. But I was so determined to get to the end, I forgot to enjoy the journey it takes to get there.

Just like so many times in my life, I'm so busy to get to the next thing, whether it be the next meeting, the next school event, or the next weekend, that I no longer live in the moment. So at about mile nine in the race, I stepped off the course and began to look at the other runners passing by. They were full of smiles and joy, enjoying the moment. This being the Disney marathon, they were stopping at every photo op there was, waiting in line to get pictures taken with all the characters. I had missed all photo ops up to the ninth mile. Then I realized there wasn't anything I could do at that moment about my mom, but I knew she would be angry with me for missing out on the joy of this event.

So I stepped back on the course and started running with joy in my heart, a joy of the moment. I watched the sunrise over the parks and took pictures every chance I got. I stopped worrying about my finish time and started enjoying the journey. With tears of sorrow and tears of joy streaming down my face, I was able to cross the finish line by the grace of God.

But you see, I'm still in that race, the race of life. Knowing there will be a day that I get to cross that final finish line of life and hear those words I long for, "Well done, my good and faithful servant," I challenge myself daily to enjoy the moment. I have stopped looking ahead. Now I enjoy what is right in front of me. So as I take this challenge, I also put it out to you. Are you missing out on the moment? Step back, take a look, and then jump in that race that God has placed before you. Begin enjoying the journey.

Melissa Weimer - *Anderson, South Carolina*

get in the word

Hebrews 12:1–3
Therefore we also, since we are surrounded by so great a cloud of witnesses, let us lay aside every weight, and the sin which so easily ensnares us, and let us run with endurance the race that is set before us, looking unto Jesus, the author and finisher of our faith, who for the joy that was set before Him endured the cross, despising the shame, and has sat down at the right hand of the throne of God. For consider Him who endured such hostility from sinners against Himself, lest you become weary and discouraged in your souls.

John 1:5

And the light shines in the darkness, and the darkness did not comprehend it.

Matthew 25:23

His lord said to him, "Well done, good and faithful servant; you have been faithful over a few things, I will make you ruler over many things. Enter into the joy of your lord."

scripture memorization

Write out the scripture(s) in the space below and recite them ten times.

_____

_____

_____

_____

_____

_____

_____

_____

_____

_____

something to ponder

ARE YOU living in the moment?

_____

_____

_____

_____

WHAT ARE you missing in your life because you focus too much on

something else?

_____

_____

_____

_____

ARE YOU ready to run in the race for the Lord?

_____

_____

_____

_____

running observations
by dean

Slow Down and Enjoy God

RUNNING GIVES US A PERSPECTIVE ON things we can't see any other way. Seeing the world as you run is totally different than seeing the world from a car. I don't know if it is because of the activity (you are sitting down while driving) or because you are moving slower, but the world is so much more amazing on foot. If that doesn't sound plausible to you, think about this: Think about the first time you saw a beautiful sight, like the Grand Canyon, the view from the top of a mountain, or Niagara Falls. Were you standing or driving in a car? Of course, you were standing! Think about driving by (just assume there is a road to enable you to do so), and then think about walking to it and seeing it on foot. Can you imagine any time where that sight would be more pleasing from the window of the car?

Such is the gift of running. It allows us to appreciate God's creation on foot, where it is most beautiful. I will occasionally stop in the middle of a long run to look at a beautiful scene. The idea that I would pause at a location close to my home to take it in would probably never occur to me while driving in my car. I think it is because you feel so much closer to His creation when you are running.

Of course, sometimes you get up-close glances at animal life too. I have been startled so many times by rabbits, squirrels, snakes, and deer that my heart rate increases just thinking about it. Sometimes you will remember the encounter forever. For example, Debbie and I were traveling out west, and we stayed a night in Sturgis, South Dakota. I woke up early in the morning to go out for a run in the crisp, cool morning air. It was so quiet and peaceful, almost no activity in town at all. I was feeling great, enjoying the moment, when I found myself running on a path next to a stream. The path curved left and bridged across the stream. As I crossed the bridge, I looked downstream to take in the beauty of the cascading water. Then nearing the far side of the bridge, I looked up to see a deer coming onto the bridge from the side. We came within three feet of colliding! He was as surprised to see me, as I was to see him. As he ran back the way he came, I was relieved and enthralled at the same time. What a rush!

The encounters we have with God are also meaningful to our lives. Like pausing to see the beauty of the world, there are times when I feel so close to Him that I have to stop to give Him thanks for filling me so full. Other times the encounter is thrilling, like when I see Him working in a friend's life and they share their excitement with me. God is so good at revealing Himself to us in many ways. We only have to slow down long enough to take notice.

- *God's beauty is all around us and running is one of the best ways to take in that beauty.*

- *Encounters with nature can be exciting, and you never know when a run is going to turn into a trip to the zoo.*

- *Encounters with God are life changing, but we have to remain close enough to Him to recognize them when they come.*

sticky notes

_____

_____

_____

_____

_____

_____

_____

_____

_____

_____

_____

_____

_____

_____

_____

_____

_____

running intentionally:
I will lace up my shoes

I WAS A LOYAL SMOKER FOR over 12 years, only quitting while I was pregnant or nursing one of my three children. Smoking was my best friend and stress reliever. I loved it. While I have believed in Jesus since I was little and knew of his love, I haven't been very good at our personal relationship. It was more like a general belief than a way to live my life. Like most, I tried to fix things myself with my best friend, the cancer stick. Oh, how a tiny little piece of rolled up plant can ruin every aspect of your being. Honestly, it completely takes over your life. You can't go anywhere or do anything unless your pack of cigarettes is with you. How exhausting!

During that time, I was constantly searching for something that always seemed to be missing. I felt like I was a good person, consistently trying to do the right thing and help others. So why didn't I feel good about my life or myself? I know now it was because I was looking to cigarettes to calm my nerves, to rescue my stress, to fix my bad day or hour or minute. When what I really needed to do was look to Jesus as my healer, stress reliever, and friend—to ask for help from the one who can handle anything.

When I finally decided to quit, I began every single day, before my feet even hit the floor, praying: "God, please take this habit from me. Take away every urge to smoke. Please take it from my mind before I even try to think about it." Every day, every four hours, sometimes every two. And I quit. It was only through Christ that I could.

Being relieved of such a weight of addiction was amazing. I had energy and a newfound clarity of mind. The more I leaned on Jesus, the more I wanted to show God how thankful I was that he rescued me from my own self-destruction. So I laced up my shoes, uploaded a 5K app, and started training. I figured if I could quit smoking with him, I could run three miles with him too. I used my training as a time to worship, focusing my mind on rebuilding what I had torn down with selfishness. He met me right there—so faithful, so true.

You should have seen me the day my legs hurt more than my lungs. I was running down the street with tears in my eyes and my hands raised like Rocky. Oh, what a day! Fourteen weeks after I began, I ran my first 5K. But as we all know, life gets busy. Being a wife and mother, it's way too easy to put my needs and wants off until everyone else is taken care of. Fast-forward five months, and there my running sits in the waiting bin. Thanks to some devoted friends, I eventually decided to join our church's Run for God group. I am now running consistently and love that I have a group of people who run after God's heart right alongside me. God has shown me that running is very similar to my everyday walk with him.

I started running to worship and show my appreciation, but the enemy wanted to distract me from my goal. Now unless I stay focused, I'm sure to fail. When I'm running, I have to keep my focus on Christ to relieve my stress, to comfort my pains, and to run with me to the end. Most often, the greatest rewards in life come out of the most painful experiences we have. Who am I to wince at that, knowing what Jesus endured for us? Instead, I choose to step towards the resistance, hoping to learn something new with each new experience.

RUN

Today I choose to lace up my shoes, to meet You where You call.
To strengthen my focus, step over that line, and open my hands to it all.
I'll bring excuses; You'll set them free.

To be with You today is all that I need.

With each step I take my tenacity grows.

I'm running towards intention – where Your love overflows.

Counting my breaths burning like fire, muscles scream out with seizing desire,

It's there in that moment,

You rescue my doubt, revive my objective, and force failure out.

Somehow 'inadequate' is no longer the truth,

My ambition's restored and I'm running with You.

Your lungs are my lungs and Your feet are my feet,

What once bestowed strife, now appealing to me!

Oh, how I'm taken with Your boundless grace,

Such humbling affection in seeking Your face.

Now here comes the finish line miles from the start,

And each time I cross it, there's a change in my heart.

Natalie Tillett *– Wylie, TX*

get in the word

1 Corinthians 10:14
Therefore, my beloved, flee from idolatry.

Romans 5:3–5
And not only that, but we also glory in tribulations, knowing that tribulation produces perseverance; and perseverance, character; and character, hope. Now hope does not disappoint, because the love of God has been poured out in our hearts by the Holy Spirit who was given to us.

scripture memorization

Write out the scripture(s) in the space below and recite them ten times.

_____

_____

_____

_____

_____

_____

_____

_____

_____

_____

_____

_____

_____

_____

_____

something to ponder

IS THERE SOMETHING IN YOUR LIFE that you are holding back from allowing God to control?

_____

_____

_____

_____

DO YOU ACTIVELY SEEK HIS PLAN for your daily life? If so, how? If not, how can you start?

_____

_____

_____

_____

JUST LIKE WITH RUNNING, CONSISTENCY AND perseverance is key to being successful at developing a growing relationship with Jesus. How are you doing in both areas? How can one help the other?

running observations
by dean

Every Run Has a Purpose

Every time you lace up your running shoes you should have an intended purpose, even on easy days. We often think about what we're trying to accomplish when we head to the track to do 400 repeats, but most runners don't think past those special workouts. We may even think about the endurance we are trying to build with the long run, but we sometimes miss the point of the regular six mile run at two minutes slower than race pace. I hear people refer to these runs as "junk miles," and while I think there is a place for this term, it's definitely overused.

For example, the day after a hard workout is an important time to run easy. We can look at these miles as "filler" miles, but they are vitally important miles. During a run like this, I focus on running as easily as possible, paying attention to my breathing patterns, stretching out my stride a few times to lengthen and loosen the muscles, and work on relaxing my upper body while I run. In addition,

I am monitoring my body, intentionally taking inventory of each major muscle group which helps me to catch encroaching problems early. That feedback will help determine what my run is like the next day. If my body is tired, I will run easy the next day too. If I feel unexpected energy, I may go into the next day's run at a faster pace.

Before every run, decide what you are trying to accomplish and at least begin with that in mind. Obviously, there are times you discover those plans are not going to work and change them on the fly. Although this is a little unnerving for some, I think it is critical to be able to make those changes. For example, if you are going to run a hard-effort tempo run and you find during your warm up that your hamstring is unusually sore, you may want to focus on running easy.

When I pick up my Bible, I should have something in mind. Sometimes I will look for an answer to a question. Other times, I will dig into a particular story or book. Being purposeful about reading and studying is critical to getting the most out of my study time. Paul talked about keeping Christ in the center of all we do, and purposeful Bible study and prayer are the best ways to learn how to keep Him in the middle of all conversations and interactions with others. It is amazing how God can place the perfect scripture in your mind at just the right time, when you have been faithfully studying His Word.

- *Every run should have an intended benefit as your goal.*

- *Allow room for changes. Sometimes things don't go as planned, and being able to amend the plan is vital to success.*

- *When you study your Bible, having a goal will help you get the most out of your time with Him.*

sticky notes

_____

_____

_____

_____

_____

_____

_____

_____

_____

_____

_____

_____

_____

_____

_____

_____

running: my enemy, my friend

"Why in the world am I doing this?"

"I feel pretty good right now."

"I feel like I am going to die."

"That was a great run."

"That was a...well, rather exhausting run."

"I feel like I could run for miles!"

"I feel like I couldn't run for another ten feet!"

ANYBODY THAT HAS PICKED UP RUNNING as a sport has felt and expressed all of the above and more. Growing up, I played nearly every sport imaginable: soccer, basketball, football, floor hockey, tennis, racquetball, hacky-sack (is that a sport?), skiing, snowboarding (a bit), biking, and others. Although many of these sports involve running—some of them quite extensively—running is not the goal. It is one of the many components of that sport.

After reading the intriguing account of the running of the super-athletic Tarahumara Indians in the book Born to Run by Christopher McDougall, I started to run with my wife sporadically. I even went out and actually purchased a pair of running shoes. We ran at a track at times; other times we ran on back-country roads. We started to really enjoy getting outside and running. We weren't in a hurry to break any records or run fast. We just enjoyed the exercise, the outdoors, and each other's company.

Later that year, we ran our first 5K in the great city of Chicago. In 2013, my wife and I ran on and off but with no regularity. When we moved to South Jersey in the late summer, our running pretty much came to a halt. As 2014 approached, I knew it was time for more.

One of my goals for this year is to run thirty minutes a day, three times a week. It has been during these mostly early morning runs that I have embraced running as my enemy and my friend. You see, there are times when running seems like torture. At other times, it seems like you are gliding on air and could run indefinitely. My body screams, "I hate you!" and "I love you!" within the same run. In other words, I hate running, and yet I love running.

It reminds me of this dreaded flesh that we are stuck with until Christ redeems our bodies (*Romans 8:23*). The Apostle Paul stated, "For no one ever hated his own flesh, but nourishes and cherishes it, just as the Lord does the church" (*Ephesians 5:29*). And yet at another time, the same man said, "For I know that in me (that is, in my flesh) nothing good dwells" (Romans 7:18). He realized the dual relationship a Christian man has with his own body/flesh. At times I nourish and cherish my flesh; at times I loathe my flesh. And just like running, the battle is not won by the body or the flesh; it is won in the mind.

You can run much farther than you think you can (yes, even you). Ask any running coach. Once an athlete gets into shape, running is more a mental battle than anything. In order to persevere while exhausted, to continue running when faint, to press toward the finish line without quitting, you must be mentally tough, and the very arena in which the battle is waged can become your friend. Why? It will strengthen you for future runs. Likewise in the Christian life, the battle is not won by how you perform outwardly. By and large, the Christian race is won and lost in the mind. The wise man in Proverbs truly said it best when he said, "For as he thinks in his heart, so is he."

So to those of you who are about to quit in this race called the Christian life, revamp your thought life. Strengthen yourself mentally. Meditate on Scripture. Think Godly, positive thoughts. You will become stronger, and you will look back on those tough days as your friends. For you fellow runners, if you see someone alongside the road with a half-frown, half-smile on his face, you will know it was me thinking about my run—my enemy, my friend.

Josh Miller – *Woodstown, NJ*

get in the word

Ephesians 5:29
For no one ever hated his own flesh, but nourishes and cherishes it, just as the Lord does the church.

Romans 7:18
For I know that in me (that is, in my flesh) nothing good dwells; for to will is present with me, but how to perform what is good I do not find.

Proverbs 23:7
For as he thinks in his heart, so is he."Eat and drink!" he says to you, But his heart is not with you.

scripture memorization

Write out the scripture(s) in the space below and recite them ten times.

_____

_____

_____

_____

_____

_____

_____

_____

_____

_____

_____

_____

_____

_____

_____

_____

something to ponder

SHOULD YOU run even when you don't feel like it?

_____

_____

_____

_____

WHAT AREAS of your life do you have a "love/hate" relationship with?

_____

_____

_____

_____

DO YOU AVOID AREAS IN YOUR life that you should address due to the

immense challenge?

_____

_____

_____

_____

running observations by dean

Don't be a Hater

DO YOU RUN BECAUSE YOU LOVE to run? Or do you hate it and only run because you know it's good for you? These are good questions for you to answer because I believe our mindset towards anything we do will set the stage for ultimate success or failure. If you answered the first question with a resounding "yes," you are on your way to success. If you answered the second question with a "yes," I believe you can change the way you think about running.

The way we approach anything will have an impact on our level of proficiency. If we dread going out to run every day, we will fulfill our negative expectations. In the same way, if we go out to run with the attitude that it is going to have a lasting impact on our health and well being, we will fulfill the positive expectation as well. Sure, we will have days when running will be tough, but those days should be few. If we can make our daily expectation positive, we will have a more positive result.

Your ultimate success in many things, including running, is defined by you. If you feel that you need to be fast to be successful, it is you who puts that pressure on yourself. There is nothing wrong with that feeling, but understand that you have the opportunity to define success for yourself. For example, you may define success as being able to complete four runs of at least three miles every week. It's all up to you to decide what you want to get out of running. I often see runners who feel they have to keep up with their friends in order to be successful. Really? Who says so? If you feel that you dread running, maybe redefining what you expect can help take some of the pressure off.

Your feelings about running may be linked to how you feel about yourself. You may run because you want to lose weight, or to lower your blood pressure, or to firm up some loose areas. Whatever the reason, just make sure you are running because you love yourself and not because you hate yourself. It will make a difference in the way you approach your run every day. Understand that you are doing something good for yourself and enjoy it!

I sometimes look at Bible study as something I have to do. Do you dread Bible study? Is it something to check off your To Do list? Once again, our expectations are important. If we expect God to do big things in our daily time with Him, it will happen. Of course, just like running, there are days when you have to make yourself follow through, but those days get you to the big days. Do it because you love yourself. After all, God does.

> • *You define what success looks like for you. Don't let anyone determine what your goals are.*

> • *Run because you love yourself, not because you hate yourself.*

> • *We should expect God to do big things.*

sticky notes

Week

my faith and running saved me

MY FAITH AND RUNNING SAVED ME, but before I share my story I have to be honest. Running was not always good to me. I will never forget my experiences running in junior high and high school. For me it was always pure agony. I would instantly get shin splints. I believed that some people were simply not designed to run, and I was one of them. But something changed for me in 2010.

It began in 2010 when I went to pick up a prescription at my local drug store. As I waited for the prescription to be filled, I noticed a small chair with an arm cuff that measured blood pressure. I had never measured my blood pressure before, so I gave it try. I remember asking the pharmacist if something was wrong with the machine when it stated my blood pressure was in the "contact a doctor NOW" zone. Long story short, I was placed on blood pressure medication and told I would probably have to take it the rest of my life. My doctor also suggested I lose some weight.

At 225 lbs., I never thought I was out of shape, but I took the doctor's suggestion as a challenge. I immediately changed my eating habits, bought a treadmill, and started walking every day. I didn't stop walking for 18 months. You might recall that scene in the movie Forest Gump where he started running one day and simply never stopped. That was me on a treadmill. If I didn't log 30 minutes or more on the treadmill every day, I would not feel good.

On October 6, 2011, I lost my job. I was a C-level executive working for a very successful company when a private-equity group acquired us. A new CEO meant a new management team. My daily prayers included a request that God would point me where he wanted me to go. I never let my faith be diminished. "Even the youths shall faint and be weary, and the young men shall utterly fall, but those who wait on the Lord shall renew their strength; they shall mount up with wings like eagles, they shall run and not be weary, they shall walk and not faint" (*Isaiah 40:30–31*).

As weeks of looking for a job turned into months and months into a year, I recognized that I was becoming my own worst enemy. I was going through the full gamut of human emotions, including doubt, frustration, anger, and depression. I felt like a broken cog not fitting into society. I felt everyone around me was on a fast-paced conveyer belt moving forward, and I had fallen off, never to get back on. "No temptation has overtaken you except such as is common to man; but God is faithful, who will not allow you to be tempted beyond what you are able, but with the temptation will also make the way of escape, that you may be able to bear it" (*1 Corinthians 10:13*). This passage provided me optimism. I decided to put a new focus on my walking and set new physical challenges.

God has blessed me with good physical health and physical exercise gave me motivation to reach my goals, while reading the Bible kept me calm with circumstances. During my first day of unemployment, I woke up the same time I always did. I told myself I would continue to do this despite having nowhere to go. I figured why break my early morning routine of walking. But our treadmill was located in our master bedroom, and my wife has never shared my passion for early morning wakeup. It was 5:00 a.m., and that's when I had an epiphany. Why not go outside and walk? What a concept! Why hadn't I thought of this before? My daily walks turned into five and six mile jaunts. I had another epiphany. If I could run instead of walk, I could complete my workout in half the time.

In January 2012, I was visiting my mom who lives in the Southwest. On a brisk, but beautiful early morning day, I was walking towards an intersection light in the distance and wondered if I could run to that light without stopping. I did. Once past the light I picked out another and then another. Before I realized what happened I had turned around and ran all the way back to my mom's house. I jumped in the car and drove the route I had just run to see what the distance was. I was in total disbelief. I ran almost 2 miles without stopping! This was life changing for me. With a newfound confidence and the spirit of an Olympian, I naturally set my sights on the Atlanta Peachtree Road Race. Why not? I have lived in Atlanta since 1991 and had watched this race on television for many years.

For those who are not familiar with the Peachtree Road Race, it is one of the largest 10K races in the U.S. with 60,000 runners participating. It has become a traditional July 4th event in Atlanta since 1970. I showed up on race day July 4, 2012, not knowing anything about running in an organized race environment. I was doing this solo, but I loved the challenge. I could not have imagined what I was about to experience as I walked upon the scene at the staging area about two hours early. The entire scene was almost a sensory overload with loud speakers playing patriotic songs, tens of thousands of participants and spectators everywhere, helicopters in the sky, banners flying, and the emotions of everyone around me almost palpable. This was so much better than watching from a couch at home. I decided instantly I would do this each and every year!

One of the things each of us learns as we get older is that our health is one of the greatest treasures God grants us. "Or do you not know that your body is the temple of the Holy Spirit who is in you, whom you have from God, and you are not your own? For you were bought at a price; therefore glorify God in your body and in your spirit, which are God's" (1 Corinthians 6:19–20). I have lost too many family members, friends and co-workers to take life and my health for granted. Running has given me confidence in my life when I needed it the most. It has provided me a platform to compete against my own personal goals. What other sport gives you the opportunity to come together with like-minded people, each competing in their own race together and getting the reward of crossing a finish line with people cheering you on as if you were an Olympian competing for gold?

Now I run 5–6 miles 3–4 times per week. I have shed 50 lbs. I run in the top 10% of my age bracket. I am once again a C-level executive. I love running. I love God. God is truly awesome.

Steve Hallock – *Dahlonega, GA*

get in the word

Isaiah 40:30–31
Even the youths shall faint and be weary,
And the young men shall utterly fall,
But those who wait on the Lord
Shall renew their strength;
They shall mount up with wings like eagles,
They shall run and not be weary,
They shall walk and not faint.

1 Corinthians 10:13
No temptation has overtaken you except such as is common to man;
but God is faithful, who will not allow you to be tempted beyond
what you are able, but with the temptation will also make the way of
escape, that you may be able to bear it.

1 Corinthians 6:19–20

Or do you not know that your body is the temple of the Holy Spirit who is in you, whom you have from God, and you are not your own? For you were bought at a price; therefore glorify God in your body and in your spirit, which are God's.

scripture memorization

Write out the scripture(s) in the space below and recite them ten times.

_____

_____

_____

_____

_____

_____

_____

_____

_____

_____

something to ponder

HAVE YOU experienced some moments of weakness when you needed God's strength?

_____

_____

_____

_____

HAVE THESE experiences caused discouragement and kept you from meeting your goals?

_____

_____

_____

_____

HOW ARE you honoring God with your body?

_____

_____

_____

_____

running observations by dean

When Negative is Positive

I REMEMBER READING, YEARS AGO, ABOUT an older elite runner who would run his first couple of miles at a jog to loosen up before running at a normal pace. I have to tell you, it sounded strange to a twenty-something year-old runner. Why waste your time running so slow when you should be training? With age comes wisdom. Since turning 40, I have learned the wisdom of that method. I have learned that it is not how you start your runs that make the difference; it's how you finish.

Today, nearly all my runs start with my slowest mile first. A few years ago I began intentionally running the second half of my runs faster than the first half. This is known as a negative split. At the start of a run, you have fresh legs, so you normally start out fast early in your run, and then tend to slow down and run slower toward the end of your run.

I believe making a habit of running negative splits makes you stronger. You can benefit from this method no matter how much you run. I believe running negative splits prevent injuries as well. When you take the time to get your muscles warmed up before running at a faster pace, your body is better prepared to absorb the impact. In addition, your body is working at its highest efficiency when it is most tired. If you're running races, it helps you prepare for the fatigue you will encounter later in the race.

Another form of negative splits is the progression run. For a progression run, you run easy as a warm up and then you run each successive mile faster than the one before it. It is more difficult than a simple negative split run because you have to develop a sense of pace to be successful. One of the benefits is learning to get feedback from your body to determine your pace. It's also a good "in between" workout that's not an all-out effort, but it leaves you feeling good about your run. I usually just happen to run progression runs. I will get three miles into a run and realize that I am running each mile faster, and then adjust my thoughts to continuing the effort. I really think it's kind of fun.

Just like running, we encounter negatives and positives in our daily lives. I usually start my day off very positive. I read some Bible verses and pray, and then on my drive to work, I'll listen to praise music. It helps me to stay positive when I begin the day this way. However throughout the day, I sometimes get pelted with negative issues. These things can wear you down and cause you to take your eyes off of God, but when I finish the day strong with more Bible study, more praise music and the company of my Godly wife, I find that my heart and mind get back on track. That strong end to the day has the same effect as a negative split run. It strengthens me for those really tough days where Satan is working overtime to get to me.

- *Negative splits in training will help you become a more patient runner.*

- *Running negative splits makes you stronger in the latter parts of races.*

- *The last thing on your mind during any task sets up expectations for the next time. When you finish on a strong note, it leaves a positive impression.*

Devotions • VOLUME 1

sticky notes

_____

_____

_____

_____

_____

_____

_____

_____

_____

_____

_____

_____

_____

the beauty of
unplanned stuff

ONE MORNING WHEN I AWOKE, I listened for the sound of the waves.

"The tide is out," I thought. There would be enough hard sand on the shore to run. I opened my eyes and saw a flash of lightning. "So much for running."

I wanted so much to go watch the sunrise as I ran. It is such an important part of why I love the beach. I hear God in the perfect symphony of the sunrise, the crash of the waves, the footprint of my running shoe in the sand, the sound of my breath, the fatigue of my legs, and the quiet of my mind. Instead, I pulled out my Bible and read about Gideon and how the Israelites, time and again, underestimated God and wandered away to do their own thing (*Judges 6–8*). I read a devotional based on Jesus feeding the 5,000 with five loaves of bread and two fish and how the disciples still questioned how the next group of people would be fed (*Matthew 14*).

Then I put on my running clothes and opened the door to witness the most amazing sunrise. A thundercloud hung at the horizon, the sky blazing with bright pinks and oranges. I stepped out onto the beach and looked to the south. It was just the way I wanted to begin my run. It was quiet—very few people, no high-rise condo buildings, nothing to interrupt the solitude. The beach was smoother too—an easier run—but if I wanted to watch the sunrise, this amazing work of art God was painting before my eyes, I would have to go north.

I could already see people littering the beach that way. I looked at the sky again and began to run north. The sunrise was absolutely beautiful. Bright oranges, pinks and purples surrounded the clouds, the sun rising above them, casting out streaks of blazing orange. My lesson for the morning, however, was not in the sky. As I skipped through tide pools like obstacle courses, looking for a dry place to put my foot, I thought about how life is like this. It's not a nice, smooth beach of sand. Sometimes I have my pace set, I'm running through the days of life, and I come to a rough patch. It forces me to change my pace, choose my steps more carefully, and seek out the Creator of my path to make sure the next step is the right one. Slowing down and changing course are not always bad things. My ways are not his ways (*Isaiah 55:7–9*). I looked up at the sunrise and recognized the beauty was worth having to change my pace.

There was a man fishing. He made eye contact and wished me good morning. I smiled and returned the greeting, anxious to get back to my pace and my thoughts. He wanted to talk more, so I stopped. We talked about the sunrise, the spectacular lightening show he witnessed in the sky that morning, and a little about himself. I wished him a good day and returned to my run. I thought about how much my life is like this encounter. I will be in the middle of something, pursuing my goals or deadlines, when God puts someone in my path for me to bless. The beauty of the sunrise, just like the beauty of reaching out to someone in need, was worth the break in my pace.

I reached the part of the beach with the high-rise condo buildings, which did not add to the beauty of the morning. However, when I looked right instead of left, I saw the massive ocean. Life is like that too, right? There is so much ugliness in the landscape of our lives. I can easily be drawn into focusing on it, or I can choose to see the beauty God has placed in my life. God says He works all things together for the good of those who love Him *(Romans 8:27–29)*. It doesn't get any more beautiful than that.

I had to turn around. My legs were tired and my body weak. I'd made very few good choices that week when it came to eating, and my body was feeling the effects of a lack of fuel. My life is like that too. Sometimes I choose to focus on the wrong things: worry, negativity, and fear, among others. I run out of fuel for my day. God tells me to pray without ceasing (*1 Thessalonians 5:17*). Jesus says He is the bread of life (*John 6:35*). What does my life diet consist of?

As I finished my run, I started to notice the people around me. A couple, walking together, looked as if they were miles apart. The young mother was trying to enjoy the sunrise while her two young boys were running along the beach, evading their father's attempts to wrangle them. She looked tired and distracted. What had brought these people to this place in their relationship? What choices or decisions had they made? What would they do differently if they could? I know what regret and disappointment feel like. Thank You, Jesus, that all things become new in You (*2 Corinthians 5:17*). I no longer have to wish I could change the past. I only have to focus on what the Master has planned for right now.

I finished my run strong, thankful for the beauty of the morning, the beauty of life, and the beauty of the unplanned stuff of life: the rough patches, the distractions, and the people. I was thankful for the positive things that fuel my days and the grace that forgives my past. Most of all, I was thankful for a God who speaks into my life through the beauty of a sunrise and the unplanned stuff of a run.

Bonnie Burnside – *Creston, OH*

get in the word

Isaiah 55:7–9

Let the wicked forsake his way,
And the unrighteous man his thoughts;
Let him return to the Lord,
And He will have mercy on him;
And to our God,
For He will abundantly pardon.
"For My thoughts are not your thoughts,
Nor are your ways My ways," says the Lord.
"For as the heavens are higher than the earth,
So are My ways higher than your ways,
And My thoughts than your thoughts."

Romans 8:27–29

Now He who searches the hearts knows what the mind of the Spirit is, because He makes intercession for the saints according to the will of God. And we know that all things work together for good to those who love God, to those who are the called according to His purpose. For whom He foreknew, He also predestined to be conformed to the image of His Son, that He might be the firstborn among many brethren.

John 6:35

And Jesus said to them, "I am the bread of life. He who comes to Me shall never hunger, and he who believes in Me shall never thirst."

scripture memorization

Write out the scripture(s) in the space below and recite them ten times.

_____

_____

_____

_____

_____

_____

_____

_____

_____

_____

_____

_____

_____

_____

_____

_____

_____

_____

_____

_____

_____

_____

_____

_____

_____

_____

_____

_____

_____

_____

_____

something to ponder

WHAT ARE THE OBSTACLES THAT HAVE been in your path lately? What is God trying to show you by changing your pace?

_____

_____

_____

_____

WHO HAS GOD PLACED IN YOUR path recently? What gift do you have that you could use to help them?

_____

_____

_____

_____

WHAT ARE you focusing on daily? Are you giving your spirit the fuel it needs?

_____

_____

_____

running observations by dean

Races Aren't Just Races Anymore

I REMEMBER ONLY A LITTLE ABOUT my first road race. The Riverdale Road Race was a 10K race, and I don't know that I had ever run that far prior to it. You would think it would be a memorable experience, but races just weren't very memorable back then. I remember getting a t-shirt and a medal for placing in my age group, but I don't remember anything else. We just finished, waited for awards and went home. Boy, how times have changed!

A race is an experience now. Race directors are constantly trying to one-up each other by being creative and incorporating new experiences into race day. If you have experienced today's races, you would be appalled to know that there may have only been two or three water stops in a marathon 30–40 years ago, and that's only if you could find a marathon to run. Today, there are water stops every mile or two with community groups running them and entertainment to give you a mental lift when you need it. While the cost of entering a race has increased, the fun has multiplied.

There are many themed races these days, including mud runs, obstacle course runs, costume races, and color runs, to name a few. There are races that incorporate eating things like doughnuts or hot dogs during the race. If you can't have fun at one or many of these races, you are either a stick-in-the-mud or taking life too seriously. Adding some fun events to your running schedule will break up running routines and give you something different to look forward to.

A couple of decades ago, only fast, serious runners ran in road races, particularly marathons. But over the years, average marathon times have slowed. Why? Because more and more people are realizing that you don't have to be an elite athlete to push yourself and achieve big things. (There are double amputees running marathons now.) While it is great to watch elite athletes compete in a race, the moment to cherish is when someone loses 40 pounds and participates in a race that they never thought they could complete. It happens more every year, and the race organizers are recognizing it too. In many races, especially the longer distances, everyone receives a medal when they finish. Not only is the fun-level up in racing, so are the fringe benefits.

Race organizers have finally realized runners are really hungry people. This realization has led to a plethora of available food at the end of the course, and many have bagels and coffee available before the start. I've seen everything from energy bars to pizza. As author and public speaker Fran Lebowitz once said, "Food is an important part of a balanced diet."

With numbers and diversity increasing at racing events, they have become so much better. The truth is that there are many reasons to attend a race. Many are there to challenge themselves and run as fast as they can. Others are there to socialize and enjoy the company. Still others are there to contribute to a cause and stay in shape. Where else can you find a group of people with widely diverse goals, participating in a single event and having so much fun?

God created diversity in our world, not so we could segregate ourselves into similar groups, but so that we could learn from each other, help each other, and reach out to fulfill The Great Commission (Matthew 28:16-20). We don't think anything about going to a running event to hang out with people who have only one thing in common, but it seems so difficult to do the same thing in other circumstances. If we look at it from God's point of view, we realize that he puts different people into our paths for the express purpose of sharing the Good News.

- *Races used to be a mundane meeting of mostly fast runners who would run and go home, nothing more or less.*

- *A lot of thought goes into today's races to account for everyone's wants and needs, whether they are an elite runner, a recreational runner, or a dedicated walker. This diversity has made it better for everyone.*

- *God intends for us to embrace the diversity of people around us and to share His Word, not only with those like us, but also with those who are substantially different.*

sticky notes

_____

_____

_____

_____

_____

_____

_____

_____

_____

_____

_____

_____

_____

_____

_____

_____

_____

_____

_____

_____

_____

_____

_____

_____

Week 6

what do you rely on?

I AM AN INTERVAL RUNNER. I run three minutes, walk one, and repeat. I rely on technology. I have a great app on my phone that tells me to run three minutes fast then one minute steady. It also has cool features, such as keeping my pace, tracking my route, measuring my distance and elevation, and playing music, all at the same time. Today, as I was running, I realized I had been distracted by my awesome praise and worship music and was running longer than three minutes. So I stopped and checked my technology. I had missed the interval five minutes ago. It was still tracking, but the little voice had stopped talking. No worries, I had back up technology, my watch. I set my watch to beep at my intervals so I could continue.

As I continued my run, God convicted me. Do I rely on God as much as my technology? I use technology for everything, but there are so many times that my computer shuts down, my GPS takes me the wrong way, or my phone drops signal. When you accept Jesus in your life, you receive his Holy Spirit and plug into God's Word. He will never shut down on you, lead you the wrong way, or drop the signal. Psalm 119:105 says, "Your word is a lamp to my feet and a light to my path."

Like my running app that tells me when to run and when to walk, God's Word does the same. I know that when I put more faith in my God than in technology, the paths before me are wonderful. I challenge you to rely on the Lord more than you rely on technology. You will see the difference. I leave you with one of my favorite verses: Isaiah 40:31, "But those who trust in the Lord will find new strength. They will soar high on wings of eagles. They will run and not grow weary. They will walk and not faint."

Melissa Weimer – Anderson, SC

get in the word

Psalm 119:105

Your word is a lamp to my feet and a light to my path.

Isaiah 40:31

But those who wait on the Lord
Shall renew their strength;
They shall mount up with wings like eagles,
They shall run and not be weary,
They shall walk and not faint.

scripture memorization

Write out the scripture(s) in the space below and recite them ten times.

_____

_____

_____

_____

_____

_____

_____

_____

_____

_____

_____

_____

_____

_____

_____

_____

_____

_____

_____

_____

_____

something to ponder

DO YOU rely on God more than technology?

_____

_____

_____

_____

ARE YOU ready to put God first?

_____

_____

_____

_____

WHAT ELSE keeps you away from God?

_____

_____

_____

_____

running observations
by dean

Positive Addiction

ADDICTION IS DEFINED AS "THE STATE of being enslaved to a habit or practice or to something that is psychologically or physically habit-forming, such as narcotics, to such an extent that its cessation causes severe trauma". That makes it sound as if having an addiction is always bad, but I would say that there are times when addiction can be good.

Many people struggle, sometimes every day, with personal demons that are destructive to their lives. It is so prevalent that all of us have either struggled ourselves or know someone who has. But what if we turned the concept of addiction on its head? What if we looked at addiction to things that strengthen us, build us up, inspire our purpose, and make us happy? Is that possible?

William Glasser, M.D., in his book called Positive Addiction, explores this very subject. He cites many activities that can be considered positive addictions. For example: prayer, yoga, art, crafts, and, of course, running. According to Glasser, in order to be considered a positive addiction an activity has to have six things: 1) It should be non-competitive and should last about an hour a day. 2) It should be something that is fairly easy to do. 3) You shouldn't have to depend on others to do it. 4) You have to believe that it has some physical or spiritual value. 5) You need to believe that you can improve at it. 6) It must be an activity that you can do without criticizing yourself for doing it. Do those things sound familiar?

There is much research showing the positive effects of running. Some of those positive effects are: a higher level of energy, weight control or weight loss, more confidence, a need for less sleep, and increased mental strength. A good habit, like running, can be as addictive as bad habits, but can be rewarding instead of self-destructive. Of course, getting past the stage of forcing yourself to go out and run regularly to the stage of wanting to go out and run every day doesn't happen overnight. Glasser points out that it takes about a year to get to an addiction stage. No matter the stage, running provides many benefits.

The only caution is to stop short of allowing your running to replace God as your number one priority. He tells us that He is a jealous God who expects us to make Him our most significant concern (Exodus 20). The Bible tells us in Matthew, Mark, and Luke that we are to love Him with all of our heart, all of our soul, all of our strength, and all of our mind. There is really no room for anything or anyone else at the top of the list. When we place Him first in our lives, our prayer life, Bible study time, and helping others become positive addictions.

- *Addictions, although traditionally known as negative, can also be positive.*

- *There is a lot of research showing that running has many positive consequences.*

- *Loving God with all our heart, soul, strength, and mind will lead to the positive addictions of a deep prayer life, absorptive Bible study, and helping those in need.*

sticky notes

_____

_____

_____

_____

_____

_____

_____

_____

_____

_____

_____

_____

_____

_____

_____

Week

when we sell ourselves short, we sell God short.

SEVERAL YEARS AGO I MADE A fitness goal to run a 5K. I wasn't sure where to start, so I just put on my old running shoes and went out the door. I ran for a solid 20 seconds. It was ridiculous, but with my goal in mind I didn't quit. I came home from my first run—I mean walk—and researched how to run a 5K.

After I found a running plan, I put on my shoes every day and followed the plan—for seven months. My solid 20-second run turned into two-minute runs, then five, then seven (you get the idea). I was gaining confidence. I was thrilled. The day I ran for 20 minutes straight was a proud day.

Now that I was ready to run a race, I didn't know of any to join. I had no connections to real runners. Yet I was ready and determined to run, so I ended up coordinating a race.

One preparation for my race was to visit another race to observe and ask questions. Before that race began, I noticed how everyone was fit. They had the perfect running outfits, top-of-the-line running shoes, fancy timers on one arm, and iPods on the other. I watched them stretch in preparation to run and began to doubt myself. They lined up. I talked down to myself. They took off. I compared myself. When I saw the first runner heading to the finish line, I was in shock at his time and gave up. Mentally defeated, I determined two things: I didn't belong there, and there was no way I was running a race.

"You ran well. Who hindered you from obeying the truth" (Galatians 5:7)? Pause. Self-doubt is deadly, isn't it? The words I say to myself keep me from the Lord. They weigh me down. They keep me from the truth. They consume me with thoughts of myself and leave little room for my Lord. That's pride. That's sin. So I determined to turn from them and run. I chose to listen to the voice of truth. It shouts louder than my insecurities, keeps me humble, and keeps me focused on the race that is set out before me.

Today I choose to believe who God says I am. I choose Jesus. I choose to run my race. "Let us lay aside every weight, and the sin which so easily ensnares us, and let us run with endurance the race that is set before us" (*Hebrews 12:1*).

I used to think that pride was puffing myself up, but God has revealed this truth to me: Pride is looking inward for confidence instead of upward. My pride has caused me to compare and doubt myself. It's caused me to give up what God has called me to do and believe lies. But the truth is that if we trust whom God says we are, allowing Him to be our strength, then "all things are possible."

Tara Tanner – *Martinsville, IL*

get in the word

Galatians 5:7
You ran well. Who hindered you from obeying the truth?

Hebrews 11:6
But without faith it is impossible to please Him, for he who comes to

God must believe that He is, and that He is a rewarder of those who diligently seek Him.

Hebrews 12:1

Therefore we also, since we are surrounded by so great a cloud of witnesses, let us lay aside every weight, and the sin which so easily ensnares us, and let us run with endurance the race that is set before us.

scripture memorization

Write out the scripture(s) in the space below and recite them ten times.

_____

_____

_____

_____

_____

_____

_____

_____

something to ponder

WHAT PRIDE do you need to lie aside in order to run your race?

_____

_____

_____

_____

IF SOMEONE WERE TO TELL YOU that you could trust God with everything, what would be your most honest response? Is there anything you can't trust God to handle?

_____

_____

_____

_____

DO YOU FIND YOURSELVES TRUSTING THE Lord for success, but not failure? Are you leaving the results of all your work in His divine hands?

_____

_____

_____

_____

running observations by dean

There's a Place for Everyone

ONE OF MY FAVORITE THINGS ABOUT middle school and high school cross-country is that there is a place for everyone. In most sports, you have to try out for the team. I've seen a lot of stressed teenagers waiting on the posting of the final team roster for basketball, baseball, or any number of other sports. In cross-country, there is room for everyone on most teams. Of course, there is a top seven, usually considered the varsity team, but anyone can run on the junior varsity. Being all-inclusive makes the team diverse and, consequently, a lot of fun. There is no other sport where you can regularly see a group that includes the class valedictorian alongside a thickheaded wrestler. (No, I'm not classifying wrestlers as thickheaded in general.) The cool thing is the better runner could be the wrestler or the valedictorian.

The definition of camaraderie is a spirit of good friendship and loyalty among members of a group. The noun is borrowed from the French word camarade, which also gives us the word "comrade." It is a perfect word to describe the atmosphere that envelopes a cross country team. The bond that comes from working out together day after day and cheering for each other runs deep. I remember a father of one of the runners on my son's cross country team explain to me, with a lot of emotion in his voice, how hard they worked and how inspirational it was to him. Imagine how teammates feel.

The general running community is a lot like a cross-country team. There is a place for everyone. Whether fast or slow, you're always welcome to participate in local races and running clubs. It's always great to see the elite finishers talking with the mid-packers after finishing a race. There's a common bond no matter what the ability. There is an understanding from both sides about what it takes to do what they do. For the elite, the intense workouts that refine their speed are not really all that different from a long run by someone who struggles for every step. Substantively they are different, but the difficulty level could be identical.

There are also those who really don't work all that hard. They just enjoy running and the benefits of staying in shape without ever pushing themselves as hard as they can. They are accepted like everyone else, because there is a place for everyone!

God's kingdom is another place where everyone is welcome. It doesn't matter where you came from, what you look like, how much money you have, who your family is, or what you have done in the past. As much as Christians know that everyone is welcome in the kingdom, I'm always amazed that there are people who don't understand it. It is up to us to make sure everyone hears the truth. God loves us all, runners and non-runners alike. It's a message that needs to be shared with everyone.

- *Everyone is welcome in the sport of running, no matter the ability.*

- *The camaraderie shared by runners is special and creates lifelong bonds.*

- *Everyone is welcome in God's Kingdom, and it is up to us to spread the message.*

sticky notes

_____

_____

_____

_____

_____

_____

_____

_____

_____

_____

_____

_____

Week

the role of community

RUNNING ISN'T REALLY KNOWN AS A team sport. I first started running because I was utterly terrified of any sport involving large amounts of coordination. Shoot a ball through a hoop? Not really. Put one foot in front of the other? I can handle that. The individual nature of the sport and the concept of going at my own pace and striving for personal goals attracted me.

I had been running for about ten years and completed races ranging from one mile to a half marathon distance when Run for God first popped up on my radar. I tossed the idea out to a friend at church, and it took off from there. We decided to host a Run for God class at our church with my friend and me as co-leaders.

I could not believe the number of people who were interested in attempting a 5K race. We had over fifty individuals come out for the first meeting and group run. I had concerns initially. I had participated in training groups before, but this was my first experience leading one. As the class progressed, many people dropped out due to injuries, recoveries, or sicknesses, which prevented them from catching up in their training, and some simply decided that the program wasn't for them.

The group that remained, however, shared something special. They didn't try to go it alone. They learned how to rely on the encouragement and support of the group to push through difficult times. They resolved to do their best, even if that meant walking on race day.

Over and over, class members mentioned how much easier it was to run together than to go solo. Many members sought out running buddies. Over the course of the 12-week program, I was amazed to see what they could overcome. Individuals who struggled through the first 60-second runs were running three miles by week nine. Individuals who never saw themselves as runners began running faster than a nine-minute pace and were looking at future races before we even finished the program. People who caught the flu or had injuries that took them out of training for several weeks still came back to finish the program. Many reported weight loss, improved sleep, and a healthier respect for the food they put in their bodies.

The most successful people were the ones who stayed plugged in. They appreciated encouraging words and passed them along to others. They recognized that even though we all have different time or distance goals, we have the same hurdles to overcome each day. We all need words of encouragement to help us through a lousy day at work, a hectic schedule, or a poor night's rest, any of which could leave our legs feeling dead before an evening run. We are better together.

The same applies to our walk with Christ. We pursue our individual relationship with Him with personal discipline, but we need other believers to have a truly healthy and successful faith. I can be a runner while logging countless miles alone. I can be a better runner when I am connected to a group of people who share my values and push me to strive for higher goals. In the same way, we can accept Jesus as our Savior and then read His Word on our own, but we will be healthier and stronger Christians when we connect to a group of believers who share our values, encourage us, and hold us accountable for how we live our lives.

The Bible is clear about the need for fellowship in the church. We are told to meet together, encourage one another, and even to confess our sins to one another. Just as it helps motivate us to run toward a goal with others, it also helps us remain faithful to Christ to fight our battles and take our stands with others, knowing we are not alone. Just as hearing about another runner's workout can inspire us to make the time for one of our own, so friendly accountability can also encourage us to keep practicing spiritual disciplines like prayer, scripture memory, and fasting. An encouraging friend can help us rebound after a running setback. A faithful friend can refocus us and help us overcome the spiritual setbacks. And just as keeping company with experienced runners can help us set higher goals, so being around mature Christians can inspire us to continually seek the kingdom of God and His righteousness.

At the end of our program, we had over twenty people complete a 5K race. Everyone who made it to the starting line also made it to the finish line, and each one had an individual story to tell of the challenges they faced. Staying connected makes a difference, both in our pursuit of running goals and in the pursuit of our Lord and Savior Jesus Christ.

Rebecca Taylor – *Jacksonville, FL*

get in the word

Hebrews 10:25
Not forsaking the assembling of ourselves together, as is the manner of some, but exhorting one another, and so much the more as you see the Day approaching.

1 Thessalonians 5:11
Therefore comfort each other and edify one another, just as you also are doing.

Ecclesiastes 4:9–10

Two are better than one, Because they have a good reward for their labor. For if they fall, one will lift up his companion. But woe to him who is alone when he falls, For he has no one to help him up.

scripture memorization

Write out the scripture(s) in the space below and recite them ten times.

_____

_____

_____

_____

_____

_____

_____

_____

_____

_____

_____

_____

_____

_____

_____

something to ponder

WHAT ARE SOME OF THE POSITIVE words a fellow runner has shared with you that have helped you overcome discouragement or a setback? How can you pass that encouragement along to another runner? How is this a reflection of Jesus Christ to others?

_____

_____

_____

_____

IN THE STORY, THE CASE IS made that our spiritual walks are both individual and team efforts. In what ways is your spiritual life just between you and God (individual)? In what ways does it involve your church or parachurch organizations (team)?

HOW CONNECTED ARE YOU TO A local body of believers? Are there areas of your spiritual life (prayer, Bible study, accountability, etc.) that would benefit from increased involvement in a church? If so, what are some practical steps you can take to get active in ministry?

running observations by dean

Join the Cheerleading Squad

DON'T YOU LOVE IT WHEN SOMEONE is cheering for you? You feel a piece of what it is like to be a rock star on stage. Most of the time, the supportive voice you hear is familiar to you. Other times that voice belongs to someone you don't know. But it doesn't matter; they both make you feel good.

One of the most inspirational moments I can remember was at the end of a Run-for-God-sponsored race when nearly everyone who had already finished gathered at the finish line to cheer for the last competitor. I am sure she will never forget that finish. We all became cheerleaders that day. So why don't we do more of that? Why don't we all pick up virtual pompoms and cheer for everyone?

When I run my cool down I like to begin at the finish line and run the last mile of the race backwards, cheering for everyone who is still finishing. Sometimes I enjoy it more than the race itself. It is one of those times I can cut loose and have some unabashed fun supporting people I don't know. It doesn't matter what you say as long as it is positive and uplifting. Do you know them? Call them by name. Don't know them? Call them by their number, shirt color, hairstyle or anything else you can come up with. Just say something and do it enthusiastically! Remember you're part of the pep squad, not the cheerleading competition squad. We want folks pumped up. We're not worried about what the judges think of our cartwheels.

Whether or not some of those runners come to you after the race to thank you for the mental lift you provided them, you can take heart that you made a difference to someone. Make it a habit to spend some time lifting up your fellow competitors.

Over time you will find more and more people cheering for you when you run. Crazy people are memorable people, so they will remember you when you cheer for them. As soon as they get the opportunity, they will return the favor. I know some people at the races simply because we have forged a supportive bond. Some of us don't even know each other's names, but we know that we support each other. We wave or give a respectful nod to acknowledge our uncomplicated relationship.

As Christians, God calls us to support each other in many important ways, and sometimes the bonds made through simple interaction lead to conversations that build life-changing relationships. I firmly believe God places people in my path with which he intends for me to share His love. Why would a running event be any different?

- *We all love to have someone cheer for us. Turning that around and directing it toward others makes them feel special.*

- *An uplifting word from someone you don't know can be as encouraging as a word from a friend.*

- *We are called to share God's love. What better way to do it than through being a cheerleader for someone else?*

sticky notes

_____

_____

_____

_____

_____

_____

_____

_____

_____

_____

_____

_____

_____

_____

9
Week

run uphill!

THE FIRST 30 MINUTES OF JANUARY 1, 2013, I ran my first 5K with my husband. We started at midnight and ran through the Christmas lights at a beautiful local park's "Festival of Lights." With my adrenaline high, I was thrilled to be starting a new year with a new and healthy lifestyle.

I remember running up two tough hills near the end of the race. Most of the people around me either slowed their run or started walking. I was tired, almost out of breath, but determined. I passed several people on those hills, just because I kept running. I felt incredible. After the race, I decided to make that my motto: "Run Uphill!" I had it engraved on my wristband, along with my personal emergency information. Sometimes I remember it or look down at it while I'm running. It encourages me to keep running no matter how hard the hill is. Those words motivate me to face my challenges, because "Run Uphill!" is more than a running motto. It has also become my life motto.

One reason I was able to pass other runners on the hills was 90% of my training had been uphill. I trained primarily on a treadmill. I had set it at an incline when I first started to run. Though small and slow, every step I took was uphill. My husband hadn't trained this way; much of his training was outdoors on flat roads. Even though he had already participated in a few 5Ks and usually had better endurance than me, the hills in this race set us apart. He had to stop and walk, while I kept going.

I realize that I am in training for my Christian life every day. I train by studying the Bible, spending time with God in prayer, and learning from other believers. I train in a controlled environment, but I don't know what hills (difficulties) will come my way next. I should make sure I am training at a high intensity, always driving upward and forward. The more I learn about God and the more in tune I am to His voice, the easier it will be to rely on His strength and conquer the trials of life. I should train diligently and then run with confidence, both physically and spiritually. While we shouldn't be in spiritual competition with other believers, it's easy to tell that there are Christians who live more victoriously than others. Often the hills of life are the events that distinguish victorious Christians from defeated ones.

Thankfully, we don't have to rely on our own power to conquer those hills. God supplies us with the power we need, but we still have to fight the good fight of faith and run our own race. I had to put forth some extra effort to get up the hills in that 5K. I later made a list of some ways I can put forth the effort to run uphill in other real-life situations. Running uphill means:

To try harder than normal

To do right, when wrong is easier

To get out of my comfort zone and get the job done

To accept the challenge, take responsibility, and be a leader

To avoid passivity

To not let others drag me down

To have a confident, optimistic attitude

To look to Jesus, who endured the cross and the shame that He despised, because He knew the joy that would come at its completion.

Hannah Jones – *East Bend, NC*

get in the word

Hebrews 12:1–2

Therefore we also, since we are surrounded by so great a cloud of witnesses, let us lay aside every weight, and the sin which so easily ensnares us, and let us run with endurance the race that is set before us, looking unto Jesus, the author and finisher of our faith, who for the joy that was set before Him endured the cross, despising the shame, and has sat down at the right hand of the throne of God.

2 Timothy 2:15

Be diligent to present yourself approved to God, a worker who does not need to be ashamed, rightly dividing the word of truth.

1 Corinthians 15:57

But thanks be to God, who gives us the victory through our Lord Jesus Christ.

scripture memorization

Write out the scripture(s) in the space below and recite them ten times.

something to ponder

IS YOUR spiritual training intense enough to prepare you for life's battles? How could you kick it up a notch?

_____

_____

_____

_____

WHAT SPIRITUAL hills have you faced lately? How could you have been better prepared?

_____

_____

_____

_____

WHAT DOES running uphill mean to you?

_____

_____

_____

running observations
by dean

The View Is Always Worth the Climb

ANYTIME MY WIFE, DEBBIE, AND I are traveling, I love to wake up early and go for a run in a new city. I can remember times when I would notice a hill that, once climbed, would afford a great view of the city. I like to climb that hill, even though I know it will be difficult to get all the way up, because the view is always worth it. It's one of the few times I will stop in the middle of the run to look around me.

On the days you don't feel motivated to workout, remember that the view is worth the climb. You will reap tremendous benefits from getting out there and completing your workout. Sometimes running the workout I don't want to run yields the best results. I've often thought the reason for this is my low expectations. I am more relaxed than normal, letting it all hang out, and so I find myself gliding along more easily than I thought I would.

Whether metaphorical or real, I never pass on the opportunity to climb to the top of the hill because I know what the result will be. After all, I may never be back to that city again, or I may never be in the same place in my training again. I have to take the opportunity while I can. On the few occasions I have not made the climb, I usually regretted it. The only caveat is reserved for those times when your body is truly not ready for the workout or the climb because of injury, fatigue, or illness.

You can't be the best you can be without working hard, but how do you stay motivated? Imagine the results. When you find your motivation waning and you're talking yourself out of a tough run, envision the view you will see at the top of the hill. The hard work is always worth it.

In the same way, speaking the truth in love and telling unbelievers about Jesus are important habits to build. Sometimes I want to speak up but have trouble finding the words, and other times I reflect on how I spoke up with a less than lovely tone. Just as working through tough workouts yields a more efficient runner, spending time with our Lord yields a more effective witness.

- *Remember that focusing on your goal helps to keep you motivated on those days when it is tough to get out the door.*

- *Anything worthwhile in life requires climbing a hill, whether physical or metaphorical.*

- *Being the most effective witness you can be requires effort, but the view is worth the climb.*

sticky notes

_____

_____

_____

_____

_____

_____

_____

_____

_____

_____

_____

_____

_____

_____

_____

_____

spiritual base

Last week I began a forty-week training plan that will hopefully land me at the Chattanooga Ironman finish line in under twelve hours. I've become familiar with training for an event like this. I have read about it, studied it, been certified to coach it, and endured it.

The first thing you will learn about any kind of endurance training is that you must first establish a base. A base is a period of training when you will exercise at an intensity that may seem easy, monotonous, and just a waste of time. Why do I say that it may seem to be a waste of time? Because as athletes we have an inner desire to always do better, to push ourselves to the limit, and, as runners, to just get faster. Base work accomplishes none of this; at least that is what we athletes often think.

Many runners never get faster, because their hard days are not hard enough and their slow days are not slow enough. Many times you will fall into one category or the other, but rarely into both. Base work builds endurance and lays the foundation for all of your other training. Sure, you can do speed work every day of the week. You can even do 100 meter sprints until your heart is pounding out of your chest, but without a base level of fitness you'll find it very hard to complete a 5K or 10K, much less a half or full marathon. I once read a study that stated many NBA players will run 4.5 – 6 miles in a game at high intensities with no problem, but ask those players to run six miles straight, and they'd find it a challenge. Why? Because basketball players do not build a base level of running fitness, nor do they need it. They train those fast twitch muscles to do exactly what they are designed to do, go fast, and neglect those slow twitch endurance muscles.

Speed work is great. It pushes you outside your comfort zone and makes you a better runner. But without a good base period, even the best speed work plan will not sustain you. If all you've done is speed work in training for an endurance race, you will blow up, hit the wall, and burn.

So let me get to the point. Today I was running one of those dreaded six mile, low intensity, Zone 3 training runs. For those of you who don't understand what that is, just take your comfortable running pace and add about two minutes per mile to it. It's a slow run. It's almost embarrassingly slow, and I was having a battle in my mind as to whether or not I should speed up. The runner in me wanted to pick up the pace to my comfort zone and not look like the turtle rolling down the sidewalk, but the trainer in me was hammering home the point that base work is a must. Without it, my 140.6 mile race might end at 70.3 or sooner.

At this point the Lord began speaking to me about my spiritual base. Don't you just love it when God turns an idea back on you and applies it to your walk with him? He began to show me that just as I must have an athletic base when competing in endurance events, so I must also have a spiritual base to compete in life.

A spiritual base is time spent in prayer and God's Word. This is the base by which we should all build our spiritual lives. While I love to read books or hear sermons on how to be more spiritually fit, these resources are like speed work. They will make you more knowledgeable, but without a strong base, they are useless.

If you have a deep, daily relationship with God, then hearing a great sermon or reading a great spiritual book is like sharpening the edge of an industrial size log splitter. That log splitter has a base big enough to get the job done even with a dull edge, but sharpening it makes the job easier. If you don't have a deep, daily relationship with Christ, then hearing a great sermon or reading a great book is like sharpening the edge of a razor blade. Yes, it's very sharp, but it won't cut through an oak log for lack of base strength.

So I challenge you today to join me in building a spiritual base that will handle even the biggest job. Make prayer and time in God's Word the backbone of your spiritual life. Yes, it's okay to sharpen your edge, but only after your base can back it up.

Mitchell Hollis – *Dalton, GA*

get in the word

John 1:1
In the beginning was the Word, and the Word was with God, and the Word was God.

2 Samuel 22:29–30
For You are my lamp, O Lord;
The Lord shall enlighten my darkness.
For by You I can run against a troop;
By my God I can leap over a wall.

Hebrews 4:12
For the word of God is living and powerful, and sharper than any

two-edged sword, piercing even to the division of soul and spirit, and of joints and marrow, and is a discerner of the thoughts and intents of the heart.

scripture memorization

Write out the scripture(s) in the space below and recite them ten times.

_____

_____

_____

_____

_____

_____

_____

_____

_____

_____

_____

_____

something to ponder

HOW DOES SPENDING TIME IN GOD'S Word differ from listening to a great sermon?

_____

_____

_____

_____

HOW DOES talking to God enable us to gain more from that great sermon?

_____

_____

_____

_____

HOW SPECIFICALLY do you make time with God and the study of his word your spiritual base?

_____

_____

_____

_____

running observations
by dean

Running in the Dark

HERE'S A QUESTION I HEAR OFTEN: Why would anyone like to run? I suppose most people feel about running the way I feel about shopping. I would rather rub alcohol into a cut than visit an outlet mall, so I get the complaints.

I run usually during daylight hours, but occasionally I have to run in the dark, because not running on any day is not an option. I was never able to "just say no" to running. I recall one of those days when I was headed down the street to run in the dark around 9:00 p.m. I live close to a track, so when I run at night, I like to run on the track where there is lighting and therefore safety. But unless I am running intervals or something similar, I like to run on a road or trail.

On this particular night, my desire to run on the road overcame my fear of running in the dark. We don't have much traffic where I live, so it is easy to move to the other side of the road when approaching cars can't see me. If they are coming in both directions, I will get off the road and wait for them to pass. (I have a strong desire to avoid being run down by grandpa's Cadillac only to be found by some wild animal who hasn't eaten for two days.)

The other big problem with running in the dark is dogs. For a runner, dogs can be scary. I have learned over the years how to deal with them, so when you can see them, they're not a problem. While I was running in only little moonlight that night, I heard a growl from the shadows. I could not see the growler, but I could tell that he was getting closer, so I stopped. Dogs will stop when you stop, but only temporarily. I stared out into the darkness trying desperately to see the dog, but I could not. He sounded angry and large. I think I offended him in some way. He was letting me know in no uncertain terms that I was not allowed anywhere near his space, which must have included the road. Now what?

I started talking to him. No, I take that back—I shouted at him. As he got closer, I shouted louder in case he didn't hear me. Then I began to walk to let him know that I was not personally invested in that piece of real estate and I was fine with him being the sole ruler. He followed me. Oh no, he was stalking me in the dark. I thought of related movies, like Cujo and Pet Cemetery. I don't know why I didn't think of Lassie or Benji or even Scooby-Doo. I kept moving and shouting and after 40 terrifying seconds that felt like five minutes, I was rid of the dog. I went back to the track with my heightened senses and finished my run.

When we live life without God or even stray away from Him, we're running in the dark and scary things lurk in the darkness. We can avoid it by living according to His will. He will provide something much better than a track with some streetlights. He will provide unmatched illumination. "For You are my lamp, O Lord; the Lord shall enlighten my darkness" (2 Samuel 22:29). We never have to run in the dark while the Lord lights our way.

- *Running in the dark can be scary.*

- *Sometimes we have to choose alternatives we don't like to remain dedicated to our goals.*

- *God wants us to run the race of life with his illumination.*

sticky notes

where did she go?

I LIKE BOOKS. I'M PROBABLY IN the middle of reading four or five different books right now. I start to read each one then set it down, and another catches my eye. I usually finish the books I start, but sometimes I come back to a book forgetting I had ever started it. Anytime I'm in a bookstore, I'm in danger of walking out with new reading material. If I bought books as often as I'd like, I'd be broke. For that reason, I often borrow them from friends, visit the library, or buy them used.

At the end of last year, I decided to start a devotional book that had five lessons a week, thought-provoking questions, a place to journal, and a place to record my runs for the week. I decided to buy it used online when I found it for about 10 percent of the list price. I was kind of surprised when the book came and I found someone had actually written in it. Usually when I buy a used book online, I expect margin notes or highlighting, but someone had used it as intended and was pretty honest in her journaling. At least, she started to use the book as intended. The optimism and transparency in week one faded. Each subsequent week had less insightful posts and fewer miles logged. After five weeks, the book showed no signs of use.

So I've got to wonder what happened to the book's previous owner. Did she just give up after such a good start? Did she get injured and have to take some time off? Or did she just lay down her book and forget to pick it up, like so many books I've started before?

There's something about the way people are wired that keeps them from sticking to a new program that doesn't get the results as quickly or as easily as they had hoped. I'll bet a lot of us have thought about starting a new hobby and given up on it. I've led enough Run for God classes to know that we will never finish with as many people as we start. I go out of my way to be as enthusiastic as possible, encouraging every class member and warning them of the danger signals of burnout, but even with the extra effort, people drop out before finishing the program.

We've all seen this at church too, right? People will start to come to church, get involved, make new friends, and really start to make positive change in their lives. And then you ask yourself, "Where did she go? What happened to that new guy or gal?" You ask others, "Did something happen to upset them? They're gone. They dropped out of the program." I wish that didn't happen. If only we could be better at helping people get and stay connected.

In the end, it doesn't really matter that much if someone drops out of a couch-to-5K program. I'll be there as best as I can to support them, encourage them, and run beside them, but they have to do the running. If someone starts coming to church and drops out, that's a different story. That matters. We need to improve how we convert seekers to believers to followers. Starting (even starting late) in the race of faith is important – but finishing the race is the principal goal. Do whatever you can to help those around you finish and finish well!

Kent Ogle – *Webb City, MO*

get in the word

Luke 9:62

But Jesus said to him, "No one, having put his hand to the plow, and looking back, is fit for the kingdom of God."

Galatians 6:4–5

But let each one examine his own work, and then he will have rejoicing in himself alone, and not in another. For each one shall bear his own load.

2 Timothy 4:7

I have fought the good fight, I have finished the race, I have kept the faith.

scripture memorization

Write out the scripture(s) in the space below and recite them ten times.

_____

_____

something to ponder

DO YOU HAVE TROUBLE SEEING A task through to completion? What is your biggest disappointment associated with quitting a task?

_____

_____

_____

_____

HAVE YOU EVER HAD SOMETHING THAT doesn't really have an end? How can you set incremental goals and/or adjust your expectations to stay focused?

_____

_____

_____

_____

LOOK AROUND AT YOUR CONGREGATION. DO you notice the absence of anyone who used to worship with you? What can you do to help get them back in church?

_____

_____

_____

_____

running observations
by dean

Waiting for Weight Loss

I BELIEVE WE MUST BE PRAGMATIC about body weight and running. I'm a little skinny fellow of about 154 pounds, and I have seen many in my family struggle to manage their weight. Several years ago, I gained twenty pounds in one month when I had to take time off from running. It is in my genes to be overweight if I ever stop and continue my current calorie intake.

I have known many people who have started running because they wanted to lose weight. The story usually goes like this: They begin running and can't run more than 200 yards without stopping. They run every other day for two to four weeks, work up to an ability to run over a mile continuously, and can cover a couple of miles total. It hurts every time, and they are eager to see results. When they step on the scale after that time, they have not lost any weight. So they quit. The hard work obviously doesn't work for them. Does this sound familiar?

Here is a lesson I learned. I was diagnosed with a stress fracture in my femur, which is the large bone in your thigh. I couldn't run and had to take three months. I was in pretty good shape at the point it happened, so my mileage was fairly high. Did having to stop cold turkey make me gain a bunch of weight immediately? No. In fact, I didn't gain any weight for a month, and that was December, otherwise known as the month of eating. I hadn't modified my diet because my weight was holding steady, but by the end of January, I gained twenty pounds. My metabolism had taken December to slow down. Once it did, my eating caught up with me. Likewise, when I was able to start back up in March, it took a month of running at least five days a week to begin to lose the weight.

You can't rush it. You have to be consistent over time to see results. When you keep your foot on the gas, you will eventually pick up speed. The difficulty lies in having the patience and determination to keep going.

Try slowing down your pace. It doesn't have to hurt as bad as it has. If you will run at an easy pace consistently, you will successfully shed those extra pounds. It takes longer for some than others; so don't get discouraged because you know someone who lost weight with less work. God made us all a little different. Chances are if He made you have to work harder to lose weight, He also gave you the ability to work harder too.

Bible study and prayer are similar to this. We have to consistently practice them to feel the full benefits of being close to Him. When you invest the time to abide in Him, a few days away from that will not slow your spiritual metabolism. Conversely, if you don't spend time with Him consistently, you may never be able to feel His constant presence and faithfulness. Rev up your spiritual metabolism by spending quality time with Him every day.

- *Many people give up on weight loss because they try to run too fast or for longer distances than they should.*

- *You can't rush it. To get your metabolism working harder takes consistent effort.*

- *Your spiritual metabolism can be increased in the same way by spending consistent time with Him.*

sticky notes

my best running partner is God

IN THE SPRING OF 2013, A strong desire to start running again pressed in on me. I fought it using every excuse I could. A 53-year-old woman shouldn't be pounding the road, I said, a sure recipe for disaster and bodily injury. However, my persistent desire propelled me to explore the wooded trails behind our home.

For three weeks, starting with one day a week, then two, then three, I managed to eek out a 25 – 30 minute jog. Why so cautious? Because in the 15 years since my last consistent running, whenever I ran I experienced foot and hip pain within a couple of weeks. At the time I chalked it up to middle age, accepting the fact that running was no longer in my future. I dropped my dream of running a half marathon. However, despite all my self-doubt and apprehension, God had other plans. He pushed me out the door, and now one year later, I have completed two 5Ks, two 10Ks, a 12K, and 3 half marathons. I've had personal records I thought I'd never achieve, and I'm looking forward to future races, which includes my first marathon in June.

God used running to teach, guide, and strengthen my faith. He opened my eyes and heart to a deeper relationship with Him. I have learned that our daily struggles in life mirror the struggles of a training regimen. There were cold, wet, and dreary days when I didn't feel like getting out of bed, and times I wanted to give up on a tough run. However, I always knew that God was with me, encouraging me to trust Him and calling me to meet the challenge and to endure the obstacles while focusing on Him. My runs became a source of joy and spiritual growth, a time spent in prayer and praise. I came to treasure Jesus as an essential part of my runs, the best running partner God could provide. If the Lord cares this much about my running, how much more does He care about my daily life struggles? All He asks me to do is to use the same methods I used to meet my running goals.

As I began doing this, I first realized I needed to transfer my discipline in training to my spiritual growth. It became a priority for me to dedicate daily time to prayer and reading the Word. Second, I knew the only reason I succeeded in running was my focus on God during my training, especially when it became difficult. Now when the trials of life become overbearing, I immediately begin to focus on the Lord. Most importantly, if I had not listened to His voice and obeyed Him, I would not have experienced the transformation that God had planned for me: the gift of endurance, the strengthening of my faith, the ability to trust Him in all situations, and the joy of serving others by encouraging them to meet their running goals. To God be all the glory in everything I do.

Running has shown me I am helpless without God. Instead of trying to control every detail of my life, I seek God's will and know I am covered by His grace and mercy. Nothing is more important to me than God. I have no desire to run unless it is in His name and for His glory.

Kristin Shurley – *Port Hadlock, WA*

get in the word

Romans 5:3–4
And not only that, but we also glory in tribulations, knowing that tribulation produces perseverance; and perseverance, character; and character, hope.

Psalm 37:3
Trust in the Lord, and do good; dwell in the land, and feed on His faithfulness.

2 Timothy 4:5
But you be watchful in all things, endure afflictions, do the work of an evangelist, fulfill your ministry.

scripture memorization

Write out the scripture(s) in the space below and recite them ten times.

_____

_____

_____

something to ponder

IS THE DREAM OF YOUR LIFE greater than your desire to submit your life to God?

_____

_____

_____

_____

ARE YOU devoting yourself to God as you are to running?

_____

_____

_____

_____

ARE YOU using the sport of running to share God's love with others?

_____

_____

_____

_____

running observations by dean

The Magic Training Program

THE NUMBER OF TRAINING PROGRAMS AVAILABLE is roughly equivalent to the number of stars in the sky. Well, that may be an exaggeration, but there are a bunch of choices. You can find free programs online, purchase books with even more choices, or you can hire a coach to design a program for you. If you just want to run and have no interest in running any faster or easier, you don't need a training program, but I don't know many runners who don't want to run faster tomorrow than they do today. Finding the right training program is like finding the right running shoe. You usually try a bunch of different choices that feel pretty good, but once you find the right one, you know it.

The trick to finding a good program is knowing when to discard what you're doing and try something else. Just because Sally is faster than you doesn't mean that her training program will enable you to run as fast as she does. As a matter of fact, it may make you slower or even stop your training altogether. Many runners will stick to a training program no matter how they feel, thinking that improvement is right around the corner. Telling your body it feels okay when it doesn't will often lead to injury. There's a reason your body is talking to you. Listen to it. If you ignore your body's messages, you could injure yourself, and you won't maximize your ability. You must learn how to shift on the fly according to your body's demands, or you will never live up to your potential.

It's fun to discover what works best for you. The geek in me likes to figure out how to get the most out of my body. After running sporadically for most of my 30s, I began running regularly again when I turned 40. It took me four years, a stress fracture, and two more serious injuries to learn enough about my body to be able to train effectively. As you get older your body begins a revolt against anything resembling what you did when you were 20. I have never found what works for me in any full training program, and all of it is different from what worked for me when I was 24.

If the goal is to get faster and be the best you can be, you have to analyze your body's feedback before, during, and after every run. You have to learn how to keep the things that work and throw out the things that don't. If you are following a plan, you have to know when to deviate from the plan and when to push through it. That's where the fun is for me.

God has provided a plan for us in the form of the Bible. However, we all have different talents and gifts to offer back to God. Although there is an element of the plan that is non-negotiable, some details are up to us to fill in. We can be the best we can be when we learn to listen to Him and follow the Holy Spirit's direction for our lives. He's providing the direction. We need only to follow it.

- *Just because it works for someone else doesn't mean it will work for you.*

- *To be the best runner you can be, you have to listen to your body effectively.*

- *Our spiritual training plan is written out in the Bible, but how we use our spiritual gifts is up to us to discern.*

sticky notes

_____

_____

_____

_____

_____

_____

_____

_____

_____

_____

_____

_____

_____

Week

food for thought

WHETHER WE ADMIT IT OR NOT, most of us know how to stay healthy. We understand that our bodies need physical activity each day for our muscles to stay strong. We also understand that our bodies work more effectively with healthy food choices. The more I run, the more I am reminded of the importance of good nutrition. I am also starting to better understand the importance of spiritual nourishment.

In John 6, Jesus has a large crowd following him, because they had seen his miraculous signs (*John 6:2*). The crowds are hungry and tired. Andrew finds a young boy with five loaves of barley and two fish. Starting with that, Jesus feeds 5,000 men that day and collects leftovers. But the teaching wasn't over. Jesus comes back at the end of chapter six to speak to the crowd again.

His subject they all know well—hunger. He reminds them of the miracle He had just performed. The people were hungry, so Jesus took what they had and multiplied it, filling the need in their lives at that moment. He explains that physical food will never satisfy us forever. We will always grow hungry again. But Jesus tells the crowd about another kind of food. He states in John 6:35, "I am the bread of life. He who comes to Me shall never hunger, and he who believes in Me shall never thirst."

The Word of God nourishes our soul and empowers our life as Christians. Spiritual disciplines such as fasting, prayer, and Scripture memory create an intimate relationship between us and Jesus. "How sweet are Your words to my taste, sweeter than honey to my mouth" (*Ps 119:103*). Spending time with Jesus is as essential for spiritual growth and contentment as eating and breathing is to our physical bodies. We will die without Him, but many of us are weak spiritually and don't understand why.

Let's use our physical bodies as an analogy. Our bodies require constant energy from food. We eat at least three meals a day, seven days a week. We are "starving" if we go for a few hours without eating. In fact, research is showing that eating every two to three hours during the day will maintain blood sugar levels and keep cravings at bay. Small amounts of food throughout the day seem to be the best way to energize our bodies and allow us to work at our full potential. We could probably skip a few meals without trouble. If, however, we began skipping entire days of nourishment, we would feel the effects. We would become sickly and weak. We would not feel our best or work at our full potential. So if our bodies require twenty-one meals a week, plus snacks to stay well, how do we expect our souls to live on three meals of living bread a week?

Christians tend to believe that going to church a couple of times a week should provide enough nourishment to satisfy, but we wouldn't want to live off of only three physical meals a week, regardless of how healthy those meals are. Why should we expect to be spiritually healthy if we only "eat" spiritual food on Sundays and Wednesdays at church? More than that, we aren't eating much at church. The pastor or teacher has spent time in the Word studying and praying. They have feasted on the Bread of Life. We sit at their feet and consume the crumbs of their relationship. Many of us live off a couple of crumbs a week and wonder why we are frail, unsatisfied, and ineffective believers. Should we not be feasting every day? Wouldn't we be more spiritually healthy if our nourishment was continual throughout the day?

Being in the Word daily and spending quality time with Jesus are essential to living a life of faith. Relationships take time. The Bible is clear that "the devil walks about like a roaring lion" (*1 Peter 5:8*). If you have ever watched a show about nature, you soon realize that lions do not go after the strong. When a lion is stalking its prey, it will carefully choose the antelope or gazelle at the back of the pack. It will pick the one that doesn't seem quite as strong as the others. The sick, the weak, the one that won't be able to fight back, the one that can't run as fast—that is lion's prey.

When Satan attacks our homes, families, churches, or communities, are we strong enough to fight? Are we grounded in the Word of God? Have we been feasting on the Bread of Life? Do we have the strength and energy to fight the schemes of the devil? Do we have the stamina to flee temptation and run the race of truth that we have been called to? Or do we tire easily? Are we crippled by our lack of spiritual food?

If we are living on mere crumbs each week, we cannot expect to be strong enough to fight the good fight. What we eat determines our energy, stamina, and endurance. Healthy food is better at developing muscles than junk food. The same is true for our spiritual food. We must be spending time in the Word of God daily. The more time we spend in the Word, the more we realize how weak we were before. The more time we spend, the more we learn about the character of Christ. The more time we spend, the more we will experience and the stronger we will become! We must develop spiritual muscles (disciplines) in our lives. We must feast on the Bread of Life continually. Then we will go from being prey to being vessels used by the Creator of the Universe. Taste and see.

Jennifer Gonzalez – *Silverton, TX*

get in the word

John 6:7–14

Philip answered Him, "Two hundred denarii worth of bread is not sufficient for them, that every one of them may have a little."

One of His disciples, Andrew, Simon Peter's brother, said to Him, "There is a lad here who has five barley loaves and two small fish, but what are they among so many?"

Then Jesus said, "Make the people sit down." Now there was much grass in the place. So the men sat down, in number about five thousand. And Jesus took the loaves, and when He had given thanks He distributed them to the disciples, and the disciples to those sitting down; and likewise of the fish, as much as they wanted. So when they were filled, He said to His disciples, "Gather up the fragments that remain, so that nothing is lost." Therefore they gathered them up, and filled twelve baskets with the fragments of the five barley loaves which were left over by those who had eaten. Then those men, when they had seen the sign that Jesus did, said, "This is truly the Prophet who is to come into the world."

1 Peter 5:8

Be sober, be vigilant; because your adversary the devil walks about like a roaring lion, seeking whom he may devour.

Psalm 119:103

How sweet are Your words to my taste, sweeter than honey to my mouth!

scripture memorization

Write out the scripture(s) in the space below and recite them ten times.

_____

_____

_____

_____

_____

_____

_____

_____

_____

_____

_____

_____

_____

_____

_____

_____

_____

_____

_____

_____

_____

_____

_____

_____

_____

_____

_____

_____

_____

_____

_____

_____

something to ponder

HOW MUCH time each day are you setting aside for time with the Savior?

_____

_____

_____

_____

IF YOU ARE FEELING WEAK AND frustrated, could it be that you aren't receiving the proper nourishment? How are you going to be intentional this week about feeding your soul?

_____

_____

_____

_____

DESCRIBE THINGS IN YOUR LIFE THAT hinder your time with God. If you make a list of the top five priorities in your life right now, where would Jesus be? How will you place him first in your life this week? How can you incorporate Jesus into your everyday life and learn to draw strength from him?

_____

_____

_____

_____

running observations
by dean

Treat Your Feet

HOW MANY TIMES HAVE WE HEARD about the importance of a firm foundation? When running, your feet are your foundation. It is important to take care of your feet. One minor problem with your feet can cause problems all the way up to your lower back. The good news is that it is not hard to treat your feet right! The consequences of abusing your feet are downtime, frustration, and pain.

Don't go barefoot. We have too many choices in footwear to allow ourselves to walk around without some protection on our feet. I learned this lesson the hard way years ago when I stepped on a pair of spikes lying upside down. It was the day before a race, and I was unable to run after ripping my foot open on exposed spikes. There are many hazards lurking, just waiting to catch you barefoot. Toys lying on the floor, whether from your pets or children, are disguised devices of foot mutilation. Rocks, sticks, or any small manmade item hiding in the grass has the potential not only to surprise you, but also to inflict major pain to your feet.

Don't ignore heel pain. As you age, this rule becomes more and more important.

Plantar fasciitis is a common running injury that does not have to be so prevalent. Anyone who has had it vividly remembers the pain of stepping out of bed after a good night's sleep. If that pain doesn't wake you up, it probably means you passed out from the pain. If you catch it at the onset, you can prevent major pain and weeks or months away from running. Wearing good shoes with firm arch supports (read "no flip flops") will help tremendously, but taking action will help even more. Find a firm rubber ball, place it on the floor, put your foot on top of it and roll it under your foot. Stretching out the tendons across your arch will help to relieve the pressure that is causing the problem. The pain will usually be on the bottom side of the heel, and it helps to allow the ball to dig into the painful area to break up the tightness at the source.

Make it a habit to wear good shoes all the time. No more really needs to be said, but let me state the obvious. High heels may look pretty, but they are not good for your feet. Solid synthetic materials are not good either. Your feet need to breathe. If you must wear shoes that are not good for your feet, it is important to spend time with massages and preventive care.

- *A few other important things to remember about your feet:*

- *Keep your feet away from potentially contaminated water.*

- *Always wear socks for any vigorous activity.*

- *If you get a blister, don't pop it.*

- *Use caution when exercising in new shoes. If they hurt initially, don't expect them to get better.*

- *If you are diabetic, taking care of your feet is critical.*

Never forget about the foundation. We take our feet for granted until there is a problem, and then it is impossible to forget them. In a similar way, we can go through our days focusing on programs and rituals and forget about our foundation in Jesus Christ. Having a deep relationship with Him means we won't forget His faithfulness or worry about His provision when the tough times come. We will be less likely to become tangled in sinful habits, because we will be taking our life to Christ daily. Take care of your foundation, and it will take care of you.

- *Keeping good shoes on your feet will help to ensure a healthy body, not only your feet, but also your other running muscles, tendons and ligaments.*

- *Don't ignore pain in your feet. Get to the root of the problem, and you will get in more miles.*

- *A strong relationship with Christ will ensure that our Christian walk is as healthy as it can be.*

sticky notes

_____

_____

_____

_____

_____

_____

_____

_____

_____

_____

_____

intolerance of my sin

THE ONLY HIGH SCHOOL SPORTS I was coordinated enough to participate in were cross-country & track. Fast-forward through an 11-year sabbatical (first child and 30 lbs. added) to another time of great physical fitness. I devoted myself to Pilates and kickboxing as a stress reliever. Being young and in shape allowed me to keep up without much pain. In the next ten years, our second child came home, I underwent surgery, and I permanently damaged my foot. As I look back at the seasons in my life, I see a pattern where physical fitness and life events have played tug-of-war with my time and energy. Each life event has made my physical fitness harder, more painful, and less appealing.

I have learned at least two things over the years: I tend to be complacent about my physical health, and the only way to combat that sin is to stop tolerating it. The Lord opened my eyes last year while I watched my daughter push her body past its limit into the danger zone. She has an SVT heart condition where her heart rate will increase to 270 beats a minute at any given time. Her SVT is usually triggered by exercise, which causes the blood pressure to fall due to the lack of blood being pushed out, making her lethargic. She was pushing her heart to overwork which made it enlarge as if it were on steroids. She was ignoring the pain in order to compete, and she ended up in heart ablation surgery. Around this time, she had messed up her knee also, giving her more pain to push through in competition. She would finish a race in tears, but remain determined not to quit. Watching her showed me how complacent I was about my own body.

There are many people who struggle to exercise or conquer a physical challenge and praise God for the small victories. I want to be like them. Scripture says in Hebrew 12:1, "Therefore we also, since we are surrounded by so great a cloud of witnesses, let us lay aside every weight, and the sin which so easily ensnares us, and let us run with endurance the race that is set before us."

Although I have experienced some setbacks in the past 11 months, I have progressed from walking to running by God's grace. I just have to keep moving forward. I need to run my race both physically and spiritually, because keeping up with the young ones will kill me. By doing morning squats with our daughter and keeping up with our son, I have entered a new season of connection with our kids. An expression says, "Those who pray together grow together," but add sweat and service to prayer and another layer of growing develops. Training every day to become Christ-like is hard, but doing it together makes the journey an adventure. I pray the journey you are on includes people you love, because the race is won through perseverance and perseverance requires encouragement.

Christina McKinley – *Jetmore, KS*

get in the word

Hebrews 12:1

Therefore we also, since we are surrounded by so great a cloud of witnesses, let us lay aside every weight, and the sin which so easily ensnares us, and let us run with endurance the race that is set before us.

Hebrews 10:24–25

And let us consider one another in order to stir up love and good works, not forsaking the assembling of ourselves together, as is the manner of some, but exhorting one another, and so much the more as you see the Day approaching.

Psalm 23:4

Yea, though I walk through the valley of the shadow of death,
I will fear no evil;
For You are with me;
Your rod and Your staff, they comfort me.

scripture memorization

Write out the scripture(s) in the space below and recite them ten times.

_____

_____

_____

_____

_____

_____

something to ponder

WHAT SIN DO YOU NEED TO become intolerant of?

_____

_____

_____

_____

WHY DOES GOD INSTRUCT US IN Hebrews 10 to stir up love and good works toward one another?

_____

_____

_____

_____

WHEN THE PAIN IS LOUD AND hard, what keeps you persevering for God?

_____

_____

_____

_____

running observations
by dean

Running From Responsibility

RUNNING IS THERAPEUTIC. IT BENEFITS US physically and mentally. While running, we recharge our mental batteries outside the hectic world of deadlines, complaints, cell phones, and general negativity. Our responsibilities can sometimes weigh heavily on us and cause stress that manifests itself in many negative ways. Going for a run allows us to leave those stressors and focus our minds on something more pleasant.

In a world where people are waiting in line to get a piece of your time, running allows you to pause that line and seize some time for yourself. Clearing our minds of the busyness of life lets us fill it back up with positive, uplifting thoughts. It resets our brains, like rebooting your computer to make it perform better. Clearing your brain of the clutter makes you more efficient.

Frustration runs are great too. Sometimes you have a tough day and going out to run is a great release for the accumulated frustration. Adrenaline flows, giving you a higher than average energy level, which leads to a pretty good workout. If you let it all out, you won't have to worry about sleeping that night because you will be exhausted.

And then there is the problem-solving run. Clearing your mind allows you to think through issues or conundrums you have encountered. There have been a number of times I have paused in the middle of a project to go for a run and I come home with a solution to the problem. We have all tried to recall a fact or a thought, and after digging as deeply as we can into our brain, we just can't come up with the answer. Then, an hour later, the answer comes to us from out of the blue. Clearing our heads works.

Although we can never run from our personal responsibilities, a good run feels that way. Likewise, we cannot run from our responsibilities as Christians. James tells us that faith without works is dead. When we are His, we want to follow His will. Our obligations are many, but with God's help, it doesn't feel like a burden. It is tough to leave our responsibilities in His hands because we want to do everything for ourselves, but that's what He wants us to do. Just like running doesn't relieve us of having to complete our obligations, leaving things in His hands doesn't let us off the hook for taking care of those around us. But the feeling of letting go of either of those things is tremendous.

- *Running provides a temporary escape from the responsibilities of the world.*

- *Running clears your mind so that you can think about problematic issues clearly.*

- *Giving your concerns over to God provides stress relief, knowing that He can help you through anything.*

sticky notes

_____

_____

_____

_____

_____

_____

_____

_____

_____

_____

_____

_____

_____

_____

from suffering to salvation

NOT VERY MANY PEOPLE KNOW MY past. They aren't aware of the pain I have undergone or the addictions that have plagued my life. They don't know my struggles with sin or the fact that Jesus was little-to-non-existent in my life. They see me, as I am today, a person made new by salvation in Christ. Jesus changed my life forever and used running as a platform to mold and shape me.

While stationed in Iraq in December 2009, I used most of my free time to lift weights. Cardio training was out of the question, because I despised running. The farthest I had ever run was three miles. I remember when I found out that the Boston Marathon was coming to my base, thinking, "Who in their right mind would ever run 26 miles for fun?" Many friends were signing up for the race, friends I thought would never challenge themselves to run such a distance. I decided to get out of my comfort zone and investigate marathon running. I had a tough time deciding, until one friend explained finishers get a shirt and medal. I don't know what it was about that shirt, but I thought, "That's it. I'm doing it!"

Training was rough, especially when the sandstorms came. I suffered injuries. Scheduling training around work really began to take its toll. April approached quickly and race day finally came! I'd been waiting months for this chance to test my limits, and four and a half hours into the race, I finished. I battled blisters, 100+ degree temps, and extreme fatigue. I felt horrible when I finished—honestly, the worst feeling I've ever felt post-race. I thought this had been the worst idea I'd ever had and I would never do it again. Little did I know how God would use this race to begin something new.

Growing up as the son of a preacher had its challenges. I lived to do exactly the opposite of what my parents wanted. I fell into alcohol and tobacco at an early age. After my first deployment in 2006-2007, my life went in a downward spiral. I was in a state of spiritual starvation and angry with everyone for no reason. I knew the teachings of Christ and went to church, but never really engaged in the communion of the Holy Spirit. I tried to fill my voids with sin and overlooked the fulfilling grace of Jesus.

After my first marathon, I vowed never again to run a distance that long. I stopped all training runs for 10 months. Well, a year later I just so happened to finagle my way into the actual Boston Marathon. This was an experience of a lifetime. Because of my Iraq Marathon the year prior, the Boston Athletic Association brought me in as an honoree for Patriot's Day. I attended press conferences, went to premiere events, and was even introduced to the elite athletes. I felt downright awesome! I began to consider adopting running into my life because of the connection I felt with others and the hard work that goes into a big race such as Boston. Something was still missing though. Even though I set a new personal record (PR), I felt empty. I needed some spiritual nutrition, and God was ready to feed me.

After the Boston Marathon, I decided to step out of my comfort zone and set a goal to complete an Ironman triathlon (2.4 mile swim, 112 mile bike and 26.2 mile run). I knew I had some very bad behaviors to extinguish in my life, yet no matter how hard I tried, I couldn't shake the addictions. After months of training and living a healthy life, I gave into sin. I remember one Saturday in August when the temptation consumed me. It pushed me over the edge into realizing I needed a makeover, and Jesus stepped up to give me one. At church the following day, my Lord got a hold of me. He said my life is no longer my own and I needed to die to myself so that He could take charge. No more alcohol or tobacco for me. Praise the Lord; I've been addiction-free for over three years.

A week after my rebirth, I met a gentleman named Brian who introduced me to an organization called myTeam Triumph (mTT). It is a mentorship program for those with disabilities (called captains) where able-bodied athletes (called angels) push and pull them in endurance races using specialized racing equipment. Brian was running 135 miles to raise awareness of veterans and the sacrifices they had made. This inspired me. Before this, I only ran for me. Now I saw I could run for others. Brian and Christian, mTT's executive director, pushed me to get outside my comfort zone and run for others. I took that philosophy and literally ran with it.

I met a special captain named Katie, who has cerebral palsy. She is my inspiration. She challenged me to push beyond what I believed I was capable of. Katie and I have swum, biked, and run hundreds of miles together. She taught me that we must accept who we are and make the best of our lives.

God is always present when I run. He's in the hills that challenge my motivation. He's in the water that cleanses my soul and keeps me hydrated; He's in the shoes that protect my feet and allow me to continue to live my mission. He's always there, watching over me. I was spiritually lost, and God knew that running would help me find Him. Now I know that all the challenges he put me through were to help strengthen me, so I can live as He directs. Jesus set the example for me to follow, showing how suffering leads to salvation and new life. He sacrificed His body, so that I would be saved. He endured torture and beatings, so I would be cleansed and made new. Sacrificing my body by enduring miles and pushing through pain is how I try to imitate God. When I'm fatigued, I feel consumed by His salvation. When I endure for the good of others and run for God, I'm alive.

Race Log (4 years):
10 x 5K
4 x 10K
2 x 15K
5 x Half Marathon
10 x Marathon
3 x Sprint Triathlon
1 x 50 Miler

3 x Half Ironman

Next Race: Ironman with Captain Katie

Aaron Hunnel – *Appleton, WI*

get in the word

Ephesians 5:1–2

Therefore be imitators of God as dear children. And walk in love, as Christ also has loved us and given Himself for us, an offering and a sacrifice to God for a sweet-smelling aroma.

2 Timothy 2:10–12

Therefore I endure all things for the sake of the elect, that they also may obtain the salvation which is in Christ Jesus with eternal glory. This is a faithful saying:
For if we died with Him,
We shall also live with Him.
If we endure,
We shall also reign with Him.
If we deny Him,
He also will deny us.

James 1:2–4

My brethren, count it all joy when you fall into various trials, knowing that the testing of your faith produces patience. But let patience have its perfect work, that you may be perfect and complete, lacking nothing.

scripture memorization

Write out the scripture(s) in the space below and recite them ten times.

_____

_____

_____

_____

_____

_____

_____

_____

_____

_____

_____

_____

_____

something to ponder

IN WHAT WAYS DO YOU EXPERIENCE God when you run?

_____

_____

_____

_____

HOW DO YOU OVERCOME CHALLENGES THAT you encounter t hroughout life?

_____

_____

_____

_____

WHEN WAS THE LAST TIME YOU got out of your comfort zone and learned something new?

_____

_____

_____

running observations
by dean

Barriers to Entry

A BARRIER TO ENTRY IS DEFINED as an obstacle that makes it difficult to enter a given market. It is a term usually reserved for business, but it also applies to sports. In business, the cost of getting a license, new products, and a good selling location makes it a challenge to start operating. It's the same in sports. For example, if you are going to take up golf, you will have to buy golf clubs, balls and other equipment to get started. Then you will have to pay each time you play. Golf has a moderate barrier to entry, making it inaccessible to some. Running, on the other hand, has a low barrier to entry. The cost of getting started with shoes and clothing is fairly inexpensive. Like any other sport, you can spend a lot of money, if that's your choice, but to get started, you can get by with very little.

As I write this, great athletes from many countries are playing in the World Cup. I have heard many times that the reason soccer (or football, if you are so inclined) is so popular is that it has a low barrier to entry. That made me think about running and how it differs from soccer, because I don't hear about running defined as one of the most popular sports on earth. A couple of reasons may be that soccer is a kid's game as much as it is an adult game and we define a soccer player and runner differently.

Kid's soccer is big in the United States, but adult soccer is not as big as, say, softball. Soccer is easy to understand, and you can play a pick-up game with four participants. In most countries, no other sport comes close to soccer in popularity, but why is running not as popular? I look at it this way: all soccer players are runners, but not all runners are soccer players. You have to be able to run for nearly every sport. Plus, running is a popular exercise medium for adults. So in my book, all of this means running is the most popular sport in the world, it's just not recognized as such.

While we are on the topic of low barriers to entry, consider the kingdom of God. Jesus paid a huge price for our entry into the kingdom. The only things we have to do are believe and confess. It's such a low requirement for such a heavenly reward.

- *Running is a low-cost activity that almost anyone can do.*

- *Running is part of nearly every other sport, which makes running the most popular sport in the world. Just don't tell the soccer fans.*

- *Salvation carries a monetary cost of zero and is the most precious thing we can obtain.*

sticky notes

_____

_____

_____

_____

_____

_____

_____

_____

_____

_____

_____

_____

_____

_____

fix your eyes

I HAD THE OPPORTUNITY TO COMPETE in the Firecracker 10K race on July 4th. Race time conditions were ideal with temps in the 60s. The course was a bit hilly and challenging. Bands, singers, and even crazy guys dressed up as Elvis lined the way to entertain us. They placed water stations at intervals to refresh us. Around mile five, we had a decent hill to scale followed by a nice long decent.

The Firecracker 10K was different than the other races I've competed in this year (four 5Ks and a triathlon). It doesn't matter what race a person decides to run. All runners are interested in one thing—crossing the finish line. This reminds me of a passage from 1 Corinthians 9:24–25, "Do you not know that those who run in a race all run, but one receives the prize? Run in such a way that you may obtain it. And everyone who competes for the prize is temperate in all things. Now they do it to obtain a perishable crown, but we for an imperishable crown." I am a slow runner compared to those who won this race. Did it discourage me from running? No. I was out there to do my very best, to beat my best time at 10K, and I accomplished that goal.

In life, we have two choices. We can run the race that God lays out before us, or we can run our own race and follow our own path. The path that God lays out before us will be challenging. It will have hills and valleys, good times and bad, times of thirst and times of refreshment, but in the end our Father is there to welcome us. Hebrews 12:2 tells us to look "unto Jesus, the author and finisher of our faith, who for the joy that was set before Him endured the cross, despising the shame, and has sat down at the right hand of the throne of God." As I was approaching the end of the race, I kept focusing on the finish line. I wasn't concerned about the people around me or the people trying to run me down from behind. I wasn't concerned about the last six miles of the race. My eyes were on the finish line.

No matter what you are going through right now, may I encourage you to fix your eyes on Jesus? He doesn't promise an easy race, but he does promise a great after-race party. Keep your eyes on Jesus.

Andy Feliksiak – *Rock Island, IL*

get in the word

1 Corinthians 9:24–25
Do you not know that those who run in a race all run, but one receives the prize? Run in such a way that you may obtain it. And everyone who competes for the prize is temperate in all things. Now they do it to obtain a perishable crown, but we for an imperishable crown.

Hebrews 2:9
But we see Jesus, who was made a little lower than the angels, for the suffering of death crowned with glory and honor, that He, by the grace of God, might taste death for everyone.

Colossians 3:23–24
And whatever you do, do it heartily, as to the Lord and not to men, knowing that from the Lord you will receive the reward of the inheritance; for you serve the Lord Christ.

scripture memorization

Write out the scripture(s) in the space below and recite them ten times.

_____

_____

_____

_____

_____

_____

_____

_____

_____

_____

_____

_____

_____

something to ponder

WHAT KIND OF CHALLENGES ARE YOU facing right now?

_____

_____

_____

_____

HAVE YOU TAKEN YOUR EYES OFF of Jesus and focused on other surroundings instead?

_____

_____

_____

_____

ARE YOU WILLING TO GIVE THE Lord total control of your life?

_____

_____

_____

_____

running observations
by dean

Running the Course as It Is Laid Out

LET'S SAY YOU'RE TALKING TO A running friend, and she invites you to a race four weeks from today. You're in good shape and will have no problem covering the distance of the race. What is the next question you ask? If you're like me, I want to know about the course. Is it hilly or flat, on a road or trail? Are there a lot of turns? Is the course certified? We want to know the details. Some people like hills (I call these people "crazy"). Others prefer flat, fast courses. Some prefer trails to roads. Maybe you're trying to qualify for Boston or a better position at Peachtree, which makes course certification important. Regardless of the reason, we always want to know what the course is like before we run the race.

I remember preparing for a race recently that was all the way across the country in Bend, Oregon. I sat at my computer with a map of the course and Google Earth trying to figure out how hilly the course was. I wanted to mentally prepare for the race, and it is easier if you have an idea of what the course is like. One thing struck me during this endeavor: we can't control the course or the conditions. The only person who had the first luxury, in this case, was Max King, the course designer. The fact that I know who designed the course should give a little insight into how difficult it was.

In every race, we all have to run the same course under the same conditions. It doesn't matter how much we fret over it. None of it varies from person to person. By focusing too much on how difficult the course is, we take away from truly preparing for the race. We should be thinking about how best to tackle the challenges to get the most out of our performance. You may be a poor hill runner, but the reason for that may be you have repeated it to yourself so many times. If we think it or say it enough, we'll convince ourselves.

If we don't like something about a course, the best thing we can do is to embrace the difficulty. I know people who always run well in difficult circumstances. They seem to thrive on it. It may be more accurate to say that others often fail to run well in difficult circumstances because they have defeated themselves before the race begins. The person who thrives on poor conditions knows that others are going to have difficulties and takes advantage of it. The way we battle this tendency is by not allowing negativity to enter our minds. Sure, it's easier said than done, but it is possible for anyone.

By focusing on a hopeful outcome or your goal for the race, you focus on the reward. Envisioning yourself after a race, talking about how great the race was and how well you handled difficulties, will go a long way toward a successful outcome. The great basketball coach John Wooden once said, "Things turn out best for the people who make the best of the way things turn out."

A life with God follows the same path. There are difficulties out there that we face regularly. We can focus on how difficult our course is or make the most of it, running the race to the best of our ability. The apostle Paul often compared life to a race, and we should take his advice to run for the win.

> • *Understanding the course you are going to run is important to getting the most out of your race.*

> • *Once the gun goes off, everyone in the race runs the same*

course. We can focus on how hard the course is or on having the best performance possible.

• *The Christian walk is similar to a race. Sometimes the race is difficult, but we should still run to the best of our abilities. By focusing on things we can't control, we take our eyes off the prize.*

sticky notes

_____

_____

_____

_____

_____

_____

_____

_____

I will never be fast

I HAVE COME TO THE REALIZATION that I will never be fast. I used to be at least sort of fast, but as my years have advanced, my speed has diminished. With that in mind, it would be easy to get discouraged and give up, but then things like the following happen to keep me going.

Tonight I participated in a local "Go H.A.R.D." (Hug A Runner Day) event. It was only a mile run; totally for fun and just what I needed as I start to work back into running again.

I started out with all the other runners at an easy jog. The best part was watching the parents with their kids make their way around the course. Before long, I found myself running alone. I've noticed that happens a lot. A bunch of runners are ahead of me, a few are behind me, and I run alone. That's okay. To be honest, I am kind of comfortable in that spot. I actually like running alone.

Then I came up behind two little girls who had sped past me earlier. They were walking now. I encouraged them a couple of times to keep going. They would take off at top speed, only to have me plod up behind them in a few seconds.

Finally, I came alongside the smaller one (I'll call her "pink kitty" since she wore a pink kitten hat). I told her I'd run alongside her until we reached the end. She started to kick on the jets again, but I told her to slow down—we'd just go slow.

She was doing her best. She looked up at me and said, "My heart hurts! It feels like it's breaking!"

I nodded, "I know. That's your heart growing stronger. Don't stop. Don't give up. You can do this."

We ran beside each other while I chatted about her cool hat and her school, encouraging her often. She was a fast runner for a 5 year old. "I don't think I could have run that fast when I was 5," I said.

She looked up and asked, "How old are you?"

"I'm 54. Pretty old, huh." She nodded. (Funny, at the moment it felt pretty good to be that old.)

Step by step we ran together. "Not much farther," I said.

As the finish line approached she wanted to speed up, but I told her to hold back until the final turn. We got into that turn, and I told her I wanted her to run as hard as she could. I figured she'd leave me behind when she kicked in those afterburners, but we weren't done. She gave it a burst of speed, but then I could see her slowing. I had to speed up and run beside her again, egging her on.

Pink Kitty crossed the finish line at full speed, so proud of herself and what she had done. She had finished her mile run.

I was pretty happy too. Not because I had run my fastest mile (far from it), but instead I helped someone else reach her goal.

The Christian walk is a lot like this run. Sometimes I feel my best days are behind me, that I'm not nearly as fast as I once was. Only now, I have a better reason to run. I get to come alongside others who are just starting their race, those whose hearts feel like they are breaking, and encourage them with the knowledge they will get stronger.

I can help them get their minds off the pain. I can remind them to slow down and take one step at a time. I get to watch them do things they never thought possible.

I'll never be fast like some of them, but this is my race, the one that allows me to meet people all along the way to say, "You can do this." This is why I run. Care to join me?

Donna Sumrall – *Hattiesburg, MS*

get in the word

1 Thessalonians 5:11
Therefore comfort each other and edify one another, just as you also are doing.

Hebrews 10:22–25
Let us draw near with a true heart in full assurance of faith, having our hearts sprinkled from an evil conscience and our bodies washed with pure water. Let us hold fast the confession of our hope without wavering, for He who promised is faithful. And let us consider one another in order to stir up love and good works, not forsaking the assembling of ourselves together, as is the manner of some, but exhorting one another, and so much the more as you see the Day approaching.

scripture memorization

Write out the scripture(s) in the space below and recite them ten times.

_____

_____

_____

_____

_____

_____

_____

_____

_____

_____

_____

_____

something to ponder

WHO CAN you encourage today?

_____

_____

_____

_____

WHAT THINGS discourage you?

_____

_____

_____

_____

WHAT DO YOU SHARE WITH OTHERS that gives you the greatest joy?

_____

_____

_____

_____

running observations
by dean

What Is the Definition of Fast?

DO YOU KNOW SOMEONE WHO IS fast? How fast are they? Everyone has a different opinion on the definition of fast. For example, I think running a 5K in under 16 minutes is fast. (Runner's World says running a 5K in under 25 minutes means you are a committed runner.) You see, fast often means faster than me.

So, how important is it to be fast? Three words: not at all. That's one of the most beautiful things about running. We love to talk about the latest Galen Rupp race, but we also love to talk to our buddies about their races too. I can get as excited that a friend at work, who is new to running, ran under 30 minutes for a 5K as I do that Rupp set an American record in the indoor two mile.

Being fast only gets you a little name recognition and some hardware. The real benefits of running come in the form of better health and lasting friendships. I have tremendous respect for those who spend more time on the course than I do, but work just as hard. It may be easy to get motivated when you are going to run with the leaders of many races or compete for age group awards, but the people I have the most respect for are the ones who are just there to participate, push themselves as hard as they can go, and hang out with a great bunch of people. Do they see this as a competition? No, they avoid that distraction.

Don't get me wrong. Competition is fun and I love it. It used to drive me through every race, but when I made the decision a few years ago to focus on people who were not my direct competition, the races became so much more enjoyable. I feel like my running world doubled in size. My absolute favorite moments are when someone is running their first 5K, and as they cross the finish line, they become overwhelmed with emotion because they have accomplished something they never thought they could. I never get tired of that one. Eight years ago, I missed it every time.

Similarly, if we were solely focused on keeping up with the Joneses, our jobs, or anything else, we would miss out on big moments with people around us. Not only that, we would be in danger of making an idol for ourselves. By focusing on the things of God, we see so much more. When we attend church on Sunday and Wednesday, but leave God out of every other day, we're not living the full life that He intends for us to live.

- *It is not important to be fast unless that is the focus of your running. There is nothing wrong with wanting to be as fast as you can be.*

- *Competition can get in the way. It's great to enjoy the local rivalry, but don't forget about everybody else.*

- *Focusing on God opens up a wide world that we miss while focused on ourselves*

sticky notes

_____

_____

_____

_____

_____

_____

_____

_____

_____

_____

_____

_____

_____

_____

_____

_____

_____

_____

run the race God has set before you

ONE SUNDAY MORNING DURING THE MEET and greet time at church, two ladies commented on my upbeat personality. One woman said that I am always so bubbly, and another said that I always smile. I didn't have time to tell them that I don't always wake up that way. Some days I have to talk myself into that smile. I also have to remind myself daily to be grateful for all I have and force myself not to dwell on things I don't need.

Every morning, I mentally prepare myself to face the world. I hit snooze a few times. I get up, go into the bathroom, and look at the scared person staring at me in the mirror. I make breakfast and pack lunch for my son and myself, but during this whole process, I am in prayer. If you were sitting in my kitchen watching me, you might think I was doing what any normal mom does as a morning routine. If you were to look closer though, you would see that I was quietly talking.

I give my fear and anxiety over to God. Jesus says I don't have to carry that burden, so I try not to. I thank God for the food I am preparing, the home we live in, the little boy laughing at cartoons in the other room, the heat, electricity, and the most basic of things that I take for granted every day. By the time I am ready to walk out the door, all of the worldly junk that fills my mind has finally been cleared. When I get to my porch, I am able to greet my neighbors with a smile.

Most people don't understand how I can be so positive all the time. It is simple. I choose not to worry about what I can't control. I choose to give the negativity, illness, worry, and stress in my life over to God, but I didn't learn to do that on my own.

In January 2013, my sister convinced me to join a local Run for God 5K challenge. Scared and worried about embarrassing myself, I agreed to try it. I ran track in junior high and high school, and I was so bad my parents begged me to quit at the end of my freshman season. Run for God was not what I expected at all. Everyone was so warm and friendly. The program is tailored to reach people of all faith levels and fitness levels, and God did what God does. He met me where I was and carried me to the finish line.

The Run for God class prepared me to begin a journey back to God. Each week I read the story and listened to people's responses to the discussion questions, and I thought, "Why am I so angry all the time? I have a good life in spite of being a single mom. I have enough money for all the things my son and I need, a wonderful family, and a good job. Why can't I just be happy?" During week three of our Run for God class, the discussion was titled "Running Your Own Race: Running the Race God Has Set before You." I knew then that it wasn't my sister who led me to the class, but God.

My sister is extremely athletic. She runs much faster than I do, but when we trained together for the 5K, she never left my side. She pushed me through each work out, running beside me step by step. She refused to allow me to quit or fail. A week before our race, the words "run your own race" rattled around in my head. My sister would have stayed with me through the whole course if I had wanted her to, but I decided it was time for me to trust God and let Him carry me to the finish line. I told her to go run her race, meet her time goals, and I would run mine.

I was scared out of my mind when the gun went off, but I turned on my mp3 player and went on my way. I became discouraged in the first half mile because I felt as if hundreds of people were passing me. I knew I had to change my focal point, so I concentrated on my breathing and paced myself to the beat of the music. Around the one-mile marker, I started seeing the leaders of the race looping back. I passed people from my RFG group as they headed back to the finish line. They were over half way done with the race and I had at least a mile ahead of me. They were throwing me high five's and yelling, "Good job!" I felt overwhelmed by their love. God was showing His love through them.

My sister's house is about half way through the course, and when I reached it, I cried. My son was sitting in the front yard with my mom. He yelled and waved a sign that read "GO MOMMY!" It took about 300 feet for me to pull myself back together, but I picked up the pace and started the loop back. As my music carried me, I felt a second surge of energy take me into the last mile. Then I saw my sister, who had already crossed the finish line, running toward me. She ran the last mile with me, encouraging me to stay strong. She stepped off to the side about 200 feet from the end, and in the photo of me crossing the finish line, you can see her in the background with her hands around her mouth, yelling at the top of her lungs.

Faith and God's great love carried me through that race. Run for God taught me that anything is possible with God on my side and faith in my heart. I smile and have a happy heart today, because I am running God's race.

In Galatians, Paul says they are focused on the wrong things. Christ gave them a mission. He has given each of us a mission. I had to run a 5K to realize my mission, and now that I am running my race, I don't plan to ever look back. Every morning I wake up, praise God, and ask Him to show me what path I need to run. Without Him, I would be lost on the trail.

Katie Hendricks – *Carrollton, OH*

get in the word

Galatians 5:7–8

You ran well. Who hindered you from obeying the truth? This persuasion does not come from Him who calls you.

Joshua 1:9

Have I not commanded you? Be strong and of good courage; do not be afraid, nor be dismayed, for the Lord your God is with you wherever you go.

Philippians 4:13

I can do all things through Christ who strengthens me.

scripture memorization

Write out the scripture(s) in the space below and recite them ten times.

_____

_____

_____

_____

something to ponder

WHAT ARE YOU WITHHOLDING FROM GOD? What burdens do you carry that you should give up to Him?

_____

_____

_____

_____

WHEN WAS THE LAST TIME YOU stepped out of your comfort zone and allowed God to carry you through your fears?

_____

_____

_____

_____

DO YOU SPEND TIME WITH GOD each day, asking Him about your mission in order to avoid allowing Satan a foothold for distraction?

_____

_____

_____

running observations
by dean

Thank the Volunteers

RACES ARE GREAT FUN! IT DOESN'T matter if it is a local race with 100 participants or a party moving down Peachtree Street in Atlanta called "The Peachtree Road Race." There are mud runs, color runs, and foam runs. Some races are plotted through downtown areas, some through the woods. Some have tons of awards; some are no-frills. There are 5Ks, 100 milers, triathlons, and duathlons. There is a race for everyone. Whether a race requires a lot of planning or only needs someone to draw a line in the dirt, they all have one thing in common—volunteers.

Many volunteers are runners themselves and understand what you are going through as you run. Many of them get up early on Saturday mornings to help their community or the race's charitable beneficiary: Boy Scouts, Girl Scouts, or ROTC for example. Almost any race that takes place on the roads will employ the services of the local police department, and although they may be paid for their services, they usually volunteer to do the work.

Race directors have a huge responsibility to bring their event together for everyone to enjoy. Have you ever wondered how the portable toilets show up for the event? Yes, the race director has to pay attention to every detail, and at most events they have curve balls thrown at them all day long. They must make decisions quickly, because more questions are coming in another three minutes. Usually when I want to talk to the race director on race morning, I have to wait in line.

On race day, those who hand out drinks, tell you where to turn, and protect you from traffic have put love and time into their roles under a director's supervision in order to give you a great experience. If you are not one who already tells the volunteers how much you appreciate them, tell someone the next time you race. For most events, volunteering means giving up a day to a cause, and you are part of that cause. Remember that whenever something doesn't go well for you. These people care about doing things right. I once ran a marathon and was going to receive the first place masters award. When they called out the winner, the time was fifteen minutes slower than my time. Imagine my shock. I calmly walked to the front to explain what had happened, and the race director sent me a trophy in the mail the next week. Problem solved, and I didn't need to get upset about it.

Like a race, God has set up a course for us to follow. He is standing at the corners telling us which way to turn. He has aid stations along the way to help with any need. He waits for us at the finish line with something much better than a medal—everlasting life.

- *Races are full of volunteers trying to make your day the best it can be.*

- *The volunteers really like to hear appreciation from participants, so thank someone at your next event.*

- *God wants us to run His course. He said it would not be the easy course, but it will be worth the effort.*

sticky notes

_____

_____

_____

_____

_____

_____

_____

_____

_____

_____

_____

my Lord's patient faithfulness

"FOR I KNOW THE THOUGHTS THAT I think toward you, says the Lord, thoughts of peace and not of evil, to give you a future and a hope" (*Jeremiah 29:11*).

I thought knowing Jeremiah 29:11 would be enough, but looking back at my past, I realize its deep truth. As a 220 lb. couch potato who ate junk food and would not even utter the word exercise, I read that verse and thought that on some far away day (like maybe in heaven) I would have hope and a future. I knew what it said, but I didn't believe it. Then I came to a medical crossroad where I had to make lifestyle decisions to avoid the onset of diabetes. I was already on blood pressure medication at the time and did not take the doctor's warning seriously enough to change anything.

Later on, we moved to a new town, got a new doctor, and heard a much worse diagnosis—type 2 diabetes. The doctor agreed to let me try lifestyle changes, but once again I fell short. Feeling defeated, I wondered what plans God had for me, not realizing that the answer was in front of me. My new doctor was an Ironman. With my shopping bag full of medications, I left the drug store and headed across the parking lot to work.

I worked as a fitness technician, so I had all the tools I needed but was not using all of them. My boss approached me about teaching the weight management program, and I needed to try it myself, so I could be more effective as an instructor. As I rose to the occasion, the inches started melting off me. Then I saw a poster for a half/full marathon and found out they accepted walkers. I raised the funds I needed, trained, and travelled from Ontario, Canada, to San Diego, California, in 2005 to walk my first half marathon. Over the next six years, I tried a couple of times to train without success. In 2011, I trained for and ran a 5K race that April. Following that success, I packed my running shoes away for six months. Then in October, I rallied myself to try again and ended up walking two half marathons in June and September 2012.

That September, our church in Ontario, Canada, started a Run for God group. I coached the walkers for the fall and spring sessions. During the spring session, the Lord led me to get involved in myTeam Triumph. In July, I went to Iowa with two other girls from our group along with several ladies from another Run for God group in Michigan. We participated in the Bix 7 race and spent an afternoon in mission work. These wonderful Run for God girls inspired me to continue pursuing my goals. They believed in God's plan for me.

Years ago, I could not have imagined the joy I would feel in sharing my faith and being encouraged by the many Christian runners and walkers I've met. God has been faithful to me. He has patiently waited for me to realize the plan He has had for me. I now am keeping my shoes laced and moving forward, knowing all is possible with the Lord by my side.

Vicki Burgess – *Ontario, Canada*

get in the word

Jeremiah 29:11

For I know the thoughts that I think toward you, says the LORD, thoughts of peace and not evil, to give you a future and a hope.

Psalm 136:1–2

Oh, give thanks to the Lord, for He is good!
*   For His mercy endures forever.*
Oh, give thanks to the God of gods!
*   For His mercy endures forever.*

John 14:27

Peace I leave with you, My peace I give to you; not as the world gives do I give to you. Let not your heart be troubled, neither let it be afraid.

scripture memorization

Write out the scripture(s) in the space below and recite them ten times.

_____

_____

_____

_____

_____

_____

_____

_____

_____

_____

_____

_____

_____

_____

_____

_____

_____

_____

_____

_____

_____

_____

_____

_____

_____

_____

_____

_____

_____

_____

something to ponder

DO YOU really believe in God's everlasting faithfulness?

_____

_____

_____

_____

DOES RUNNING THE RACE THAT GOD has set before you appear to be too big for you to accomplish?

_____

_____

_____

_____

DO YOU FEEL ALONE AS YOU face the changes you are making and as you work towards your goals?

_____

_____

_____

running observations by dean

The Padawan Becomes the Master

I KNOW MANY RUNNING FAMILIES IN which everyone or nearly everyone runs. You'll see the entire family show up for local running events. Not many activities allow a whole family to participate on equal footing, but running does. It certainly makes it easier for everyone to understand why it is important to do things like getting up early on a Saturday morning to get a long run in before it gets too hot.

A running friend of mine has a son who runs middle school cross country and track and gets better each year. My friend, who is over 50, is a fast runner who wins awards at most of his races. Until recently, his son had never beaten him. On the day he did, his son referred to the Star Wars Jedi as he passed by, "The padawan has become the master." My friend was so proud.

My wife, Debbie, has run off and on for most of her life but has had difficulties with it. She has taken up many other activities to keep herself in shape. Last year, she attended one of my beginning running classes. Now she runs, and I love it. For the first time, we are able to run miles together. To share running with her is a highlight for me. I've also enjoyed running with one of my sons when he was in high school cross-country. Passing on my running experiences was a lot of fun for both of us. I can imagine how much fun it would be to run with your entire family.

Another running friend of mine has a mother who took up competition in her eighties. She has even held a few state records for her age, so it is never too late to share running with your family. For those who have relatives who feel like they can never run, there are thousands of examples that prove nearly anyone can run. Look them up and share some of them.

Sharing a race with friends is great, but it is even more special to share running with those you love the most. Having someone else in the family run with you can encourage you deeply. In the same way, having the support and friendship of your church family blesses you greatly. Like brothers who help during adversity, our church family can walk with us as we walk with Christ, but it is much more fulfilling to have that kind of relationship with your family at home. Both of my boys were saved on my front porch. I can't think of anything more precious than sharing Jesus Christ with them.

- *Sharing running with family builds memories that will last a lifetime.*

- *Having family members who run helps them to understand those uncommon things you do related to running.*

- *Sharing the successes and questions of your faith with family will deepen your relationship with God.*

sticky notes

Week 20

on becoming a grace-filled runner

I HAD RUN THE SAME ROUTE dozens, maybe hundreds, of times, and yet this morning felt different. My legs were almost as heavy as my heart. I was only a mile in. The sun had not crested the horizon. I chugged up the hill and stopped, collapsing on the curb of a country road, defeated.

It wasn't like me. I'm not a quitter. My very nature defines me as a leader who is persistent and tenacious, a perfectionist to the core, but early that morning, this perfectionist crumbled before the Lord. For many months prior to that run, I'd been living, working, running in my own strength. I woke extremely early to log miles. I counted calories and turned my body into a machine that delivered results. I scheduled my runs religiously and calculated my pace, splits, and other nerdy runner variables. I constantly thought about exercise and how to better myself as a runner. As I sat there on that curb, watching the sunrise and calling out to the Lord, I was weary of striving. That's when I heard, "My yoke is easy and my burden is light. Cease striving and know that I am God; I will be exalted."

It wasn't instantaneous or pretty, but I gradually learned to walk (and run) in His grace. I gave up the legalistic practices that bound me. If I needed to miss a workout, I remembered that the Lord's grace was sufficient for me. When I felt myself start the striving again, I knew my focus had shifted and needed to be placed back upon the Lord. After all, it is only because of Him that I am able to run or do anything in this life.

Years later as the mother of two little ones, I still love running, but my schedule (if one can even call it that) looks completely different. I run two or three times a week, most often pushing a jogging stroller. We stop frequently to pick up a dropped toy or check out a beautiful flower. I have no idea what my pace is on most runs or even how far I've gone. Counting calories has been replaced by my desire to fuel well and feed my family healthy meals. I still occasionally struggle with that old perfectionist, but my prayer continues to be that my life, running included, will be enveloped by His grace. He will be exalted, not me. May my life and my running glorify Him as an expression of thankfulness for His freeing, life-giving grace.

Kristen Townsend – *Fredericksburg, TX*

get in the word

Matthew 11:30
For My yoke is easy and My burden is light.

Psalm 46:10
Be still, and know that I am God;
I will be exalted among the nations,
I will be exalted in the earth!

1 John 5:4
For whatever is born of God overcomes the world. And this is the victory that has overcome the world—our faith.

scripture memorization

Write out the scripture(s) in the space below and recite them ten times.

_____

_____

_____

_____

_____

_____

_____

_____

_____

_____

_____

_____

_____

_____

something to ponder

IN WHAT WAYS ARE YOU STRIVING today? How can you turn those things over the Lord?

_____

_____

_____

_____

DOES YOUR life reflect the grace you've been given? What does that look like for you?

_____

_____

_____

_____

HOW CAN your running schedule better exalt Him?

_____

_____

_____

running observations by dean

Form Follows Function

WHAT DOES PERFECT RUNNING FORM LOOK like? Every sport has a technique that becomes the model that we refer to as perfect form. If you are a golf fan, you have seen Jim Furyk play. Golf is a sport where form is critical to good performance, and Furyk doesn't display perfect form. But he gets the important stuff right. Similar to a golf swing, some elements of running form outweigh others. Not everyone can look like Olympian Ryan Hall while running, but we can get the important elements right.

Being comfortable is important, but it's also the number one contributor to poor running form. Most people just go out and run and never give a thought to form, so they find their comfort zone, and with much repetition it becomes their personal default form. Instead of this, you want to develop a comfortable form within the guidelines of an efficient form. Here are a couple of ways to improve. First, run fast. Typically, running fast forces your body into your most efficient form. Second, run barefoot. If you want to feel what it is like to run as efficiently as you can, take off your shoes and run strides on the grass. Do you land more towards the front of your foot and less on the heel? Today's shoes with their big, thick heels tend to encourage us to land on our heels, which is not the most efficient way to run.

Many flaws come from being lazy with our form. It's akin to our seated posture. It is easy to sit with our shoulders hunched over. In the same way, it is easy to run without being upright. The next time you are out running, think about being as tall as possible. You will feel more energy. You'll think you are bouncing from one foot to the other more quickly than you used to. Now bend forward slightly from your feet and your body position should be in proper alignment. Just remember that the forward lean is from your feet, not from your hips.

Be careful not to over-stride. Your feet should land under you, not out in front of you. A stride that is too long is inefficient and can lead to injury. A better way to speed up is to increase your cadence.

And finally, relax. I see a lot of runners who are too tight in the shoulders, arms and neck areas. Relax your arms and shoulders. You will be amazed how much relaxation will speed you up as you transfer that energy to the task at hand.

In the New Testament, we read over and over again about the Pharisees' tight focus on rules and the formality of their religious rituals. God wants authenticity, not trite repetition. In running, there are basic elements of form that are important, but not every detail is critical. We just need to run. With the Lord, we just need to worship. How we worship varies from one person to the next, because what matters most is our heart.

- *Running in bare feet on the grass can give you a feel for what good running form feels like.*

- *Running with good form will make you feel more energized.*

- *We need to focus on the important elements and not get bogged down in the details. That's true for running and for worship.*

sticky notes

_____

_____

_____

_____

_____

_____

_____

_____

_____

_____

_____

_____

_____

_____

Week

"are you okay? you've lost a lot of weight."

A FUNNY QUESTION I GET ALL the time now is whether I'm okay because of my weight loss. Here's the reason they ask. I've been a leader much of my life. As a former high school and college athlete, both football and track captain, I led by example. I grew up in church and lived a life free of the challenges that many teens and young adults encounter today. Fast forward 24 years, I was tired all the time, no energy, achy joints, overweight and generally unhappy. I had no reason to be unhappy. God had blessed me with a wonderful wife. We stood by each other through a battle with infertility and were rewarded for our faithfulness with two children through adoption. I felt blessed for the life I had, but I was still unhappy.

The unhappiness had to do with what I had become. My once fit body was now an embarrassment to me. My body as God's temple (*1 Corinthians 3:16*) had fallen in disrepair from years of neglect. Keeping up with my three-year-old son had become extremely difficult. I watched my daughter play on the playground with her friends and their fathers, because I was too tired to run around with them. It was time to do something.

In July 2013, I learned about a course that our church was going to offer. It was called "Run For God – The 5K Challenge." I thought I would give it a try, but there was no way I'd run a 5K at the end. I told my wife about the group, and to my surprise she said she was thinking of joining too. (I say, "to my surprise," because she was and is in great shape.) Even though I was my high school's track captain, I never ran distance. I was a sprinter and took pride in the fact that I successfully avoided running any distance over a mile all through my high school career. I couldn't imagine running 3.1 miles.

The day of our first meeting I weighed in at 245 lbs. I was six foot two inches tall, with an 18" neck, 48" chest, and 40" waist. I struggled through the first workout. The 60-second run was difficult for me, but I made it. Each workout challenged me enough to do good, but not enough to break my will. Week after week, I stuck to the program and found myself wanting, even needing, to run. It had become a time I could escape my world and draw close to God (James 4:8). I also found myself shedding weight. I started feeling better, my disposition changed, and my strength was being renewed (*Isaiah 40:31*). Not only would I "mount up with wings like eagles," but I would "run and not be weary."

My first 5K was October 4, 2013. By race day I had lost 40 lbs. I completed my race, but I wasn't done. I had been sharing my story on Facebook and discovered I had a large group following my progress. Many said I had inspired them to start running. I had become a leader again. Since my first 5K, I've run in two additional races and am registered for three more. I've logged almost 400 miles since I started tracking them in September 2013. My new goal is to complete a half marathon.

I'm still 6'2", but now I weigh 185 lbs. with a 16" neck, 42" chest and 33" waist. My dramatic weight loss has become an opportunity to share my faith and story with people I encounter through my occupation. I believe God has given me these results so I can witness. God has used "Run For God – The 5K Challenge" to change my life, so now others are experiencing the program because of the change they see in me.

Todd Myers – *Oregon, IL*

get in the word

1 Corinthians 3:16

Do you not know that you are the temple of God and that the Spirit of God dwells in you?

James 4:8

Draw near to God and He will draw near to you.
Cleanse your hands, you sinners; and purify your hearts,
you double-minded.

Philippians 1:6

... being confident of this very thing, that He who has begun a good work in you will complete it until the day of Jesus Christ;

scripture memorization

Write out the scripture(s) in the space below and recite them ten times.

_____

_____

_____

_____

_____

_____

_____

_____

_____

_____

_____

_____

_____

_____

_____

_____

_____

_____

_____

_____

....

something to ponder

WHAT DOES it mean to you that you are God's temple?

_____

_____

_____

_____

HOW DO you draw near to God?

_____

_____

_____

_____

HOW WILL you witness to someone today?

_____

_____

_____

_____

running observations
by dean

There's No Such Thing as Bad Weather

BILL BOWERMAN WAS A TRACK AND field coach who trained 31 Olympic athletes, 51 All-Americans, 12 American record holders, 24 NCAA champions, and 16 four-minute milers in his 24 years at the University of Oregon. There are many famous quotes attributed to him but my favorite has to be: "There is no such thing as bad weather, just soft people." It's a pretty direct statement, maybe even harsh, but it has a ring of truth to it.

Of course, there is such a thing as bad weather. I wouldn't want to minimize the effects of bad weather events, but that wasn't really what Mr. Bowerman was talking about. He was talking about commitment. Of the many levels of commitment, we all must choose one. We certainly don't need the same level of commitment as an Olympic athlete who lives and breathes running, but if we don't have some expectation for ourselves, we tend to flounder and do less than we want. We don't reach even the vague goal we had in the back of our minds. If we decide what we are going to do and hold ourselves to it, we will fulfill it.

There is nothing wrong with running in the rain (except for lightning) as long as you don't mind people thinking you're crazy. Running in the snow is kind of fun as long as it's not too icy and slick. Cold and hot weather can be tough, but you can plan around it for the most part. In the summer I will often run early in the morning, which requires me to plan the day before. Other times I will wait until the sun is going down. For cold weather, a treadmill is a reasonable alternative. I never skip my run because it is too hot or too cold.

When you allow yourself to use weather as an excuse, other reasons to skip a workout come just as easily. I've seen a lot of missed runs because "something just came up." Of course, if your level of commitment is such that you are okay with skipping the occasional workout, that's fine, but most runners are bummed out when they miss a run. It delays their training goals. All it takes is a higher level of commitment.

If we know we're not going to get hurt by getting a little wet or a little cold, we can handle being uncomfortable. Even if you wouldn't trust your weatherman to bring you a cup of coffee, he is usually accurate about temperature and precipitation. Planning around rain or high wind is definitely possible when you know it's coming. For me, I like to act like a kid when I run in the rain. Try stomping through puddles like a five year old without having any fun. I don't think it's possible. Choose your level of commitment and stick to it.

Of course, God expects our commitment to Him. Not only that, He expects our highest level of commitment. Jesus said we should love God with all our heart, soul, and mind. According to John 3:16, God holds nothing back from us, so we should hold nothing back from Him. We reap tremendous rewards by being fully committed to our Lord.

- *Being committed to running means dealing with less than ideal weather.*

- *With a little planning, we can minimize the effect of weather.*

- *God gave us His Son in return for our highest level of commitment.*

sticky notes

_____

_____

_____

_____

_____

_____\

don't limit what God can do

WHILE TRAINING FOR MY FIRST MARATHON I felt some pain in my right knee and decided to go see my doctor. I wanted to be sure my knee was okay to run the next day. He said I probably had a small stress fracture.

He asked, "Why are you running a marathon—to prove a point?"

"I'm raising money for melanoma cancer research in memory of my brother and his wife," I said. They had both passed away from melanoma 16 months apart.

The doctor got choked up and said, "If I were you, I'd still run it."

I started to cry. I had thought he was going to tell me not to run it. Instead, he told me to take a week off of training and then see how it goes. So after a week I got things started again with a 13.5 mile run.

During this run, the chorus to a worship song ran through my mind. It was a wonderful time with God. My knee felt okay afterward, so I resumed my training. I found a running group that did run/walk intervals. I did 20 miles of slow running with these ladies, and my knee felt good. No pain. I thought for sure I didn't have a stress fracture until the dull ache returned a couple runs later. It was five weeks until the race, and I decided my knee needed more rest. I told a couple of running friends, who suggested riding my bike instead, but I got mixed reactions from others.

Some said, "Don't run the marathon and risk injury." Others said, "Taking a break is a good idea, but you need to do more runs before the marathon." Others were supportive of my plan.

At this point, I wasn't sure what God wanted me to do, so I sought the Lord for some answers. One day while reading my Bible, that worship chorus came to mind. The song is entitled "Oceans (Where Feet May Fail)." I had been hearing it a lot on the radio, so looked up the words and wrote them out.

"Spirit lead me where my trust is without borders.

Let me walk upon the waters, wherever you would call me.

Take me deeper than my feet could ever wander,

And my faith will be made stronger, in the presence of my Savior."

This song is all about trust, not putting God into a box, not limiting what God could do by my lack of faith. I started searching Scripture. I wanted to know if He wanted me to run this marathon. If I took a break from training, would I still be able to run the race? I came across the end of Isaiah 41:13. "Fear not, I will help you." It leapt off the page at me. I felt a peace wash over me. At that point I wasn't worried about how many miles were left in my training program. I had to give my knee complete rest from any impact. Absolutely no running.

"I got the message, Lord."

After four weeks of rest, I tested my knee out again. The pain I had left was very minor. I ran four miles plus a slow jog and some walking for another four and a half miles. My knee felt a little achy afterward, but after a couple days the pain was completely gone.

Rain fell the weekend before the race, and I did the last eight-mile training run with my running buddies. On the way to the park, the clouds parted, the sun shone through, and a double rainbow hung over the park. As I got out of the car the rain started again. My friends and I took off down the trail. They were faster than me, but I let them go ahead and ran alone with my mp3 player. I wasn't alone after all; I was running with God. Every step of that run in the rain was a blessing. I felt no pain, and I worshipped God. The following week I felt no pain, and by race day I was ready to go.

During the race, I ran with the ladies' running group I mentioned earlier. We ran/walked 12 miles together, and mile after mile the water stations were out of sports drink. I darted across the street to see if there was a water station on the other side. Nothing. I pressed on alone, resigned to the possibility that it would just be my mp3 player, my God, and me. Then "Oceans" started playing.

I prayed God would help me rely on Him. It was a sunny, 80-degree day, and I needed electrolytes. A friend caught up with me at mile 14, and said, "If you can hang on until mile 16, I have some friends waiting for me. They can help you." When we found them, they gave me a water bottle and shoved a handful of electrolyte tablets into a baggie. They were angels of mercy! As we approached mile 19, I said I was cramping up and could no longer run. I told my friend to go on ahead of me, knowing God would take care of me.

I started to walk and continued praying and worshipping. As I passed mile 21, I felt a renewed strength and started running again. I felt like I was soaring. Isaiah 40:31 says, "But those who wait on the Lord shall renew their strength; they shall mount up with wings like eagles, they shall run and not be weary, they shall walk and not faint." That was me. I finished strong, thankful to God for His help and provision.

On the back of my running shirt, I put Romans 5:3–4. "And not only that, but we also glory in tribulations, knowing that tribulation produces perseverance; and perseverance, character; and character, hope." God used my training and this race to teach me perseverance in the midst of my suffering. He wanted to mature godly characteristics in me, and in the midst of it all, I learned to trust in Him more deeply and press on in hope.

Anna Dwinger – *Orange, CA*

get in the word

James 1:6
But let him ask in faith, with no doubting, for he who doubts is like a wave of the sea driven and tossed by the wind.

Philippians 4:19
And my God shall supply all your need according to His riches in glory by Christ Jesus.

Isaiah 58:11
The Lord will guide you continually,
And satisfy your soul in drought,
And strengthen your bones;
You shall be like a watered garden,
And like a spring of water, whose waters do not fail.

scripture memorization

Write out the scripture(s) in the space below and recite them ten times.

_____

_____

_____

_____

_____

_____

_____

_____

_____

_____

_____

_____

_____

_____

_____

something to ponder

HAVE YOU ever gotten mixed messages from well meaning friends?

_____

_____

_____

_____

IN WHAT ways can we hear God's voice speaking to us now?

_____

_____

_____

_____

WHEN YOUR faith and trust have been challenged, how have you handled it?

_____

_____

_____

_____

running observations
by dean

Waves and Rainbows

HAVE YOU EVER HAD ONE OF those days when you start running through your routine and out of the blue you start feeling great? As a runner, this is one of the most enjoyable surprises you'll find. The feeling of floating along at a great pace with little effort will energize you like nothing else. Sometimes that feeling comes during a race, and you surpass your personal goal by more than you thought possible. Runs like that give you confidence to keep going and work even harder to improve. They brighten your mood for a good 24 hours.

On the other end of the spectrum are the days when you feel as if your legs weigh 100 pounds each. You try to push through, but it never comes together. You run along at a pace that is thirty seconds to a minute slower than your average pace, but you labor much harder than you normally do. You question your training schedule, and begin to think about changing course. It tears down your confidence.

These are memorable experiences, but they are anomalies. They are outliers we should discard when we are evaluating where we are in our training plan. That bad feeling is like a wave coming to the shore. It is temporary and needs to be understood in context. It will crash on the beach and dissipate. That good feeling is like a rainbow set in the sky, so appreciate it for what it is—beautiful and temporary.

I love the good days, the bad days, and everything in between. I believe we have to take each day and appreciate it for what it becomes. It is easy to find joy in the good times, but if we want to be successful, we have to find joy in the tough days too. Otherwise, we run the risk of letting those days have a negative effect on us. When we allow too much negativity, it will have a detrimental effect on our training. Looking at tough days in a positive light is difficult to do. It takes a change of our normal state of mind, and the best person to help with changing our state of mind is Christ.

In 2 Corinthians 4:18, the Bible tells us this: "... while we do not look at the things which are seen, but at the things which are not seen. For the things which are seen are temporary, but the things which are not seen are eternal." When we fix our eyes on the things of God, we have a perspective of what is important. When we understand what is important, we can see through the bad days and simply enjoy the good days, whether we're looking at running or anything else we do.

- *Some days are better than expected. Some are worse. That's okay.*

- *Both the good days and the bad days are temporary and should be understood as such.*

- *When we have our thoughts planted in the right place, we can find joy in both the good days and the bad days.*

sticky notes

crashing into God's purpose

"EVERYTHING HAPPENS FOR A REASON," I assured myself while lying on the floor in my pitch black, silent bedroom. After crashing twice in a cycling race, both times hitting the back of my head, my life changed. Before March 19, 2011, I was a traditional collegiate student-athlete: healthy, self-sufficient, logical, and goal-oriented. Now I felt lost and alone in life with a traumatic brain injury.

As an engineering student at Penn State University, I had a plan for my future. Then I was consumed by symptoms caused by sports-induced concussions: pounding headaches, mood changes, fatigue, memory loss, and crippling brain fog. Inability to form coherent thoughts became my new norm. I was also functionally blind. My eyes worked, but only half my brain functioned properly. I could not interpret many of the normal eye signals, consistently leaving me with a skewed perception of the world.

Exercise? Forget about it. I struggled to have the balance and motor skills to walk around the house, let alone run or ride my bike. After two years of unsuccessful rehab, I was angry, anxious, and depressed. I always had a plan, but now I was fumbling through life without direction. "Why me? What about my future?" I asked myself. Throughout my healing process, I learned only one person knows the answer to these questions, God. He always has a plan.

Growing up, I was an athlete, not a Christian. I did not love God and did not think God loved me. I zoned out at church, slept through Sunday school, and hated youth group.

I thought the Lord, like my pastor, spent His days judging me for my sins. My goal was merely to avoid His wrath.

I loved endurance sports. I ran cross-country and track, swam on numerous swim teams, and even did some sprint triathlons. In high school, I discovered track cycling, a discipline similar to Tour de France style road cycling with a few important differences. Races are shorter, between 5K and 20K, fields are smaller, a 24 person maximum, and all races are on a 333 meter, 30 degree banked concrete track. Bikes have no gears or breaks and reach speeds over 55 km/h. Speed up, pedal faster; slow down, pedal slower; simple yet grueling. I craved the personal improvement just as much as I loved competing against the other cyclists. Since I live near a U.S. Olympic training center, I raced against the best cyclists in the country and the world every week. Competition was top-notch, and I loved, even idolized, the experience. Dangerous high-speed crashes are part of cycling. It seemed as if every time I crashed I hit my head.

I will never know how many concussions I sustained, but after four years of racing and many crashes, my brain was on the brink of collapse. After those final two crashes, I began my journey through traumatic brain injury. I saw many doctors, wrestled through rehab, and held personal pep talks about determination over the next two years. I developed a plan, maintained unrivaled focus, and worked with relentless fortitude to heal myself. Despite being the perfect patient, my symptoms and functional ability rapidly declined.

My brain was so injured I had to labor to do basic activities I once took for granted, including reading, interacting with people, and feeding myself. I slept all day just to save up the energy to eat dinner with my family. I rode an emotional roller coaster from depression to confusion through anger and into hopelessness. I withdrew from college and much of life. After over a thousand hours of rehab, my ability to function improved marginally. I was not responding neurologically. My brain had to fight for every impulse.

I returned to school in an attempt to shock my brain into responding, but it had the opposite effect. I was back to square one with that nagging thought, "Everything happens for a reason." It was not fair. I did everything the doctors ordered but my brain didn't heal. What was I doing wrong? Then the Holy Spirit moved within me and it clicked—I was trusting the wrong person. God is in control of the future, not doctors. He put me in this position, according to His plan. By embracing God's presence, I began a lifelong journey of ups and downs with Him by my side. Whatever He wants, I want.

Instead of being anxious, I brought all my worries and praise to God. I prayed for healing, for doctors that understood me, and a better outlook on life. After a few months, my prayers were gradually answered. Headaches subsided, brain fog began to clear, and amazing doctors appeared in my life. I became thankful for His gift of life, grateful for His sovereignty, and overwhelmed by His unending love.

Today, three years post injury, I can walk a 5K and am relearning to run. I continually praise God for the gift of movement. Once I began to make measurable neurological progress, my Lord answered my prayers about the reason this happened to me.

"I designed you," he said, "but I made you too independent and self-sufficient to seek my presence in ordinary life. I have known since the beginning of time you would need this disruption to become a Christian. First, I took away everything you relied on for support: your healthy body, sound brain, education, athletics, and friends. Then I let you be independent and try to heal yourself. Once you had nothing left, you needed my help and deliverance. It was time to build you up in Jesus Christ, showering you with my love, peace, sovereignty, trust, and strength."

God allowed my injury so He could be my Lord, friend, and gateway to eternal life. I am currently working hard every day in rehab and in my relationship with God to regain full mobility. God has taught me about His character and the power of prayer through athletics and injury. I don't know what He has in store for my future, but I know one thing, He always has a plan.

Catherine Probst – *Yardley, PA*

get in the word

Isaiah 55:8–9
"For My thoughts are not your thoughts,
Nor are your ways My ways," says the Lord.
"For as the heavens are higher than the earth,
So are My ways higher than your ways,
And My thoughts than your thoughts.

Romans 12:12
Rejoicing in hope, patient in tribulation, continuing steadfastly
in prayer...

Psalm 32:8
I will instruct you and teach you in the way you should go; I will
guide you with My eye.

scripture memorization

Write out the scripture(s) in the space below and recite them ten times.

_____

_____

_____

_____

_____

_____

_____

_____

_____

_____

_____

_____

something to ponder

DO YOU HAVE FAITH THAT GOD has a plan for you? How has God's peace and love reassured you along your journey?

_____

_____

_____

_____

HOW HAS GOD'S PLAN DIFFERED FROM your plan? How has God used a devastating event in your life to bring you closer to him?

_____

_____

_____

_____

WHY SHOULD we trust God to guide us through life?

_____

_____

_____

running observations
by dean

Unknot Those Muscles

HAVE YOU EVER HAD SOMEONE RUB your shoulders or upper back and found a really painful spot? Those knots in your muscles appear all over your body. They are typically caused by overwork, injury, or even sitting down too long, which causes muscles to contract into a small mass of hard tissue. We may not feel one until we put pressure on it, which may partially explain the explosion of foam rollers and other trigger point devices. Sometimes when I use mine, I find areas that are much more tender than I thought. Muscle knots will affect your running, if you ignore them.

When a muscle is very tight for a long time, the blood flow can be interrupted a little, making recovery more difficult. Applying heat will relax the knot a bit and get your blood flowing again. While using heat exclusively may not completely heal the muscle, it will make it easier to massage the area. Try a heating pad, a hot bath, a rice sock, or a damp cloth warmed in the microwave. Just be careful to avoid steam burns.

Pressure is the best way to work out these knots. That's why rollers work so well. Don't have a roller? Try a tennis ball (or your hands). If it's a tough spot to reach, like your back, you can use that tennis ball against a wall or maybe exchange massages with your partner or a friend. I once had an inflamed piriformis muscle, which is a small muscle located deep inside the layers of gluteal muscle, running close to the sciatic nerve and causing pain all the way down my leg. I sat on a tennis ball while driving back and forth to work for two weeks, and the problem was solved.

When those methods do not work, I am a big believer in massage therapy. It took me years to get up the courage to go to a massage therapist, but it was one of the best running-related decisions I have ever made. The massage itself did not feel good, but the relief that followed was wonderful. Expect a little soreness, but nothing as intense as the muscle knot. Remember to drink a lot of water following a massage. As a matter of fact, hydration is important at all times when battling these knots.

One last consideration is stretching. The knots are caused by muscles that contract, so stretching those muscle fibers will loosen them, depending on their severity. It is one more reason why stretching after every run is important. You won't feel some of the knots forming, so stretch regularly for best results.

Life happens, and as it unfurls, we have pointed moments that cause us intense emotional pain. They're like painful knots in your muscles, constantly reminding you that something is not right. The remedy for those life moments is Scripture reading. Finding the right Scripture reference for those times is like a therapeutic massage working out the emotional knot.

- *Knots in your muscles can cause you to alter your running stride to avoid the pain, which will eventually lead to injury. Keep them worked out.*

- *Pressure applied directly to the painful spot will help to release the knot. You may need to massage the knot several times to keep it worked out.*

•*God provides His word to us to reveal Scriptures that can help to work out our emotional knots.*

sticky notes

_____

_____

_____

_____

_____

_____

_____

_____

_____

focal point

HAVE YOU EVER WATCHED A BEAUTIFUL sunrise or sunset while running? They remind me of God's great creation and my part in it. He gives me the strength to get up each day and the passion to run. For years, I ran cross-country and track for the praise of my peers, medals, and personal records. I competed for selfish reasons, and when I didn't like the outcome, my emotions did not glorify God.

In college I decided to create a focus point when I ran. I would put crosses on my shoes so when I looked down, I would be reminded of what Christ did for me. I would memorize Scripture and repeat it as I ran. Romans 8:18 was one of my favorite verses to get my mind focused. I would look at the trees or clouds and think of who created me. I would touch the cross necklace around my neck to remember Christ's sacrifice for my life. I even stamped the fish symbol inside of my forearm with "JESUS" printed in the middle. It didn't matter if I ran a PR or came in last; I thanked God each time for the ability to run that day.

In this way, I changed my focus from my needs to God's glory during my run, and that changed everything. My emotions were linked to giving God praise. I wasn't overcome with disappointment when I fell short of my goal. I no longer cried for my selfish desires because God showed His faithfulness to me in an amazing way.

What do you focus on when you run? How can you turn your gifts and passions into God's glory? Run in such a way that will gain you a heavenly prize. Medals, trophies, and records will all fade away someday. Get rid of the things that entangle you and try to take your joy. Run a race for God and give Him the praise by focusing on the eternal each day.

Kristen King – *Circleville, OH*

get in the word

Romans 8:18

For I consider that the sufferings of this present time are not worthy to be compared with the glory which shall be revealed in us.

1 Corinthians 9:24–27

Do you not know that those who run in a race all run, but one receives the prize? Run in such a way that you may obtain it. And everyone who competes for the prize is temperate in all things. Now they do it to obtain a perishable crown, but we for an imperishable crown. Therefore I run thus: not with uncertainty. Thus I fight: not as one who beats the air. But I discipline my body and bring it into subjection, lest, when I have preached to others, I myself should become disqualified.

Hebrews 12:1–3

Therefore we also, since we are surrounded by so great a cloud of witnesses, let us lay aside every weight, and the sin which so easily ensnares us, and let us run with endurance the race that is set before us, looking unto Jesus, the author and finisher of our faith, who for the joy that was set before Him endured the cross, despising the shame, and has sat down at the right hand of the throne of God. For consider Him who endured such hostility from sinners against Himself, lest you become weary and discouraged in your souls.

scripture memorization

Write out the scripture(s) in the space below and recite them ten times.

_____

_____

_____

_____

_____

_____

_____

_____

_____

_____

_____

_____

_____

_____

_____

something to ponder

WHY DO you run? What motivates you?

_____

_____

_____

_____

WHAT IS your focus point? How can you focus on God during your run?

_____

_____

_____

_____

WHETHER YOU win or lose, how can you best give praise to God?

_____

_____

_____

_____

running observations
by dean

Energy Sappers

RUNNING TAKES A LOT OF ENERGY. In order to run as far and/or as fast as you want to run, it is important to be as efficient as possible. I see runners do a number of things that sap more energy than they think. I want to focus on running a race at peak level, running as hard as you can and getting the most out of your performance. Admittedly, some of these are not huge energy sappers, but some are big. Taken together as a group, they can mean the difference between reaching your goal and falling short.

First of all, extra movement can take energy. Head movement is one I see a lot, especially in runners with long hair. I'm not sure why (I have almost no hair), but there is a definite connection. Not all folks with long hair do it, but many do. Not only does it take energy to move your head back and forth, but it distorts your vision too. Keeping your head still and relaxed allows you to focus on muscles that move you forward.

Arm movement is another one. Moving your arms is essential, but many people have a lot of sideways movement to their arm swing. If you draw a line down the middle of your body, your arms should not cross that line. Again, energy should be directed forward.

Another common energy sapper is tension in muscles that do not contribute to running. The most popular of these is in the shoulder area. When you use energy to keep your shoulders raised, you are using redirected power from your running muscles.

Many small movements that can redirect your momentum include talking while running and looking around at the scenery unnecessarily. They may not make a big difference, but they could keep you just shy of your goal.

A few form issues include slouching, carrying your hips too far back, and bending over as you go uphill. Runners tend to slouch or lean forward when they get tired. Practice staying upright when you run hard, and it will begin to feel strange to lean forward. This will allow your hips to stay forward too. The next time you go out to run, try slouching just a little and see if it makes you feel slower. I think it does.

Runners seem to have a natural tendency to lean forward uphill. I don't know why, but I think we feel like we're getting there faster if we look like we're about to hit the finishing tape. Don't do it. It saps a lot of energy from your quads to lean forward on the hills. The next time you run up a hill, check your posture. Notice how your quads feel when you lean forward.

The final and most significant energy sapper is attitude. I talk a lot about the power of your mind, and I believe some people have a slow pace not because they can't speed up, but because they believe they are slow runners. Recently I ran a 5K and was struggling mightily in the first mile, when a good friend made a comment that made me smile. That smile energized me. Of course, the energy was there the whole time, awaiting discovery. I ran my second mile faster than the first, which is unusual for me. A negative attitude can be a big energy sapper.

God gives us many delightful things to enjoy. So many, in fact, they can take the focus off of Him while we're busy. Anything that takes away from our personal relationship with the God of the universe is an energy sapper. Many of those energy drains are small, but when put together, they add up. I have to focus on eliminating those things or I find my relationship with Him weakening. Making Him your first priority will help to ensure this doesn't happen.

There are a number of physical habits that can cause us to focus our energy on things other than the task at hand. Being aware of those and eliminating them will make you more efficient.

> • *Attitude can be an energy sapper or an energy builder. Which one are you practicing?*
>
> • *To prevent relationship weakness with God, we should aim to glorify Him in all we do.*

sticky notes

_____

_____

_____

_____

_____

_____

rest

ALARM SET—CHECK. WORKOUT CLOTHES LAID OUT—CHECK. Water bottle in refrigerator—check. Phone charged and ready to go—check. New running app—check. I had the makings of a great run, ready to go for the morning, but I did not count on being up four times with our new puppy. I did not count on insomnia and getting only a few hours sleep. So when my alarm clock went off at 5:15 a.m., I gave myself permission to turn it off and roll over for another hour of sleep.

I don't enjoy not following through with my plans, even the plans that involve only me. But I have learned over the years, as I am sure you have learned, that things have a way of not always working out in the way you expect.

Have you ever heard that old phrase about the best-laid plans? My curiosity got the best of me, and I did a web search to find out exactly what the rest of this phrase is and where it came from. "The best laid plans of mice and men often go astray" comes from a poem entitled "The Mouse" by Robert Burns. It means exactly what we all think it means. Plans change when you least expect them to.

Fitness professionals agree that rest days are important to schedule during your week; just as important as workouts. Even though my stubborn self was not thrilled with facing the fact that I would not be going for my morning run that day, I understood that perhaps this was the way God wanted it to be. I obviously needed that extra hour of sleep. Jesus tells us in Matthew 11:28, "Come to Me, all you who labor and are heavy laden, and I will give you rest." With the extra sleep, I was able to rise refreshed and spend my quiet time reading my devotions and praising God for the gifts He has given me - a home, warm bed, extra quilt my grandmother's best friend made for us, hot coffee, and endless opportunities to run another day.

Julie Dossantos – Fort Pierce, FL

get in the word

Matthew 11:28

Come to Me, all you who labor and are heavy laden, and I will give you rest.

Exodus 33:14

And He said, "My Presence will go with you, and I will give you rest."

Psalm 62:1–2

Truly my soul silently waits for God;
From Him comes my salvation.
He only is my rock and my salvation;
He is my defense;
I shall not be greatly moved.

scripture memorization

Write out the scripture(s) in the space below and recite them ten times.

_____

_____

_____

_____

_____

_____

_____

_____

_____

_____

_____

_____

_____

something to ponder

WHAT PART of your schedule could you give up in order to give yourself extra time for rest?

_____

_____

_____

_____

ARE THERE busier times in your life, where you know you need extra rest?

_____

_____

_____

_____

WHAT GIVES you rest?

_____

_____

_____

_____

running observations by dean

Recovery Run

I LOVE RECOVERY RUNS. THERE IS no pressure to accomplish any particular goal except to cover a certain distance or time. The idea is to work some soreness out of your legs and you don't have to run hard to do it. As a matter of fact, you have to run slow.

I always run a recovery run the day after a hard run. Running hard will take its toll on your body, and it needs rest. I believe active rest is best that day after a hard workout or race. An easy recovery run makes perfect active rest. If I were going to take a day off, I would prefer it to be the day after a recovery run. Your legs get stiff with lactic acid build up from running fast, and an easy run will help to alleviate that soreness.

So how do you go about a recovery run? Easy. That's the key. A couple of minutes slower than your regular pace is not too slow. At the fastest, thirty seconds to a minute slower than your average run is appropriate. Run slow, take it easy, and enjoy the lower effort. Think of it like lying on the beach, or relaxing to a good movie. I always think about recovery runs as a reward for working hard the day before.

Recovery runs will help prevent injury. Keeping your legs as loose as possible is an important part of keeping yourself on the healthy track. After the run, take time to stretch. Pay attention to particularly sensitive muscle groups and spend a little more time gently stretching them.

If it is important to run easy the day after a hard workout, it is even more important to recover from a race. The longer the race, the longer the recovery needs to be. My rule of thumb is a day of easy running for each mile of the race. A lot of other folks will back me up on that. For a 5K, I will take a recovery run the day after the race and run easy at least two more days before getting back to hard running again. For a marathon, I will take a week for recovery runs and then run easy for another two to three weeks.

"Therefore, if anyone is in Christ, he is a new creation; old things have passed away; behold, all things have become new." (*2 Corinthians 5:17*). It's a good way to look at recovery runs. Each race is the end of a journey, some short and some long. Either way, new beginnings are always intriguing. Any time we are tested and become tired and worn, it is good to remember that we are new creatures in God's eyes.

- *Recovery runs are a reward for working hard. Enjoy them without guilt.*

- *As a rule of thumb, run one easy day for each mile of a race to ensure your body is ready to get back to hard running.*

- *Each mountain we climb, whether a race or difficult life circumstances, new beginnings are welcome. But nothing beats the new beginning of becoming a new creature in Christ.*

sticky notes

testing my hope in the Lord during a marathon

"EXAMINE ME, O LORD, AND PROVE ME; Try my mind and my heart" (*Psalm 26:2*).

I participated in the Oklahoma City Memorial Marathon on Sunday, April 28th, 2013. This verse from Psalms is the one that God led me to focus on during this event. I wanted to be tested. I wanted to be proven, good or bad, not just physically but mentally as well. Psalm 34:4 says, "I sought the Lord, and He heard me, and delivered me from all my fears." Right before the marathon, I wrote a story about how I was going to ask God to test me. I wanted to learn what I needed to do to improve my relationship with my Lord and Savior. He answered me in an unexpected way.

I had a plan for running the marathon. I spent the last few weeks preparing myself mentally; gaining some much needed strength from our Run for God class. My classmates put forth a level of effort that gave me a much-needed spiritual boost. A print shop made me a shirt with Psalm 26.2, and I had "I am Second" printed on my race bib to remind me who is first. I had a fail proof plan to remind me why I was doing this. On race day, we attended the OKC memorial for a deeply moving sunrise service with a sermon that wrapped up by comparing God to the wind. You cannot see either one, but you feel the effects both have on you.

When the starting horn sounded, I took off at a nice easy pace. I ran with a friend until we arrived at the first mile marker, and then I told her I would catch back up to her at the finish line. As I slowly sped up to a comfortable pace, I worried more about my race than thanking God for the next mile. I was reviewing my preparation when a clear thought entered my mind: "I have been preparing you for this your whole life."

I should have been focused on my faithful Lord, so I prayed for a word to dwell on over the next mile. The first word that came to mind was grace, so I thanked Him for His saving grace and helping me through my future failures. That mile went smoothly. On the next mile, I dwelt on perseverance. I thanked the Lord for the perseverance He was giving me, and before I could finish, a song by Plumb came on entitled "I Need You Now," reminding me where I would get that perseverance.

The course turned into some neighborhoods, and I started noticing the crowds and their signs. Around mile 14, the course ran by Lake Hefner, and my digestive system started to bother me. I didn't know how to handle problems with my stomach. I'd never had them before, so I stopped eating energy chews to help. Big mistake. No longer thinking about God's will, I prayed at each new mile for the runners who were sidelined with pain, cramp, or injury.

I started walking intermittently to relieve cramping muscles, but I didn't turn to God for perseverance for a while. Finally I realized I needed the intrinsic motivation that can only come from God, not encouragement from a stranger or a funny sign. In the Lord's strength, I carried on. The cramps and digestion problems did not disappear, but they did become manageable.

Once I rounded the final corner and noticed my family and friends cheering me on, I knew I'd made it, but my calves were cramping so tightly they felt like baseballs. My youngest daughter came out of the crowd, took my right hand, and started to run with me. But my calf stopped me. Her worried eyes were a painful sight. I prayed a quick prayer for God to see me through and was able to run again by His grace. Holding my daughter's arm up as we crossed the finish line made all the pain worth it. They asked for a finisher's picture, and I took it with her.

I failed my Lord numerous times during that race. I allowed my cramps and stomach trouble to open the door to self-doubt and bad judgment. Just as in everyday life, I had the choice to trust in Him or struggle on my own. As He does every day, He provided me His grace when I did not deserve it. I failed in my test, but I learned a lesson I will not soon forget. He told me He had been preparing me for this my whole life. I just need to believe in His training.

Tony Hopkins – *Okay, OK*

get in the word

Psalm 26:2
Examine me, O Lord, and prove me; Try my mind and my heart.

Psalm 34:4
I sought the Lord, and He heard me, and delivered me from all my fears.

Jeremiah 29:11
For I know the thoughts that I think toward you, says the Lord, thoughts of peace and not of evil, to give you a future and a hope.

scripture memorization

Write out the scripture(s) in the space below and recite them ten times.

_____

_____

_____

_____

_____

_____

_____

_____

_____

_____

_____

_____

_____

something to ponder

IN WHAT areas of your life do you need to seek God's will?

_____

_____

_____

_____

WHAT STRUGGLES HAVE YOU NOT GIVEN to God to help you

persevere through?

_____

_____

_____

_____

WHAT IS distracting you from placing your trust in God?

_____

_____

_____

_____

running observations
by dean

What Were You Expecting?

HAVE YOU EVER HAD A BAD running day? Maybe you had a bad race and substantially missed your goal. Maybe you realized halfway through a long run that you were going to suffer a great deal if you didn't cut it short. Perhaps you were on the track trying to run fast and realized today wasn't your day. We have all had bad days. They are not limited to running related issues, but we will stick to running here.

Bad days unfold in different ways. Some runs begin innocently enough. You start off feeling good, only to find out a mile or two later that you lost that feeling. Sometimes it waits until the near-end of a long run. Other times bad days are clear from step one. No matter how it develops, bad days are a bummer. I think the worst bad days are the ones where you think you are going to have a good day and it just doesn't work. The difference is the expectation.

Falling short of a race goal may be due to overblown expectations. While it is great to go into a race with high confidence, your optimistic goal may be just unrealistic. You may find after the race that you lacked the preparation needed for your goal. I often find myself discounting the missed workouts or the tweaked hamstring, not wanting to admit their significance. Of course, sometimes you perform at higher levels than you thought possible, so you think, "I'll probably do it again." That only encourages you to overestimate next time. When you understand this, you'll overcome the down days more easily.

Many things outside of your control can cause a bad day. Our job is to pay attention to the things we can control and do all we can to ensure the best outcome possible. We must fairly assess where we stand prior to a race or training run. We will still have some good and bad days, but if we understand ourselves correctly, we can set realistic goals.

Preparation is key to everything we do in both running and faith. If we spend time in prayer and study, we will be better prepared to handle tough situations when they arise. We don't want to be caught trying to cram in those last minute prayers because we have neglected to pray on the good days. It is akin to squeezing in some last minute runs to make up for a lack of preparation over the last few months. Think of your prayer life this way: If Jesus came back and told you that you would be granted everything you prayed for last week, how would the world around you change?

- *We all have bad running days, which can be caused by both controllable and uncontrollable circumstances.*

- *The key is to control the things we can control and not worry about the things we cannot.*

- *What would be different today if all your prayers from the last week were granted?*

sticky notes

_____

_____

_____

_____

_____

_____

_____

_____

_____

_____

_____

_____

_____

_____

Week

the missing piece

I HAVE ALWAYS BEEN ATHLETIC. I played softball and basketball from my very first opportunity at 5 years old. As an adult I continued to play softball (even while pregnant), until I was hurt several years ago during a collision. I tried tennis, which I love, but it didn't mix well with my work outside of the home. I typically filled in my fitness gaps with walks and occasional classes at the gym, but I abandoned the idea of participating in an organized sport.

As a young athlete, I didn't struggle with weight much. I could eat what I wanted, and my activity level took care of the rest. But in my mid-thirties (after my accident), I had to start watching my weight. The walks and the classes weren't doing the job. A friend told me about a smartphone app that counted calories, helped with meal selection, and tracked exercise. It had every food imaginable and many restaurants. I used it for a few months, and it opened my eyes to the true nature of food. I discovered that everything has calories. I mean, cauliflower has calories—who knew? My scale was finally moving in the right direction for a change, but something was missing from my life.

I am an athlete. An athlete needs a challenge or a competition, so I began tinkering with the notion of running. I used to hate it. I loved the saying, "If you see me running, you'd better run too, because someone or something is chasing me." When I ran, I had no guideline to follow. I would just get out there—arms flailing, chest burning, sides cramping, and nose running. I would finish up in complete misery. I had no idea what I was doing, but something kept pushing me to try.

That's when "Run for God – The 5K Challenge" came into my life. I was apprehensive at first. What does running have to do with God? As I followed the program, I found running to be the most tangible parallel to walking out my Christian faith I have ever experienced. Some days I feel as if I could run 25 miles and not break a sweat. On other days, taking a jog to the mailbox seems impossible. Such is my Christian walk. Sometimes I think I'm walking so close to the Lord I can smell His honeysuckle breath, and other times I wonder if I am even saved. Through the program, I learned it is faith that keeps me going, faith that doesn't let me quit, faith that never gives up in both physical and spiritual running. By faith I know if I train properly, regardless of my feelings, I will be ready. By faith, I know God is with me, even when He feels distant; rooting for me, cheering me on, and telling me, "You can do this."

Running, my missing piece, has improved my life in ways I never dreamed. First, I am in better health in my late 30s than I was in my twenties. I eat better, and I am pleased and a little shocked at how my body has responded to running. I never imagined I would see my high school weight again. Second, I have found contentment in having myself as my only competition—conquering my fear, winning against doubt, and occasionally grabbing a PR. Third, I've had many opportunities as a student and a facilitator to minister and receive support, to encourage and be encouraged, to laugh or cry, and even to be angry.

What started off as a simple running program has transformed me, and I am excited to see where the roads will lead. I recently celebrated the first anniversary of my initial 5K and I'm participating in the RFG half marathon study now. I am running the race that is set before me. I may never get a medal, but I will get my prize.

This journey has not been easy, but we were not promised it would be. God promised to give us the strength to endure, the faith to continue, and divine fellowship until the end. Enjoy the journey.

Lainie Gresham – Carrollton, GA

get in the word

Isaiah 43:7

Everyone who is called by My name,
Whom I have created for My glory;
I have formed him, yes, I have made him.

Proverbs 16:9

A man's heart plans his way, but the Lord directs his steps.

Proverbs 18:15

The heart of the prudent acquires knowledge, and the ear of the wise
seeks knowledge.

scripture memorization

Write out the scripture(s) in the space below and recite them ten times.

_____

_____

_____

_____

something to ponder

GOD CREATED US ALL FOR HIS glory, each of us with our own gifts, personality, talents, and tools. What has God created you for? Have you been hiding it due to your season of life, loss of confidence, or lack of motivation?

_____

_____

_____

_____

HOW HARD is it for you to let God surprise you and change your path?

_____

_____

_____

_____

ARE YOU teachable? Are you able to admit you need help? Are you looking to see who and what God has put before you in order to bring you closer to Him?

_____

_____

_____

running observations by dean

Why Is It So Hard to Be Simple?

SOMEONE ONCE SAID, "LIFE IS SIMPLE; it's just not easy." When we hear it, we can feel its truth. Isn't running the same? It doesn't get much simpler than putting one foot in front of the other in a monotonous, repetitive cadence. Think about it: Running a marathon is simple; just keep moving for 26.2 miles. How hard can it be?

No matter how long you have been running—six months or thirty years—you know running can be dreadfully difficult at times. Since we tend to make things more complicated than they are, I think it is helpful to remind ourselves from time to time that running is not rocket science.

I talk to a lot of people who say, "I'm just not a runner," or "I used to run, but I just can't do it anymore." Why do they feel this way? I think it's because they look at running as something to be endured rather than something to be enjoyed. Sure, there are tough days to endure, but those days can be scarce if you go about it properly.

I enjoy running immensely, and you want to know what I think about when I run the hardest and dig the deepest? I think about running. I focus on the task. I know a lot of people who try to zone out or keep their minds occupied with something else while running hard. I think that's a way to endure a hard run, but I want to enjoy it, and the only way I can do that is to get totally absorbed by it. Don't get me wrong. I like to listen to a little music, spend time in prayer, or just think about other things while running an easy routine, but when I'm running hard, I keep nothing else in my head, nothing to complicate the task at hand.

I believe some of the best things in life reside at the corner of Simple Street and Hard Avenue. If you can boil things down to their simplest level (easier said than done), it is easy to enjoy them. Running is one of those things. Eric Liddell of Chariots of Fire fame once said, "I believe God made me for a purpose, but He also made me fast! And when I run I feel His pleasure." Eric understood the simplicity and the joy of running. I truly believe that God made us to run. It may not be everyone's cup of tea, but many of us understand what Eric Liddell was saying, whether we're fast or not.

The Gospel is another one of those things that is simple and hard. It is simple to understand that Christ died for us and conquered death in order to atone for our sins. It can be hard to live in a world with many temptations and people who will persecute you for your simple faith, but we can't focus on enduring this world. We have to see the simplicity in the Gospel and share it with the same joy that Eric Liddell felt when he ran. If you have ever felt the delight of the Lord in using you to lead someone to salvation, you have felt the deepest joy there is. We make sharing the Gospel seem hard, but shouldn't it be simple?

   • *Running may be hard at times, but it is simple.*

   • *Don't look at running as something to be endured. Enjoy it.*

   • *The Gospel is simple, but we tend to make sharing hard.*

sticky notes

---

turnover in my walk with Christ

TURNOVER, YOU MAY KNOW, IS THE act of bringing the rear roll-off foot forward, which assists the opposing foot with a counterbalance for propulsion. Without it, the body remains stagnant. I say all this to note how turnover illustrates my walk with Christ. Let me explain.

Ten years ago I got hit with depression. No turnover. I don't mean I felt really sad for days. I mean I almost let it take my life. Sitting in a running car in a closed garage seemed like a good way to go—peacefully, quietly. Fortunately God had a plan for me, and it wasn't to isolate my wife, Julie, and our three boys. Since medicines were a joke and I felt I was exhausting my options, I starting running. I suspect I'm like a lot of people who found the path of recovery by running down the road. I found the time I spent running was excellent for communing with God. I used that one-on-one time to discover Him and learn how to be healed. My turnover had started.

By our Father's grace and mercy, I learned how to put one foot in front of the other. I intentionally planned my training runs when I knew I would be the most depressed. I returned from them encouraged and uplifted rather than down and out. Once I was making excuses for putting off my training runs, and Jane Seeley, editor of Marathon & Beyond, responded, "So what's a few hills?" Those words stuck with me, because they are a great metaphor for life. The path from depression to destiny certainly has its share of hills, but when I'm focused on what's most important (faith, family, & friends), I can manage the hills.

I'm a Clydesdale runner through and through, which means I am genetically disproportionate to the models on the cover of your favorite running magazine. I'm not setting any land speed records here. Having left depression behind, I was excited to be anywhere God would have me, at any pace. The occasional 5K quickly gave way to my first marathon! I started serving in the church and went on a few mission trips to the Dominican Republic. After losing months of my life to dark isolation, God was increasing my turnover faster than I ever imagined. I clung to Romans 5:1–5, which tells us that suffering produces perseverance, which builds character, which leads to hope. Try to fathom the power of God's perfect love for us. We have an all-consuming hope that can overwhelm our hearts with a desire for His will.

I continued on with a few more marathons and grew daily as a Christian. A friend eventually talked me into running the Lake Tahoe Triple Half Marathon for my fortieth birthday - a half marathon a day for three days. What I didn't know at the time I registered was that God had more plans for my turnover. I was to witness the beauty of His creation, become His hands and feet to the other runners, and also be introduced to the next phase of His plan—leading a Run For God ministry in my church.

Our Lord brought me out of darkness and into the most breathtaking views I've ever seen in order to give me a Romans 5 moment of hope through my suffering (and if you have run the course, you know I mean suffering). He turned my cul-de-sac faith into a conduit. It reminded me of a quote from Dr. Tony Evans, "God will bless you when He can bless through you." Run for God is now in its third year at our church with 5K, 10K, and half marathon training groups. I have become an elder and am co-facilitating a men's class.

God has certainly redefined turnover in my life. He has my feet moving at an unprecedented pace. He has a plan of greatness for your life too. You have a unique, never-to-be-lived-again life, and He wants to be the focus of it.

Regardless of where you are or where you have been in life, God has plans for you. He does not call the qualified; He qualifies the called. Are you following His call already? How comfortable are you in that pursuit? Just as in our training runs, growth comes when we're uncomfortable. Listen to God and provoke yourself to become better than you were. Moses was a murderer who freed a nation. Abraham was an elderly man who became a great father. I was a depressed, stagnant man who has become the hands and feet of Christ Jesus in my home, church, and community. If you haven't created turnover with the feet of your Christian run, start today and discover His greatness for you.

Jon Folsom – *Champaign, IL*

get in the word

Romans 5:3–4
And not only that, but we also glory in tribulations, knowing that tribulation produces perseverance; and perseverance, character; and character, hope.

Proverbs 3:5
Trust in the Lord with all your heart, and lean not on your own understanding.

2 Timothy 4:5
But you be watchful in all things, endure afflictions, do the work of an evangelist, fulfill your ministry.

scripture memorization

Write out the scripture(s) in the space below and recite them ten times.

_____

_____

_____

_____

_____

_____

_____

_____

_____

_____

_____

_____

something to ponder

WHERE ARE you with the turnover in your Christian run?

_____

_____

_____

_____

WHAT KEEPS you from not taking matters into your own hands and turning them over to God?

_____

_____

_____

_____

STARTING TODAY, how can your faith change from a cul-de-sac to a conduit?

_____

_____

_____

_____

running observations
by dean

How Often Should I Run?

HOW OFTEN YOU SHOULD RUN DEPENDS on what you want to accomplish. What will your schedule allow? Are you doing other forms of exercise in addition to running? Do you want to be competitive? Do you want to be the best you can be? You can't answer the first question until you answer the other questions.

As a starting point, traditional wisdom says you should run a minimum of three days a week, 20 – 30 minutes at a time. At the other end of the spectrum is the elite runner who runs twice a day, every day. Most of us fit in between. Training plans typically have built-in rest days. It is certainly safe to run five days a week. However, if you want to run more than that, you need to build up to it. I run every day and, as of this writing, have run every day for more than a year and a half. That may sound like a lot, but there are at least seven people in the United States who have run every day for over 40 years. You can go back and read that sentence again to confirm what you think you read. I'll wait.

You will read in many places that we need rest days, but you can define rest days in different ways. You can rest and run in the same day by running very easy, but it takes years to work your body up to a point where running every day is comfortable. You have to decide how much running you want to do, how much running your schedule will allow you to do, and then set your goals and slowly build toward them.

Once you set your goal (it's important to articulate a goal, not play it by ear), then you should pursue it slowly and consistently. If you decide from day to day whether you are going to run, you are setting yourself up for disappointment. Set a target, understanding you'll have to alter the plan at times, but also understanding you can't hit a target you can't see.

On a side note, it is perfectly okay to take a week or two off once or twice a year, but if you decide to take a month or two off, you may feel as if you're starting all over when you begin to run again.

Spending time with God is a little different. The more time we spend with Him, the stronger we get. We can't over-train in God's Word or service. One of the greatest things about running is that you can spend time with the Lord while you are doing it. Also, we can't beat ourselves up when we miss a day of Bible study. It has been my experience that the more we do, the more we want to do. Paul talked about continuing to strive for our goal, even as we pass through failures. God doesn't give up on us, so we shouldn't give up on ourselves.

- *Decide for yourself how much running you want to do and, like Nike says, just do it.*

- *Listen to your body and build toward your running goals slowly.*

- *When we spend time with God, we become stronger spiritually. We can't over-train with God.*

sticky notes

_____

_____

_____

_____

_____

_____

_____

_____

_____

_____

_____

_____

_____

_____

_____

_____

training teaches me, finishing defines me

THE APOSTLE PAUL WANTS TO KNOW and suffer with Christ (*Philippians 3:3-11*). He does not want to earn righteousness in his own efforts. He knows he could gain everything in the world and still be a pauper without "the excellence of the knowledge of Christ Jesus my Lord, for whom I have suffered the loss of all things."

Oswald Chambers said, "We are not made for the mountains, for sunrises, or for the other beautiful attractions in life—those are only intended to be moments of inspiration. We are made for the valley and the ordinary things of life, and that is where we have to prove our stamina and strength."

In Mark 9:2, Jesus takes Peter, James, and John to the mountaintop. Have you ever felt as if you were on a mountaintop with Jesus? The feeling of seeing things from God's perspective makes you want to stay there. When I compete in a race, I have the same experience as I cross the finish line. I am elated with the results persevering through my training to complete the race.

But God does not intend for us to stay on the mountaintop. We must return to the valleys, because staying up there is selfish. Jesus wants Peter, James, and John to understand this. We do our work in the valleys. How do we become better and stronger as runners? It's not when we cross the finish line. No, we grow when we gut out the last 400 meters of speed work. We learn endurance as we push ourselves up another hill. We grow in faith as we persevere in long runs.

I am who I am as a Christian by what lessons I bring out of the valley. On the mountaintop, Christ shows me how the training has shaped my character. Then I must return to work for His glory. Paul describes it like this, "that I may know Him and the power of His resurrection, and the fellowship of His sufferings, being conformed to His death, if, by any means, I may attain to the resurrection from the dead."

I am learning God has made me for the valleys. In the fellowship of Christ's sufferings, I will prove how well I can handle difficulties and demands. God wants us to take what we have gained in Christ back down into the world of lost people in order to draw them to the Savior. Paul says that in our sufferings we can show the power of faith in Christ and His glory and righteousness. So I run not for the finish line, but rather I run so the finish line will define me. Faith in the valley is what teaches me.

Oswald Chambers also said, "The life of faith is not a life of mounting up with wings, but a life of walking and not fainting."

Anonymous– *Anywhere, USA*

get in the word

Philippians 3:3–11
For we are the circumcision, who worship God in the Spirit, rejoice in Christ Jesus, and have no confidence in the flesh, though I also

might have confidence in the flesh. If anyone else thinks he may have confidence in the flesh, I more so: circumcised the eighth day, of the stock of Israel, of the tribe of Benjamin, a Hebrew of the Hebrews; concerning the law, a Pharisee; concerning zeal, persecuting the church; concerning the righteousness which is in the law, blameless.

But what things were gain to me, these I have counted loss for Christ. Yet indeed I also count all things loss for the excellence of the knowledge of Christ Jesus my Lord, for whom I have suffered the loss of all things, and count them as rubbish, that I may gain Christ and be found in Him, not having my own righteousness, which is from the law, but that which is through faith in Christ, the righteousness which is from God by faith; that I may know Him and the power of His resurrection, and the fellowship of His sufferings, being conformed to His death, if, by any means, I may attain to the resurrection from the dead.

Psalm 27:1
The Lord is my light and my salvation;
Whom shall I fear?
The Lord is the strength of my life;
Of whom shall I be afraid?

Mark 9:23–24
Jesus said to him, "If you can believe, all things are possible to him who believes."

Immediately the father of the child cried out and said with tears, "Lord, I believe; help my unbelief!"

scripture memorization

Write out the scripture(s) in the space below and recite them ten times.

----

something to ponder

WHAT DO I want to obtain in my own effort?

_____

_____

_____

_____

WHY IS staying on the mountaintop selfish?

_____

_____

_____

_____

HOW DO I want my valley experiences to point others to Christ?

_____

_____

_____

_____

running observations
by dean

Trying to Run Too Hard or Not Hard Enough?

HOW CAN YOU RUN TOO HARD? Hard running is the idea, isn't it? It surprises me to hear how people finish a race in a time that is very close to the same time it takes them to run the same distance every other day. If that is you, it means you are either running too fast during training runs or not running hard enough during races (assuming your goal is to run as fast as you can). There are those who are content with never really running hard and that's fine. It just means this isn't going to be useful advice for you unless you wish to change your approach in the future.

I spend a lot of time telling people to slow down in training. As long as you are getting your heart rate up to a good level, you're running fast enough and the run is benefitting you more than you think. There are many who train according to heart rate, staying in a range that is most beneficial to them. Most of those I have talked to about this type of training tell me that they are surprised how slowly they have to run to stay within range. At times, I have backed off of my hard training and ignored the time on most of my runs. If I don't pay attention to my pace, it is easier to focus on how comfortable I am and listen to my body for signs of weakness. I am always surprised at how little I slow down when I stop running hard for a month. I almost never use my watch for every run during the week. Easy runs should be easy.

Running easy is good for you, and running too hard every day is bad for you. Your muscles, tendons and ligaments need time to rest. Stressing them too often leads to breakdown. For those who are just beginning to run, the effect is even more intense. Take it easy on most runs. You can run hard once or twice a week and see great improvement in speed as a result.

If you are already keeping your heart rate at a reasonable level and running easy enough, but your race times do not differ much from your training runs, there may be one of two issues: 1) You are doing no hard running at all, or 2) you cannot tolerate the level of pain necessary to run faster. The first one is fairly easy to remedy, but the second, not so much. Throw in a hard run during the week, making sure you rest for at least a day or two before running hard again, and you will see improvement. Trying to move your pain tolerance level is difficult, but can be done. Just be careful doing it.

Running hard and easy can look like peaks and valleys. We have peaks and valleys in our spiritual lives, and both are important to spiritual growth. The peaks feel great and ensure we stay close enough to Jesus to want to come back. The valleys are tough, but they make us stronger and more able to get back to the peak. By staying close to our Lord, we ensure that our average altitude is as high as possible!

- *If your training runs and races look similar, and you want them to be different, try slowing down on the majority of your training runs. You may be breaking your body down.*

- *Running hard once or twice a week will help you to get faster on race day.*

- *Stay close to God to experience more peaks.*

sticky notes

_____

_____

_____

_____

_____

_____

_____

_____

_____

_____

_____

_____

_____

_____

sunshine for rainn

SOME TIME AGO, MY RELATIONSHIP WITH my Savior was a challenging one at best, non-existent at worst. Like all things in life, there is a beginning and an end. One August morning, the sun was setting on something that we valued—our furry, four-legged, family member. Her name was Rainn. She was small with the heart of an angel, beautiful inside and out. She had the spirit of a wise grandmother who was never afraid to fight for what she loved. Rainn had become terminally ill, and we had to make one of those decisions we pray we'll never have to make in life— to choose whether something that we love lives or dies.

We spent the summer praying on it, but the answer was weeks of silence. We felt angry, scared, but most of all, confused. Of all things, silence? No sign, no whisper? We set the appointment no pet owner wants to make. When the day came, we were on the road at 8:15 a.m. I couldn't help but think that by 8:45 a.m. she'd be gone, and I'd be alone. At the vet, my steps were intentionally slow. It was as though I wanted us both to savor every last moment of sunshine together. Yet as I continued what seemed to be a mile long walk up the sidewalk to the office door, I felt a sense of hope. The Lord whispered an answer to our prayers. "Today's not the day. Have faith. It's going to be okay."

We checked into the office and were faced with a new dilemma. As the vet explained the methods of euthanasia, we learned we could choose a quick and painless method in our absence, or an uncomfortable method in our presence. We resented the choices, but then the Lord brought a third option to mind.

While weighing the options, an obvious choice had been hidden by our fears of losing her. On top of her illness, she suffered from an inability to eat. Though they could not treat the illness, surgery could enable her to eat again. In her frail state, she may not survive the surgery, but if the other options were to euthanize her, what would we lose?

While she was in surgery, I found myself in prayer. I felt nothing under me, nothing to stand on but my faith in God and our Lord Jesus. I put everything I had and wanted in His hands. That warm August afternoon, our little one made it through the surgery and came back home with us. The next day, she could eat again. She ended up living a happy life for another two months in the comfort of our home.

Rainn passed away on an October morning. At the time, I was beginning my third week of the Run for God series at Harborside Christian Church in Safety Harbor, Florida. While Rainn's story may be sad to some, to me it's a symbol of hope. You see, up until that moment, I had never fully surrendered to God's will. In my own arrogance, I denied Him. In Rainn's final months, God showed me His grace and my everlasting hope. I saw that He works in mysterious ways and that even our tragedies are part of a greater plan.

On June 22, 2014, the journey that started with Rainn and involved many of the friends that I met through Run for God concluded in my baptism. By continuing to run for God, I've learned that being a Christian means looking out for others. It is kindness, grace, and humility, both on and off the racecourse. By exhibiting those qualities, we've already won our race even if we haven't crossed the finish line.

Jeremy Castanza - *Oldsmar, FL*

Hebrews 11:1

Now faith is the substance of things hoped for, the evidence of things not seen.

Lamentation 3:25

The Lord is good to those who wait for Him, to the soul who seeks Him.

Isaiah 55:8–9

"For My thoughts are not your thoughts,
Nor are your ways My ways," says the Lord.
"For as the heavens are higher than the earth,
So are My ways higher than your ways,
And My thoughts than your thoughts.

scripture memorization

Write out the scripture(s) in the space below and recite them ten times.

_____

_____

_____

_____

_____

something to ponder

DO I HOPE ENTIRELY IN GOD? Are my heart and mind surrendered completely?

_____

_____

_____

_____

HOW AM I strengthening my relationship with God?

_____

_____

_____

_____

IN WHAT tangible ways do I remind myself of God's presence in my life?

_____

_____

_____

_____

running observations
by dean

What's the Goal?

A GOAL IS THE RESULT OR achievement toward which we work. It is the aim or desired end of our efforts. Notice the general nature of that definition. There are an unlimited number of goals you can set for yourself related to running or anything else for that matter. We tend to think in terms of time or distance when we think about running goals, but there is much more.

If you've ever been to a training class on goal setting, you have probably heard of SMART goals. The letters S-M-A-R-T help you to remember to make your goals Specific, Measureable, Attainable, Realistic, and Timely. It's a good tool for setting running goals, because it clearly defines your goal and provides motivation as you work toward meeting the goal.

Having direction is important to everything we do. Running is no different. Imagine that you decide to drive to a house you have never visited. All you know is your friend lives north of you, so you get in the car and drive north. Since you don't know exactly where he lives, you have to stop and ask for directions a lot until you find someone who knows where he lives. Sounds silly doesn't it? That is what we do when we don't have a specific goal. Going out to run with no real plan will not yield optimal results. You may become frustrated, thinking you aren't getting anywhere, and eventually give up.

You may set your goal to run a set time in a particular race or to just be able to finish a specific distance, but consider these other goals. You could run at least 25 miles every week, take up cross training, or complete a set number of miles for a month or year. Be as creative as you want to be and set as many goals as you want to set.

When you set your goals, write them down. I keep a list of goal times for all common race distances in a file on my computer. I have columns for distance, goal time, and what I call my post-40 personal best. When I reach a goal, it feels good to go into the file and fill in my new time. Then, I usually set a new goal at that distance, but I have many other goals too. For example, I wanted to run 3,000 miles in a year. Done. Without setting that goal at the beginning of the year, I don't believe I would have made it. I am in the middle of a running streak where I run every day for a given amount of time or for as long as I can maintain it. The bottom line is there are many goals you can set, but the key is to decide ahead of time what you wish to accomplish and set your mind to doing it.

Once you write your goals down, find a place to display them where you will see them from time to time. Keeping your mind on your goals is important for focus. A daily reminder of what we are trying to achieve sets the goal firmly in our mind and motivates us to work towards that goal every day. I like to place them on a door or above a door that I walk through every day. Years ago, I would write my time goals down and then put them in an envelope and tape them above my door. I didn't have to see the specific goals to know what they were, but seeing that envelope every day motivated me.

I also like to set goals for myself for prayer and Bible study. Setting goals, like reading the Bible through, studying a book a month, praying for a lost person every day for a month, or anything else that helps see God's work being done will help to motivate you to keep your focus in your spiritual life. Having goals and a focus is vital to a strong relationship with our Lord and Savior Jesus Christ.

• *Training without goals is like getting in a car and trying to drive to a place without knowing where you are going.*

• *Write your goals down and place them somewhere to remind you of your target.*

•*You can set goals in everything you do.*

_____

_____

_____

_____

_____

_____

_____

_____

_____

_____

faith and endurance

WHAT ARE YOUR LIMITS? DO YOU know how far you can really go? You won't know until you have enough faith to endure the challenge.

What is faith? Faith is believing without seeing. It is trust and confidence in something or someone. Faith is very powerful, according to Jesus. You can find in Matthew 9:18–30 where Jesus heals a synagogue leader's daughter as a result of his faith. Jesus tells the man that his faith had made his daughter well. Also in Matthew 8:5–13, a Roman centurion's servant is healed as a result of faith. Jesus tells the Roman centurion, "Assuredly, I say to you, I have not found such great faith, not even in Israel" (*Matthew 8:10*). As you can see, Jesus does miracles in response to the men's faith.

Faith in God makes up your whole relationship with Him. Whenever something goes wrong, faith is that hope in the almighty God to work as He wishes.

In James 1:3, the writer says, "knowing that the testing of your faith produces patience." The word patience overlaps with words like endurance and perseverance. What is endurance? God made us physically and spiritually able to endure whatever is thrown at us, whether it's a temptation or an Ironman. Sometimes I wonder how in the world God could make our bodies so great that people can endure an Ironman race—a 2.4-mile swim, a 112-mile bike ride, and a 26.2-mile run. You may think it's impossible, but look at the thousands of people who, in my mind, are torturing their bodies to complete this intense event. Can we do the same kind of intense training for our spiritual life? You bet. Our Creator made our bodies spiritually strong. I will never forget hearing my coach say,

"You'll never know how far you can go until you've gone too far."

Challenges to our faith develop patience, "but let patience have its perfect work, that you may be perfect and complete, lacking nothing. . . . Blessed is the man who endures temptation; for when he has been approved, he will receive the crown of life which the Lord has promised to those who love Him" (*James 1:4,12*). By enduring things in life, we produce one of the fruits of the Spirit, which is spiritual strength. Like training for an intense race, trials to our faith can build us up for the glory of God our Father.

So run this race with faith and endurance and the prize will be waiting. "But may the God of all grace, who called us to his eternal glory by Christ Jesus, after you have suffered a while, perfect, establish, strengthen, and settle you" (*1 Peter 5:10*).

Miriam Burnette – *Dalton, GA*

get in the word

James 1:2–5
My brethren, count it all joy when you fall into various trials, knowing that the testing of your faith produces patience. But let patience have its perfect work, that you may be perfect and complete, lacking nothing. If any of you lacks wisdom, let him ask of God, who gives to all liberally and without reproach, and it will be given to him.

Matthew 8:8–9

The centurion answered and said, "Lord, I am not worthy that You should come under my roof. But only speak a word, and my servant will be healed. For I also am a man under authority, having soldiers under me. And I say to this one, 'Go,' and he goes; and to another, 'Come,' and he comes; and to my servant, 'Do this,' and he does it."

Matthew 9:27–30

When Jesus departed from there, two blind men followed Him, crying out and saying, "Son of David, have mercy on us!"

And when He had come into the house, the blind men came to Him. And Jesus said to them, "Do you believe that I am able to do this?"

They said to Him, "Yes, Lord."

Then He touched their eyes, saying, "According to your faith let it be to you." And their eyes were opened. And Jesus sternly warned them, saying, "See that no one knows it."

scripture memorization

Write out the scripture(s) in the space below and recite them ten times.

_____

_____

_____

_____

_____

_____

_____

_____

_____

_____

_____

_____

something to ponder

WHAT IS faith?

_____

_____

_____

_____

WHAT IS endurance?

_____

_____

_____

_____

HOW DOES patience work with endurance?

_____

_____

_____

_____

running observations by dean

Consistency Pays Dividends

MALCOM GLADWELL WROTE A BOOK CALLED Outliers where he postulated that anyone who spent enough time doing any one thing would likely become an outlier, that is, someone who fell outside the normal bell curve. People who are outliers spent at least 10,000 hours practicing their craft and thereby became great, accomplished people. For every Bill Gates there are thousands who want to be Bill Gates, but they are not willing to devote enough time to attaining that goal.

Consistency is the answer to getting better at anything you do. Running is no exception. I dodge a lot of seasonal runners who fill the sidewalks in the spring and fall. In the middle of summer and the dead of winter, they aren't outside with me. Sure, some of them are on the treadmill, and that's great, but I'm sure many of them are busy packing on a few pounds and increasing their total cholesterol, when the weather is tough. There is certainly nothing wrong in being a seasonal runner, but you can't expect to either excel at the sport or to be as healthy as you can be without consistency.

When you are consistent in your running, the cumulative effort builds up. It's something you can't feel, but it is there. Each day you are getting better, stronger, and faster. It's like making small deposits into a bank account each week. It gets to a point where you don't miss the money and before you know it, your bank account has grown. When you're consistent in your running, you will go out one day and find things clicking in a way that they never have. You'll feel great.

There is no substitute for consistency. No one can simulate consistency with something else. Hard work and consistency are nearly synonymous words in running. The hard work is getting out there for every scheduled run and following through on your commitment to bettering yourself.

In the same way, we have to be consistent in our relationship with God. Building habits of Bible study and prayer can be difficult with all the demands on our time and attention. There will be days when it feels forced, when we don't feel good about it. But at some point, it will click, and you'll find yourself worshipping the Lord God like never before. One of my favorite quotes is "You have to have bad days. Otherwise you have nothing to compare the good days to." If we are consistent through all days, we'll have more good days, whether running or studying God's Word.

- *Consistency in training is key to becoming the best runner you can be.*

- *There are no shortcuts or substitutes for consistent training.*

- *Consistency in Bible study and prayer is essential to a healthy relationship with our Lord.*

sticky notes

_____

_____

_____

_____

_____

_____

_____

_____

_____

_____

_____

_____

_____

_____

_____

Week

winning your own race

I LOOKED IN THE CHURCH BULLETIN one Sunday morning and noticed a Run for God program starting up. I hadn't run in 30 years. I asked myself if I could possibly run again. Intrigued by the thought and the fact that the program was starting close to our wedding anniversary, my husband and I decided to sign up.

Run for God became our 33rd anniversary gift to each other. We both loved running back in high school, but having avoided it for so long, I began to lean upon the verse, "I can do all things through Christ who strengthens me" (Philippians 4:13). It wasn't an easy start up. I injured myself in my first workout. My husband came to my rescue with the car, saying, "Happy anniversary, Honey." This wasn't the anniversary I was expecting. I pulled a hamstring, which set me back two weeks, and was diagnosed with fibromyalgia. But I started this running adventure, and I wasn't going to give up.

One of the first things God taught me through running was to run my own race. God has made us all so unique with different abilities and personalities. Psalm 139:14 says, "I am fearfully and wonderfully made." God knows the abilities that I have. I needed to learn to run my own race by not letting pride get the best of me and by avoiding comparing myself with other runners. I knew I should ignore what others may think of how I look, my turtle speed, or my running style. I wasn't able to keep up with them. In high school, I ran for the blue ribbon. This time my reward would be crossing the finish line to the best of my ability.

The **Run for God** program played a significant part in assisting me with my workouts, a.k.a. "storing the hay." We cheered each other on, shouting, "Keep it up," "You can do this," and my favorite one, "Only one more minute to go." I realized quickly that my Run For God buddies were there to support and encourage me. They didn't care about how I looked, my speed, or my style.

When a person has a relationship with Christ, he or she has become a runner in the Christian race. We are to run the race that is set before us, but we often compare ourselves to others in our spiritual lives. When we see pastors, church leaders, missionaries, and teachers, we try to measure our Christian walk with them. When this happens, we are more concerned about looking good to other believers than our relationship with God. This often gets us off track.

In Galatians 6:4, Paul tells us to pay careful attention to our own work, "and then he will have rejoicing in himself alone, and not in another." What Paul is saying here is to run our own race, not someone else's. How do we run the Christian race? Paul tells us in 1 Corinthians 9:24, "Do you not know that those who run in a race all run, but one receives the prize? Run in such a way that you may obtain it." This passage encourages me to keep being faithful. God's got this; so stay focused because the finish line is near. There will always be someone faster and stronger than we are, and that is all right. When we strive to be the person God made us to be, we will finish strong.

Over two years ago I started walking, which led to running. Since we started Run for God, my daughters have joined us. We all recently participated in a family race weekend. I ran a 5K with my husband, two of my daughters, and my future son-in-law. We all started at the same time, but we ran the race differently. One of my daughters started out fast and stayed fast. My husband started out his normal pace and stayed that pace. My future son-in-law ran his pace with his future bride then sped up near the finish line to pass my husband. We all ran the race with our personal style and pace. We all finished strong with the abilities God has given us.

The next day I watched one of my daughters run her first marathon. Witnessing the events of the race unfold, we were filled with great excitement and tears as we watched. Sometimes the difficulty was written on their faces, and you knew that they were looking forward to the finish line. Yet they pressed on with great determination and commitment. Almost a mile out from the finish, I saw my daughter running. Although she was still smiling, she said, "I can't feel my legs." I knew it wasn't easy, but I knew that she was going to finish strong, because her focus remained on the finish line. She received a medal for that race, which won't last, but the prize in the Christian race is eternal life. Hebrews 3:14 says, "For we have become partakers of Christ if we hold the beginning of our confidence steadfast to the end."

What does finishing strong in the Christian race look like? Living our lives while growing from God's Word one nugget at a time. Living our lives faithfully serving with our individual gifts one day at a time, encouraging others one moment at time. We will pray until God calls us home, and we will live focused on our Savior from the beginning to end. We can do this! Can't you just imagine the finish line of heaven?

Cheryl Light – *Columbia, SC*

get in the word

John 15:5

I am the vine, you are the branches. He who abides in Me, and I in him, bears much fruit; for without Me you can do nothing.

Galatians 6:4

But let each one examine his own work, and then he will have rejoicing in himself alone, and not in another.

Hebrews 3:14

For we have become partakers of Christ if we hold the beginning of our confidence steadfast to the end.

scripture memorization

Write out the scripture(s) in the space below and recite them ten times.

_____

_____

_____

_____

_____

_____

_____

_____

_____

_____

_____

_____

_____

_____

_____

_____

_____

something to ponder

WHAT ARE some reasons why we compare ourselves with others?

_____

_____

_____

_____

HOW DO we stay focused in the Christian race?

_____

_____

_____

_____

HOW DO you plan to finish strong?

_____

_____

_____

_____

running observations
by dean

Never Look Back

DO YOU HAVE A RIVAL? DO you have that person, maybe a friend, who shows up at races and it turns into a battle each time you toe the line? Maybe you win some and he wins some. Maybe you've never beaten him. Maybe he has never beaten you, but he's close. Regardless of the situation, you have an intense rivalry. Oh, you may not share openly how intense it is, but it's powerful. I can remember more than a dozen such rivalries I have had over the years.

There are general guidelines to racing that help you shave seconds from your time, as well as helping you mentally get the most from your performance. One of those rules is to never look back. When you know your rival is behind you, it can be difficult to avoid looking back to see where they are. Resist the temptation. If you turn to look behind you, your rival will see that you're worried about them. In short, you will give them hope. You want them to feel as if you are running strong and catching you is hopeless.

Worrying about someone behind you can motivate you to run faster. I remember races where I had no idea how far ahead of my competition I was, so I kept my eyes forward and ran as hard as I could. After hitting the finish line, I turned to look behind me and saw that they were much further behind than I thought. If I had turned to look behind me, I would have noticed how far ahead I was and may have slowed. My high school coach, Richard Westbrook, called it "running scared." There's a lot to be said for being motivated by fear.

There is one place where you can steal a glance back to see where you are in the race. When you turn a corner and your line of vision is clear to see behind you by cutting your eyes to the side without turning your head, I think it's okay to take a peek. It should appear like a curious glance rather than a concerned search. Make sure you remember what your competition is wearing so that you will not have to look too closely.

One of the greatest things about being a Christian is that we don't have to look back on our lives. Any mistakes we have made in our lives are forgiven by the one true God through the blood of His Son. It gives us hope to look forward and keep the finish line in mind, as Paul told us. Keep your eyes on the prize!

• *Looking back gives your opponent confidence they can catch you and could discourage you if they are closer than you think.*

• *There's nothing wrong with running scared.*

• *Keep looking forward to Christ and His righteousness, not at other Christians running around you.*

sticky notes

_____

_____

_____

_____

_____

_____

_____

_____

scratching the surface

IN MY MID-20S, I WAS BITTEN by the running bug. Entering local 5K races just wasn't enough though. I needed a goal. So after much looking, I found one that was difficult, but attainable, the Boston Marathon. My dream was to be in the same race as many of the best runners in the world, and in order to start that race, I had to earn a qualifying time, called a Boston Qualifying (BQ). A charity spot would not do. I wanted that BQ enough that I vowed never to visit Boston until I qualified for the marathon.

Over the next two years, I started running more. After the first year, I ran my first marathon, but I still had to knock an hour off of my time in order to qualify. My job as a high school teacher allowed me to take the summer and devote myself to training for the race. I even chose a marathon in Akron, Ohio, whose course profile mimicked Boston's. That summer of training was awesome. I began to see changes in my body and feel like a real runner. I headed into the race quite confident that I would lower my PR by 20–25 minutes—real progress toward that coveted BQ.

The race started off well. The rolling hills in the beginning part of the race were easy to traverse. I had planned the race and was racing the plan to a T. I even crossed the halfway point about two minutes faster than my previous half marathon PR. Right on target. But when I reached the long hill from miles 17–19, it was tougher than I expected, and I wasn't feeling too great at the top. I ate an energy gel, and everything went south in a hurry. I got sick to my stomach, and after another mile, I simply could not run anymore and had to start walking. The pain was excruciating, and all of the acid that had been building up in my legs flushed itself out all at once. In the span of about fifteen minutes, I had gone from feeling on top of the world to complete devastation. An entire season of training seemed to have been flushed down the drain. By the grace of God, I finished the race nearly 45 minutes slower than my previous marathon, and nearly scaring my wife half out of her wits when I called her from a medical tent to let her know I was okay. I put on the happy face for her and told her I was glad to have finished. But inwardly, I was crushed.

During the ride home, the most amazing thing happened. As I was trying to fall asleep, I heard this voice in my mind clearly say, "That barely scratched the surface of what I went through for you." Wow! Even though I grew up in church, went to a Christian university, and was living life how I thought a young Christian man should, it was not until that moment that I began to understand the depth of God's love. Jesus, the Son of God, took that moment of deep disappointment to speak to me. He knew how deeply that race mattered. Had I not gone through it, I would not have understood what He was saying.

He loved me enough to allow me to fail so my heart would hear His words. I am still awestruck every time I remember those words. Jesus desperately loves each and every one of us. Any pain that you experience, be it through training, injury, or life experience, barely scratches the surface of the pain that our Savior endured so that He could conquer sin and death once and for all.

Sam Ridenour – *Carroll, OH*

get in the word

Psalm 22:24

For He has not despised nor abhorred the affliction of the afflicted; Nor has He hidden His face from Him; But when He cried to Him, He heard.

Hebrews 12:3

For consider Him who endured such hostility from sinners against Himself, lest you become weary and discouraged in your souls.

Matthew 27:11–54

Now Jesus stood before the governor. And the governor asked Him, saying, "Are You the King of the Jews?"

Jesus said to him, "It is as you say."
12 And while He was being accused by the chief priests and elders, He answered nothing.

13 Then Pilate said to Him, "Do You not hear how many things they testify against You?"

14 But He answered him not one word, so that the governor marveled greatly.

15 Now at the feast the governor was accustomed to releasing to the multitude one prisoner whom they wished. 16 And at that time they had a notorious prisoner called Barabbas. 17 Therefore, when they had gathered together, Pilate said to them, "Whom do you want me to release to you? Barabbas, or Jesus who is called Christ?" 18 For he knew that they had handed Him over because of envy.

19 While he was sitting on the judgment seat, his wife sent to him, saying, "Have nothing to do with that just Man, for I have suffered many things today in a dream because of Him."

20 But the chief priests and elders persuaded the multitudes that they should ask for Barabbas and destroy Jesus.

21 The governor answered and said to them, "Which of the two do you want me to release to you?"

They said, "Barabbas!"

22 Pilate said to them, "What then shall I do with Jesus who is called Christ?"

They all said to him, "Let Him be crucified!"

23 Then the governor said, "Why, what evil has He done?"

But they cried out all the more, saying, "Let Him be crucified!"

24 When Pilate saw that he could not prevail at all, but rather that a tumult was rising, he took water and washed his hands before the multitude, saying, "I am innocent of the blood of this just Person. You see to it."

25 And all the people answered and said, "His blood be on us and on our children."

26 Then he released Barabbas to them; and when he had scourged

Jesus, he delivered Him to be crucified.

27 Then the soldiers of the governor took Jesus into the Praetorium and gathered the whole garrison around Him.

28 And they stripped Him and put a scarlet robe on Him.

29 When they had twisted a crown of thorns, they put it on His head, and a reed in His right hand. And they bowed the knee before Him and mocked Him, saying, "Hail, King of the Jews!"

30 Then they spat on Him, and took the reed and struck Him on the head.

31 And when they had mocked Him, they took the robe off Him, put His own clothes on Him, and led Him away to be crucified.

32 Now as they came out, they found a man of Cyrene, Simon by name. Him they compelled to bear His cross.

33 And when they had come to a place called Golgotha, that is to say, Place of a Skull,

34 they gave Him sour wine mingled with gall to drink. But when He had tasted it, He would not drink.

35 Then they crucified Him, and divided His garments, casting lots, that it might be fulfilled which was spoken by the prophet: "They divided My garments among them, And for My clothing they cast lots."

36 Sitting down, they kept watch over Him there.

*37 And they put up over His head the accusation written against Him:
THIS IS JESUS THE KING OF THE JEWS.*

38 Then two robbers were crucified with Him, one on the right and another on the left.

39 And those who passed by blasphemed Him, wagging their heads

40 and saying, "You who destroy the temple and build it in three days, save Yourself! If You are the Son of God, come down from the cross."

41 Likewise the chief priests also, mocking with the scribes and elders, said,

42 "He saved others; Himself He cannot save. If He is the King of Israel, let Him now come down from the cross, and we will believe Him.

43 He trusted in God; let Him deliver Him now if He will have Him; for He said, 'I am the Son of God.'"

44 Even the robbers who were crucified with Him reviled Him with the same thing.

45 Now from the sixth hour until the ninth hour there was darkness over all the land.

46 And about the ninth hour Jesus cried out with a loud voice, saying, "Eli, Eli, lama sabachthani?" that is, "My God, My God, why have You forsaken Me?"

47 Some of those who stood there, when they heard that, said, "This Man is calling for Elijah!"

48 Immediately one of them ran and took a sponge, filled it with sour wine and put it on a reed, and offered it to Him to drink.

49 The rest said, "Let Him alone; let us see if Elijah will come to save Him."

50 And Jesus cried out again with a loud voice, and yielded up His spirit.

51 Then, behold, the veil of the temple was torn in two from top to bottom; and the earth quaked, and the rocks were split,

52 and the graves were opened; and many bodies of the saints who had fallen asleep were raised;

53 and coming out of the graves after His resurrection, they went into the holy city and appeared to many.

54 So when the centurion and those with him, who were guarding Jesus, saw the earthquake and the things that had happened, they feared greatly, saying, "Truly this was the Son of God!"

scripture memorization

Write out the scripture(s) in the space below and recite them ten times.

_____

_____

_____

_____

_____

_____

_____

_____

_____

_____

_____

_____

_____

_____

_____

_____

_____

_____

_____

_____

_____

_____

_____

_____

_____

_____

something to ponder

WHAT IS the worst suffering you've ever experienced as a runner?

_____

_____

_____

_____

WHEN YOU are in the middle of it, how do you deal with suffering?

_____

_____

_____

_____

HOW CAN you make your reaction to suffering more Christ-like?

_____

_____

_____

_____

running observations
by dean

Failure is Okay

HAVE YOU EVER HAD A BAD race or a bad workout and beat yourself up for a week afterwards? Of course you have. We all have. Here are a few reasons why having bad days are beneficial.

For starters, let's look at other sports. In basketball, every time an opposing team comes down the court, the defense attempts to stop them from scoring. They fail about half the time, but that's not an indication of an impending defeat. Let's look at baseball. A batter who fails to get a hit exactly two thirds of the time will probably become a Hall of Fame member. You see, there is imperfection in every sport, and running is no different.

Here is the magical question: Did we learn from our mistakes? After all, we set a goal, we worked hard to reach our goal, race day came and we missed our goal. Me had to make a mistake, right? Well maybe. After running thousands of races over the years, I have discovered that when I miss my goal, sometimes it's my fault and sometimes I can't explain it. That's okay. I will go back and look at training logs and see if I can see if there was something that may have caused it, but if I don't find anything, I don't fret. The reason I am able to take it in stride is because the somewhat unpredictable nature of racing makes it fun. I don't always look at it that way at first, but I'll eventually get there. I believe being able to move on after a poor performance is important to running success. Dwelling on a negative outcome can cause self-doubt and confidence issues that ultimately lead to more of the same.

I love the saying, "You have to have bad days, otherwise you have nothing to compare the good days to." The successful races are that much sweeter when you have been through enough unsuccessful ones. It took me five marathons to get it right, but it was all that much more exciting when I did. The good news is you can still have the same goal next time in most cases. I have missed my post-40 10K goal by two seconds, but I still have that goal, even at 48 years old. If I don't reach it in the next couple of years, I can set a new age 50 goal!

Setbacks always take me toward Jesus, and that is always a good thing. Most of those setbacks are much more important than a race. It's no secret we fail God all the time and He forgives us when we do. If God can forgive us for our much more critical indiscretions, surely we can forgive ourselves for something as minor as a bad race.

- *It is okay to miss a goal. It doesn't mean we should stop setting goals.*

- *The inability to move on after a poor performance can have a detrimental effect on your running.*

- *If God can forgive serious indiscretions, we can forgive ourselves when we fail to meet a running goal.*

running with cancer

Running has been the tool God has used in my life to help me overcome many obstacles, including depression and epilepsy. When I found out I had breast cancer last August, I never imagined the lessons I would learn. The greatest lesson was giving thanks for cancer and other trials. I learned that thanking my Lord for hard times brings Him great glory, not to mention His unmistakable presence. It was not easy to thank Him for cancer, but with His help I can do all things (*Philippians 4:13*).

After my first round of chemotherapy I tried to keep up with my running workouts because they have always been the times when I hear God most clearly, when His presence feels most real. After my first chemo treatment, I ran for five minutes and found myself exhausted, close to passing out. My doctor ordered me to avoid running until the chemo is over. I sat on the side of the running path, crying out to God.

On May 7, 2014, I had my last chemo treatment and felt ready to run again. I ventured out on May 23 with my friend Sue, who has been walking with me and was now willing to run with me. She was a blessing, a God-sent friend reminding me of His everlasting faithfulness.

Running on this day felt like I was running for the first time. I was exhausted again and frustrated. It's hard to go from running long distances to barely pulling through a half mile. After a bit more walking and running, I wanted to sit down and quit, but my friend cheered me on, and I knew in my heart they were cheers from heaven. God was beginning to renew my strength. I am so thankful for my friend who has truly loved me at all times (*Proverbs 17:17*). Do you have friends in your life like Sue? Are you thankful for them?

The next morning while on a walk, God showed me how it was part of his plan, not a punishment, for me to stop running. He wanted to quiet me, to slow me down so that I would see Him in a new way. "Be still, and know that I am God" (*Psalm 46:10*).

Being a runner, I find remaining still to be a challenge, but I can be tranquil in His presence while I am moving. Being still means calming your heart so you can hear what our Shepherd is saying to you. For me, running is a gift He has given me, a gift that helps me serve Him with strength (no seizures, no epilepsy) in the ministry He has entrusted to me for as long as He calls.

I will remain still in God, thinking of the words in Isaiah 40:31, "But those who wait on the Lord shall renew their strength; they shall mount up with wings like eagles, they shall run and not be weary, they shall walk and not faint." The journey back to health may take time and may look doubtful, but I am putting all of my hope in Him to run with me on this journey.

Rebecca Ruth Olesky – *Easton, PA*

get in the word

Philippians 4:13

I can do all things through Christ who strengthens me.

Psalm 46:10

Be still, and know that I am God;
I will be exalted among the nations,
I will be exalted in the earth!

Isaiah 40:31

But those who wait on the Lord
Shall renew their strength;
They shall mount up with wings like eagles,
They shall run and not be weary,
They shall walk and not faint.

scripture memorization

Write out the scripture(s) in the space below and recite them ten times.

_____

_____

_____

_____

_____

_____

_____

_____

_____

_____

_____

_____

something to ponder

WHAT IS something you need to do that can only be done in His strength? Will you trust Him or keep trying it on your own?

_____

_____

_____

_____

WHAT AREAS OF YOUR LIFE DO you need to slow down in order to be still and know that He is God?

_____

_____

_____

_____

WHAT IS your hope in God?

_____

_____

_____

_____

running observations
by dean

Shoes, Shoes, Shoes

LET'S SAY YOU HAVE WORN THE tires out on your car, and you go to the store to buy some new rubber. The guy behind the counter says, "We have just the tire you need." You ask him if he needs to know what model car you drive, and he says, "Nah, they're one size fits all." I bet you decide to buy tires somewhere else. Many people hear the same thing from the running shoe store and buy them anyway.

If the place where you buy your running shoes doesn't ask you questions and/ or watch you walk or run to determine what shoe would be best for you, you should reconsider where you buy your shoes. The only exception is that you were fitted in the past and you are purchasing the same shoe again. Unfortunately—or fortunately depending how you look at it—shoe companies are regularly updating shoe models and sometimes the update doesn't feel like the previous model. Of course, keeping up with the latest technology is important, so updates are necessary.

Your running shoes are every bit as important to your running as your tires are to your car. While there are many companies who make tires to fit your car, there are only a few models from each of those companies that are suited for your car. If you use the wrong tire, it can result in poor gas mileage, stress on your transmission, speedometer inaccuracy, or poor handling. In the same way, many companies make a running shoe style that would work for you, but not every shoe a company makes would be good for you. As a matter of fact, some of them could be very bad for you and promote injury.

I wish I had a dollar for every time someone has asked me, "What's the best running shoe?" The question is asked with an expectation of a rapid response, but there is no way to answer that question quickly. I usually respond by trying to point them toward a store with staff who are knowledgeable in the fitting of running shoes. I can think of a number of injuries caused by wearing the wrong shoes, but I can't think of any serious injuries caused by wearing the wrong shirt or shorts. Oh, you may develop a serious chaffing issue, but that pales in comparison to tendonitis in your knee. This is a "leave it to the professionals" situation. You may be able to find a bargain at another store, but paying for expertise is well worth it when it comes to running shoes.

Being a Christian is similar in that you have one tool that is clearly your most important resource. The Bible is so central to our faith that it would be impossible to fulfill the Great Commission without it. I'm thankful for those whom God put in place to make a record of the events in the Bible.

- *Shoes are your most important running gear purchase.*

- *Using the wrong shoe can promote injury.*

- *The most important tool to your faith is the Bible. Don't leave it in the toolbox.*

sticky notes

run, mama, run!

IT WAS A BEAUTIFULLY BRIGHT, CLEAR, and cool morning as hundreds of spectators gathered at Robins Air Force base to watch a race. They were mostly parents and family members, mine included, who had come to watch one race. I had been training for months with my neighbor, and there we stood in the shivering cold, bundled with stashes of GU, waiting with hundreds of other runners at the starting line. For a few minutes, I began looking around at the other runners. There were those who were stretching, bouncing with excitement, smiling, and laughing while waiting for the sound of the gun to start the race. There was something deeply spiritual about that scene. The excitement warmed my heart.

When the gun fired, we waited several minutes before we started running, but that didn't stop us from moving in place in preparation for the long run ahead. As I stepped across the starting line, I could hear spectators clapping, cheering and shouting. Those wonderful sounds soon grew faint as I moved farther and farther along the road of my first half marathon. To keep myself distracted from the miles ahead, I watched my fellow runners' paces, strides, and gear. I thought about how they trained and prepared for their race, what distance they were running, and who had helped them train. I ran through many mile markers where spectators and volunteers stood ready to welcome and congratulate each of us as we passed. You could see their excitement as they tried to make sure we heard every word of encouragement. "You're doing great! Keep it up!"

The last mile was the hardest. It appeared out of reach for so long, but once I made the last turn on the course, I caught a glimpse of my father standing on the side of the road with my oldest son, who was searching for me. My eyes filled with tears. I began to wave and shout, "Hey!" When I came clear into my son's view, he ran my way smiling and shouting, "You're doing great, Mama!" and took my hand to run the last hundred yards with me. He saw no other runners. He ran as fast as he could, keeping the pace and saying softly to me, "Run, Mama, run! Run Mama, run!" Although I was growing weary, my son, whose heart was bursting with excitement, continued to stay with me till the end. As I crossed the finish line, I turned and gave my son a great big hug. We laughed and had the best time together, like there was no one else in the world but us.

"God," I thought, "this is so beautiful. Thank you for allowing me to experience this moment." A whole morning of incredible moments had merged into one. I thought of a race that we believers are running as well, a race that is different and far more important, one that requires even greater stamina, courage, and character, a race described in Hebrews 12:1–3, "... let us run with endurance the race that is set before us, looking unto Jesus..."

I realized from my experience that I am not only a runner in the faith race, but I am also an encourager to my children who are running beside me. I have helped them train; I have pleaded, instructed, threatened, punished, prayed, praised, laughed, and cried with them. I have tried to familiarize them with the course, but now the gun is up, their race has begun, and I am but a spectator. Like my son, my heart is bursting. I see no other runners. Sometimes their course will take them far from me, and yet I shout, "Run, children, run." Even if they do not hear me, I know One who will.

Occasionally, my children will grow weary, because the race is long and demands much sacrifice. They too will witness hypocrisy, and there are many voices that call to them to quit, telling them they cannot possibly win. They lose sight of their goal. They falter and stumble, and I cry, "Run, children, run!" And when they come to the last hundred yards, how I long to run beside them, saying, "Run, Tyler; run, Zachary." What if I'm gone and there is no one to encourage them to run? What if Satan convinces them they are not going to win? That is why our Lord Jesus said at the last, "It is finished." That is why the great apostle Paul said, "I have finished my course."

Oh God, hear my prayer. If they cannot hear my voice, if I must watch from beyond this arena, dear Lord Jesus, as You have run beside me so often, please run beside them and strengthen their knees that they may finish. Dear God, when they cross that eternal finish line, may I be there to embrace them and welcome them home. May we cry and laugh and spend eternity praising the grace by which we were given this victory. "Run, children, run!"

So my fellow runners, do not be discouraged! Do not give up! Do not quit! Run the race. Keep the faith, and keep your eyes on Jesus!

Tanna Friday – *Centerville, GA*

get in the word

Hebrews 12:1–3

Therefore we also, since we are surrounded by so great a cloud of witnesses, let us lay aside every weight, and the sin which so easily ensnares us, and let us run with endurance the race that is set before us, looking unto Jesus, the author and finisher of our faith, who for the joy that was set before Him endured the cross, despising the shame, and has sat down at the right hand of the throne of God. For consider Him who endured such hostility from sinners against Himself, lest you become weary and discouraged in your souls.

John 17:4

I have glorified You on the earth. I have finished the work which You have given Me to do.

2 Timothy 4:7

I have fought the good fight, I have finished the race, I have kept the faith.

scripture memorization

Write out the scripture(s) in the space below and recite them ten times.

_____

_____

_____

_____

_____

_____

_____

_____

_____

_____

_____

_____

_____

_____

something to ponder

HOW CAN we as Christians encourage each other to stay in the race?

_____

_____

_____

_____

WHAT BIBLICAL principles can we apply to keep us and our loved ones on the right course?

_____

_____

_____

_____

HOW ARE you making time for God to prepare you for the race mentally, physically, and spiritually?

_____

_____

_____

_____

running observations
by dean

My Saturday Family

I RAN OVER 20 RACES LAST year, most of them on Saturday. Races are the reward for all of the hard work you do every day of every week. The races serve as a test for where you think you are physically. They are an indication that your training is going well or that you need to try something different. I love the tension and the competition of those Saturday mornings. And as much as anything, I enjoy hanging out with my Saturday family. Seeing the same core group of people at most races makes the competition, as well as the post-race conversations, more interesting.

Some of my Saturday family members represent all the motivation I need to work hard each week. The heat of the battle during the race and reviewing the race as we cool down afterwards are so much fun. Sometimes I play those moments over in my head, when I am in the middle of a long workout and my body is trying to convince me to slow down. Envisioning a rival finishing ten seconds ahead of me gives me that motivation I need to reach down deep and get all I can out of my current session.

Others do not represent direct competition, but talking about training and racing with them is always stimulating. Those conversations often lead to ideas I can use to help me get better. It was in a conversation after a race several years ago that I learned about the effectiveness of a roller to work the knots out of my muscles. Now, I don't go anywhere without taking my tools with me. I notice a void if too many of these friends stay home.

And there are those whom I know, but I don't know. I see them, even have brief conversations with them, but I don't know their names. I still think they're awesome. Even though our interactions are strictly running related I consider them good friends. We have a common bond with each other. We share an uplifting camaraderie. Attending these events is like escaping to another world where the cares and worries of life disappear for a couple of hours. It's a good thing it is so much fun, because I don't really like getting up early on Saturdays.

I also have a Sunday family, and the two groups share some similarities. Like discussing physical condition with runners, discussing spiritual condition with my church family facilitates my growth in Christ. They are safe people with whom I can share vulnerabilities and struggles. They understand my circumstances and encourage each other. This spiritual training prepares me for sharing my faith with others, even my special Saturday family. And just as it is on race day, I can escape to a worshipful world on Sunday, where the support of other believers helps draw us closer to the Father. Spending time in the embracing arms of my church family helps me to extend my arms for the same embrace to those who need it during the week.

- *There is a special friendship that we share with those who share the same passion we have.*

- *Races are like escaping to another world if only for a couple of hours.*

- *Like the Saturday family, the Sunday family is supportive and helps you to get through the week ahead.*

sticky notes

Week

oh, the places we will go!

I'VE BEEN RUNNING PRETTY CONSISTENTLY FOR about twelve years now. When I started out, I took the route that many runners take; start off with a 5K (or ten), build up to a half marathon, and finally a full marathon. The excitement in training and running all of those races was amazing. My initial goals were first to run a marathon (check) and then to qualify for the Boston Marathon. However, after about 6 marathons, I realized that my body type (think rugby player), and my genetic gifting of a high amount of fast-twitch muscles were simply not going to allow me to shave off the 50+ minutes I would need to in order to punch a ticket to Beantown. So once the dream of Boston faded away, I asked myself, "What's next?"

I loved running and needed a goal race to keep me motivated. What parts of the running spectrum did I like? I liked running fast (who doesn't), running in the woods, and that feeling of accomplishment after finishing a grueling climb up a huge hill. All of those require the ability to be a strong and resilient runner. Thus, I tend to gravitate toward track workouts, trail races, and one very hilly half marathon in Ashland, Ohio every December.

Some of you may find that you like to be a giving runner and thus run races or join teams that raise money for causes in which you believe. Some of you may find that you like to be a joyful runner and participate in color runs or race with a lot of friends. Some of you may find that you like to compete in obstacle races like a Warrior Dash, Tough Mudder, or ultra-endurance races. Now that you've gotten through the 5K class or even the 10K/half marathon class, the possibilities are endless as are the runners you can touch with the love of Christ.

Finding your passion as a runner mirrors maturing as a follower of Christ. We decide to accept Jesus as our Lord and Savior, get off our spiritual couch and begin to walk. Soon we are running alongside Christ Jesus. We reach a point where we begin to ask, "Okay, God, what do You really want me to do with this life You gave me?" The answer is different for each of us.

Though we are all fearfully and wonderfully made, God has blessed each of us with different spiritual talents and gifts. "There are diversities of gifts, but the same Spirit. There are differences of ministries, but the same Lord. And there are diversities of activities, but it is the same God who works all in all" (*1 Corinthians 12:4–6*). The body of Christ needs preachers and teachers, but it also needs prayer warriors, those who serve in the background, those gifted in hospitality, and the list goes on. All are needed in order for a church body to function effectively.

If you are not certain what your talents and gifts are, simply ask. First, ask God where you fit into the life of the Church. He may answer you directly, or He may have you seek out somebody in a leadership position to talk and pray through the seeking process. He has used both methods with me in discovering who I am in Him and where I need to be. But just like the very first workout in the Run For God 5K Challenge, you have to have the courage to take that first step, and say, "I can do all things through Christ who strengthens me."

Samuel Ridenour – *Carroll, OH*

get in the word

1 Corinthians 12:12–14, 26

For as the body is one and has many members, but all the members of that one body, being many, are one body, so also is Christ. For by one Spirit we were all baptized into one body—whether Jews or Greeks, whether slaves or free—and have all been made to drink into one Spirit. For in fact the body is not one member but many. . . . And if one member suffers, all the members suffer with it; or if one member is honored, all the members rejoice with it.

Revelation 3:20

Behold, I stand at the door and knock. If anyone hears My voice and opens the door, I will come in to him and dine with him, and he with Me.

1 Samuel 3:10

Now the Lord came and stood and called as at other times, "Samuel! Samuel!"

And Samuel answered, "Speak, for Your servant hears."

scripture memorization

Write out the scripture(s) in the space below and recite them ten times.

_____

_____

_____

_____

_____

_____

_____

_____

_____

_____

_____

_____

_____

_____

something to ponder

WHAT IS it about running that brings you the most joy?

_____

_____

_____

_____

WHAT DO you do within the life of the Church that brings you the most joy?

_____

_____

_____

_____

DO THE talents you use in your everyday life overlap with a need of the Church?

_____

_____

_____

_____

running observations
by dean

What If Everyone Was a Runner?

IMAGINE A WORLD WHERE EVERYONE IS a runner. We would have running paths everywhere, so that we could travel on foot. We would use less gasoline, but carbohydrate consumption would be up. Showers would necessarily be available everywhere to ensure the elimination of offensive odors. Travel time would increase, but endorphin levels would be at an all-time high.

You wouldn't be late for work because of a flat tire, but you would have to leave the house earlier on "easy run" days. If you had an injury, you would be one of the oddballs who had to drive to work. Fast food restaurants would need a run-through lane, packaging your food in a backpack so that you could keep running after picking up your afternoon sustenance.

The running clothes sections of department stores would be huge and dress codes would relax to allow for more casual attire. Sales of moisture-wicking fabric would explode and bright colors would rule the dye industry. Stocks in running shoe companies would skyrocket as retail sales increased ten-fold.

Healthcare costs would plummet, except for orthopedics. Our collective blood pressure would be lower, but our tendonitis would be a regular water-cooler conversation. Heart disease would become an afterthought, while there would be a need for specialized runner's knee clinics. Obesity would be all but eliminated, but plantar fasciitis would become as common as the flu. Overall medication of society would fall precipitously while the sales of anti-inflammatories would see sharp spikes.

Everyone would understand why you're down about your latest race result. Having to reschedule a meeting because Tuesday is your track workout day would be a no-brainer. There would be fewer conversations about the weather, because—no wait; there would be more conversations about the weather and how it affected your latest run or to decide when you are going to fit in your next run. Of course, the track would be crowded, necessitating new tracks to be built so that everyone could work out at their convenience. Treadmill use would run rampant, with treadmills everywhere. Getting your run completed for the day would be easier than ever.

Local road races would be so large, we would have to run them in heats all day. We wouldn't ask our friends if they were running the race this weekend. We would ask what time slot they qualified for. Better yet, maybe they would run them by age group. They should start the older folks earlier since they like to get up before dawn anyway, and during the summer, it gets hot in the afternoon.

Isn't it great to think of all the possibilities where everyone shares the same interests? It would make conversations with anyone so much easier. Even better would be to think of a world where everyone believed in the redeeming blood of Jesus Christ. Of course, that would be the desire of God's heart. So why do we have such a difficult time trying to make His desire a reality? We will share running stories with anyone we can get to listen. When our relationship with Jesus is strong, we do the same thing, only our story is the true account of our Lord and Savior.

- *Imagining a world where everyone shares a love of running is exhilarating. Being able to share interests with anyone and everyone would bring us together.*

- *Running-themed establishments would make shopping and vacations more fun than ever.*

- *If we can share running stories with others, we have no excuse not to share our testimony.*

sticky notes

_____

_____

_____

_____

_____

_____

_____

project management

BY STRICT DEFINITION, PROJECT MANAGEMENT IS the discipline of planning, coordinating, and controlling resources and procedures to bring about a result. That's how I've been earning a paycheck for over 20 years. When most of your experience is in leading various projects, project management habits kick in everywhere, and you tend to see every new challenge in life as an opportunity to bring about a desired outcome by balancing the constraints of time, money, and quality—even with weight loss, spiritual growth, and fitness goals.

To reach a goal, a good project manager (PM) will balance all inputs, anticipate challenges, and define outcomes. Even if the project is large or has never been accomplished before, they can break everything into small incremental units that are easier to achieve. It wasn't until I viewed losing weight as a project to manage that I achieved any permanent results. I've battled food addictions and weight issues most of my adult life. Gym memberships, exercise equipment, and fad diets—all promising quick and easy results (or your money back)—usually ended in frustration and depression. Everyone knows the basic formula for weight loss: burn more calories than you take in, but it doesn't happen overnight. You don't hit your weight goal in one week any more than a beginner can run his first 5K after three workouts.

I guess it's human nature to be impatient, and although I know without a doubt that most things take time, I still hope for shortcuts and quick results. I want to burn that donut off now. I want that project finished now. I want to get that promotion now. I want to be a mature Christian now. Oops. Did I just admit I have spiritual impatience too? Yeah, if I'm honest with myself, I have to admit that I get frustrated with bad news, stagnant growth, or just failure in living up to what I profess.

I know that I have to keep working on my projects, if I want to realize the benefits. Think of the things you've learned how to do in life. Did you just wake up one morning with a new skill? Of course not. You had to learn how to do everything. Sometimes it came easily, sometimes it didn't. And things that come easily for me might not for you.

That's why I like the Run for God program so much. It presents two big goals—run a 5K and get closer to God—and breaks them down in steps that present an easy to understand approach to reaching your goals. Now that I know how to be successful, I want to help others realize their goals too. So I'm upfront with people when they express interest in joining our Run for God group. I approach it like another project to manage, explaining the resources needed, the time required, and the benefit they will realize. I challenge every new class the very first night to "give this program 30 minutes of workouts, three times a week, over the next 12 weeks, and it will change your life." Those who are intentional about their commitment to the program find it to be true.

Kent Ogle – *Webb City, MO*

get in the word

Luke 14:28–33

For which of you, intending to build a tower, does not sit down first and count the cost, whether he has enough to finish it— lest, after he has laid the foundation, and is not able to finish, all who see it begin to mock him, saying, 'This man began to build and was not able to finish'? Or what king, going to make war against another king, does not sit down first and consider whether he is able with ten thousand to meet him who comes against him with twenty thousand? Or else, while the other is still a great way off, he sends a delegation and asks conditions of peace. So likewise, whoever of you does not forsake all that he has cannot be My disciple.

Joshua 24:15

And if it seems evil to you to serve the Lord, choose for yourselves this day whom you will serve, whether the gods which your fathers served that were on the other side of the River, or the gods of the Amorites, in whose land you dwell. But as for me and my house, we will serve the Lord."

Romans 12:1–2

I beseech you therefore, brethren, by the mercies of God, that you present your bodies a living sacrifice, holy, acceptable to God, which is your reasonable service. And do not be conformed to this world, but be transformed by the renewing of your mind, that you may prove what is that good and acceptable and perfect will of God.

scripture memorization

Write out the scripture(s) in the space below and recite them ten times.

_____

_____

_____

_____

_____

_____

_____

_____

_____

_____

_____

_____

_____

_____

_____

_____

_____

_____

_____

_____

_____

_____

_____

_____

_____

_____

_____

_____

_____

something to ponder

WHAT CAN you do now that you once thought you'd never accomplish?

_____

_____

_____

_____

WHAT ASPECTS of your life do you need to be more intentional about?

_____

_____

_____

_____

HOW CAN you leverage your experiences and knowledge to help someone else?

_____

_____

_____

_____

running observations
by dean

The Learning Never Stops

AS SIMPLE AS RUNNING IS, THERE is always something new to learn. We view the sport much differently today than we did 30 years ago. The popularity of running has brought more and more curious people into the fold. They ask deep questions and dig to find answers. The reason world records continue to fall is not because people are genetically faster now, but because we understand more about training and how to prepare the body for the race.

We now have scientific studies that show us how nutrition affects performance and training. Professional runners have full time dieticians and chefs to enable them to maximize caloric intake with the proper mix of proteins, carbohydrates, fats, fruits and vegetables. Even substances like caffeine have been studied almost exhaustively to discover the impact it has on performance. All these foods and supplements interact with each other, so the research will never be complete. We will always be gaining a better understanding of nutrition and how it relates to our individual bodies.

We are learning more all the time about how cross training affects running. In the past, there were dissenting views about lifting weights and their ability to positively influence running. Today, most top athletes realize the benefits of weight training, and there are a myriad of other cross-training methods and devices that compliment running. For example, there are hybrid bicycle/elliptical machines that provide a low impact alternative to running that use the same muscles as you do when running. This enables a runner to work through an injury without the impact of running.

As an aging runner, it is encouraging to hear about the advancements in Masters Running. Times once considered off limits for the over-40 crowd are now attainable. Although some of this may be due to the fact that there are many more Masters Runners than ever before, there is also the understanding that training has to evolve with the runner. We have discovered that you cannot work quite as hard as you did when you were younger, but we are also finding that it is not necessary. We have found smarter ways to train to replace the harder ways of yesteryear.

We use terms like anaerobic threshold, VO2 max, dynamic stretching, minimalist shoes, moisture-wicking clothing, compression socks and tights, and foam roller in addition to all the old running terms. Some things have remained the same for many years, like tempo runs. They have been around for a long time and are still an important staple for many runners. On the other hand, we are learning new things about lactic acid and its role related to soreness and recovery. It is a subject we thought we knew all about 20 years ago, and now we are finding out that we were not quite right. So it is exciting to know things are changing. The learning never stops.

Gregory the Great said, "Scripture is like a river, broad and deep, shallow enough here for the lamb to go wading, but deep enough there for the elephant to swim." If learning about running never stops, how much more can be said about learning from God's Word? Although the basic stories of the Bible are simple to understand, there is more than a lifetime of learning to be gleaned from its pages.

• *There is always more to learn about running as research uncovers new training methods, nutrition advantages, and cross-training benefits.*

• *You can do your own research and then apply what you learn to what works for you. Don't become attached to new research if you find out it is not good for you specifically. Just because it works for most people, doesn't mean it works for everyone.*

• *God's Word does not evolve. There is a lifetime of learning available to you in many different translations.*

sticky notes

_____

_____

_____

_____

_____

_____

it's more than crossing a finish line; it's finishing the race!

I STARTED RUNNING USING THE C25K app on my phone. My best friend,

her sister, and I all decided we would give this a chance. We didn't think we could run, and believe me, week one day one was a challenge, but we faithfully completed the training. I wanted to run a 5K, but I wasn't a fast runner—my son would walk beside me while I ran—but I still wanted to enter the race.

I found the Run For God program in an online search, and when I saw that name, I began to weep. See, the whole running thing started because my ex-husband left me for another woman after 15 years of marriage. In the cycle of grief I experienced, I believed the lies Satan placed in my head—that he left me because I was fat. I believed this lie, and I thought if I could lose weight, he'd come back to me.

I never missed my night of running. I ran the distance, ate healthy and lost 47 pounds, but study, training, and race weren't about crossing any finish line. I was racing for the Lord. I was saying, "Lord, life is hard. I never thought I'd be where I am today. I'm scared of the future and raising my son all alone, but Lord, I'll finish strong for You! I will finish this race of life, I won't quit. I'll finish, Lord!"

I finished that 5K without walking once. I had no one at the end to congratulate me. I had no friend to run beside, but I did have Jesus. He ran beside me the whole time. When I finished, He picked me up in His arms and said, "Good job, baby girl. I'm so proud of you. Everything's going to be okay! Lonely, yes, I know, but I won't leave you alone."

I will always run for God now. That's whom I'm running for! My race isn't over yet, and I will keep on training and keep my eyes on Him.

Kelly Grimes – *Hixon, TN*

get in the word

Psalm 138:8
The Lord will perfect that which concerns me;
Your mercy, O Lord, endures forever;
Do not forsake the works of Your hands.

Romans 9:16
So then it is not of him who wills, nor of him who runs, but of God who shows mercy.

Galatians 6:9
And let us not grow weary while doing good, for in due season we shall reap if we do not lose heart.

scripture memorization

Write out the scripture(s) in the space below and recite them ten times.

_____

_____

_____

_____

_____

_____

_____

_____

_____

_____

_____

_____

_____

_____

_____

_____

something to ponder

WHAT DO all runners want to do in a race?

_____

_____

_____

_____

WHAT IS your goal when entering a race?

_____

_____

_____

_____

WHO GIVES you your next step?

_____

_____

_____

_____

running observations
by dean

Anticipating the Race

"WELL," SAID POOH, "WHAT I LIKE best," and then he had to stop and think. Because although eating honey was a very good thing to do, there was a moment just before you began to eat it which was better than when you were, but he didn't know what it was called." — *A. A. Milne, Winnie-the-Pooh*

The anticipation of a race is so exciting that it is difficult to focus on anything else. Often the excitement manifests itself as nervousness. Other times it is as if we were waiting for Santa Claus. That race has taken months of preparation running hundreds of miles, making time sacrifices, and turning down dessert a dozen times. It's exhilarating and possibly energy sapping. Learning to control your pre-race excitement is important to running a successful race.

I have found that anxiety over an event is often tied to a specific worry. Maybe you're worried about going out too fast or the massive hill at mile four or a rival who is going to show up. There are many potential worries, and each of them can either motivate you or drain your energy.

A couple of ways to combat the energy-draining worry of race day appear to oppose each other. You can focus on the problem early and build up your confidence, or you can focus on something else, like your greatest advantage or strength, effectively ignoring the problem. Whichever way you choose to handle your worries, it is important to relax in the 48 hours before race time.

Embracing the anticipation is a big part of the fun. Once you learn how to control your worries about what could go wrong, you start to focus on the challenge and what can go right. When you learn to focus your energy on the positive aspects of the race, you begin to build adrenaline reserves to unleash at race time. It is the culmination of a journey. If you have played your cards right, you'll have intense energy at the starting line, knowing you are prepared, focusing on the race. You will be ready to perform.

Of course, the anticipation and excitement we get from running any race pales in comparison to the Lord's excitement about us. Because Christ Jesus brought us into His family, the Almighty God "will rejoice over you with gladness, He will quiet you with His love, He will rejoice over you with singing" *(Zephaniah 3:16–17)*. He isn't standing on the sidelines with His arms folded, wondering why we can't run faster. He is singing about us. We are the ones He wanted in His family, and here we are now, as righteous as Christ, living our lives for His glory. God loves that. Today let's focus on our daily responsibilities in light of God's abundant love for us.

- *Keep a lid on your anticipatory excitement for the next race so you can run your best.*

- *Worrying about any particular aspect of a race will typically do nothing but use up energy you will need to run. Embrace the anticipation instead of worrying about it.*

- *As brothers and sisters with Christ, our Father in heaven rejoices over us and looks forward to walking with us throughout the day.*

sticky notes

_____

_____

_____

_____

_____

_____

_____

_____

_____

_____

_____

_____

_____

_____

_____

_____

_____

it's about more than you

IT WAS MILE 83 OF THE 2011 Run Woodstock 100 race, my first attempt at the 100-mile distance. Exhausted from having run all night on trails often resembling rivers of mud from the incessant rain and thunderstorms, I dropped into a portable camping chair and found myself unable to hold back the tears. My shoulders slumped, and I hid my head in my hands, sobbing. I was completely spent, totally empty. My support crew, which had been remarkable through nearly 20 hours of running, wasn't sure how to handle me now. A brief respite in the chair had been my reward for completing each 16.6-mile lap, serving also as a means to change socks and shoes and recharge a bit. This time, however, was different.

My wife knelt low and asked if I was okay.

"Don't make me go out there again," I muttered.

"Remember, this is about something bigger than yourself," she replied.

And with that gentle, yet profound, reminder, I pulled myself up from the chair and headed out for the sixth and final lap of what would become known as "Mudstock."

"Are you hurt?" asked Kacey, my friend and pacer for the last lap.

"Everything hurts, but no, I am not hurt."

"Well then, let's do this," she said.

For over four hours, my routine became a singular focus on making it to the base of the next hill. That meant I got to walk. With each incline I would get reduced to a walk, but each time as we reached the crest of the hill, I would hear an encouraging, yet, emphatic command once again, "Okay, you can run this."

The race started at 4 p.m. on Friday with blue skies and beautiful sunshine, but as daylight faded, the clouds rolled in, and the rain began and continued throughout the night. Many hours later on Saturday afternoon, halfway through the final lap, the clouds disappeared. Exiting the woods at the top of a climb into a wide-open space, Kacey pointed to my shadow and suggested this was God's way of reminding me that He was indeed present in this journey. Sometimes the little things matter most.

My finish line was celebrated with arms up in victory, hands clenched tightly with my wife on the one side and the inspiration for the cause—our good friend Lorrie—on the other. Lorrie has the heart of a lion, but lives daily with challenges of Rheumatoid Arthritis (RA). She would run marathons, if her body allowed it. She is an inspiration by her consistent positive attitude and her joy for the Lord, despite a daily grind that seems daunting. We ran that day to raise money for RA research. I'm not sure she realizes how important her example was in getting me to the finish line.

Within minutes of finishing, I was nodding off in the camping chair. A few minutes of treasured rest, shutting my eyes for the first time in the better part of a day and a half, were interrupted by the sound of my wife quietly crying and talking with a friend. As circumstance would have it, earlier that day her step-dad passed away. She had kept it from me, carrying that burden on her own, choosing not to let it be a distraction from the day's goal. I might have been doing the running, but she was an integral part of the team, needing to be fully present for us to achieve the finish line.

The next morning, Pam and I went to church. Despite incredible fatigue and mourning, not to mention the funeral logistics that needed to be addressed, we were drawn to worship. It was a remarkable service, filled with thankfulness and praise. It was good for both me and my wife for different reasons. The finish line was truly a big, bold dream; one that was realized only through the combined efforts of the crew, the cause, the pacers and the support of friends that were present throughout the journey.

Ultramarathoning requires such an absolute effort that all masks are stripped away from your true self. There is no energy to pretend or hide anything. It takes you to a place where you celebrate your talents, appreciate the support of those committed to you, and commune with the Lord in truly overwhelming emotion.

The finish line photo captured an expression of elation with arms held high, but if you look closely, all three of us are crying. God showed up that day in many ways. I hope my expression back to Him was of humble praise and gratitude.

Chuck Cova – *Fenton, MI*

get in the word

Philippians 3:13–14

Brethren, I do not count myself to have apprehended; but one thing I do, forgetting those things which are behind and reaching forward to those things which are ahead, I press toward the goal for the prize of the upward call of God in Christ Jesus.

Romans 12:1–2

I beseech you therefore, brethren, by the mercies of God, that you present your bodies a living sacrifice, holy, acceptable to God, which is your reasonable service. And do not be conformed to this world, but be transformed by the renewing of your mind, that you may prove what is that good and acceptable and perfect will of God.

Luke 9:23–24

Then He said to them all, "If anyone desires to come after Me, let him deny himself, and take up his cross daily, and follow Me. For whoever desires to save his life will lose it, but whoever loses his life for My sake will save it."

scripture memorization

Write out the scripture(s) in the space below and recite them ten times.

_____

_____

_____

_____

_____

_____

_____

_____

_____

_____

_____

_____

_____

_____

something to ponder

CONSIDER A TIME THAT YOU HAVE been brought to the absolute end of yourself, perhaps through illness or financial trial or a relationship challenge. At such a time, it often feels hopeless, and yet we know from Scripture that the Holy Spirit will enable us to find our way through. Reflect on how God has emboldened and encouraged you to press on. See Philippians 3:13–14.

_____

_____

_____

_____

_____

_____

_____

SEE ROMANS 12:1–2. IT HAS BEEN said that to experience running, you should run the mile, but to experience life, run the marathon. How might we relate the call in Romans to "be transformed by the renewing of your mind" to the emotional and physical ups and downs of a marathon? How do we apply those lessons to the ups and downs of life?

_____

_____

_____

_____

_____

_____

_____

_____

READ LUKE 9:23–24. IN MY EXPERIENCE, my race would have ended at mile 83 with a DNF (Did Not Finish) if it weren't for the support of friends and most especially my wife reminding me of the cause for which we were running: "This is about something bigger than yourself." Running and racing can become a selfish pursuit if our focus falls on ourselves instead of running for God's glory. Take time to reflect on your own running goals and ask yourself honestly, "For what or whom am I running? How is my running giving glory to God?"

_____

_____

_____

_____

_____

_____

_____

running observations by dean

Running and Breathing?

THERE ARE ALL SORTS OF MYTHS about how to breathe while running. The most frequently asked question I get about running from someone who doesn't run is how to breathe while running. It usually goes like this: The non-runner slinks over to me and looks around as if he is running a clandestine smuggling operation and only when he finds no one else is listening he says, "Hey, I have a question that is going to sound really stupid."

Knowing what is coming, I lower my voice and look around. I say, "I'm sure it's not a stupid question. What is it?"

"I don't know how I'm supposed to breathe when I run. How do I breathe?" I usually lower my head as if reluctant to share a deep, dark secret and say, "You wanna know the secret?" Another pause, "Whatever is comfortable to you."

You need to get oxygen to your muscles, and it is not really important exactly how you do it. Breathing in and out through both your mouth and nose is the most efficient way. Don't think about it too much. Of course, if you don't get oxygen to your muscles, you'll have to stop soon anyway.

When you first begin running, you may feel some stress on your lungs as you get used to the heavy breathing, especially in the cold weather. That feeling will pass much more quickly than the feeling in your legs. The only thing to keep in mind is to breathe a little deeper than what comes naturally in order to feel as relaxed as possible. There is a fine line between a relaxed state and chaos.

It may be worth noting that there are studies that show breathing in certain patterns may help to avoid some injuries by having the exhale begin on alternate strides. However, there are much more important factors to worry about. Just run and breathe as comfortably as possible.

We don't think about breathing every day. The only reason we think about it while running is the difficulty. Once we are comfortable with running, we don't think much about it. In the same way, God must be our spiritual breath. An old way of describing the Holy Spirit is "the breath of God." Christians have that breath within us as the new life we receive in Christ, but sometimes the pull of our flesh or the trials of the world make us wonder how we are supposed to breath as children of God. We don't want to doubt or worry, but we don't know how to let it go. The solution is to practice humbling ourselves in God's presence. Just as we pray through the pain that He will help us get to the finish line, so we pray through the trial that He will run with us, guide us, and sustain us to the end. This is spiritual breathing and the result of being transformed by a renewed mind.

- *Just relax and breathe in whatever manner feels comfortable to you.*

- *Running hard enough to breathe heavily is okay. It will make your muscles more efficient.*

- *The Christian life is about relying completely on the Spirit of God for the hills and slopes we experience. It may never become easy, but it can become habitual.*

sticky notes

the path

I STARTED RUNNING AT AGE 40 out of desperation. I never thought running was something I could do or that I would enjoy or depend upon so much. I certainly never thought it was something that would connect me to God.

In my late 20s, I went through a divorce. One of the ways I coped with the separation was hiking and walking out my emotional distress. One sad day I was plodding along, lost in thought, and stopped for a rest at the top of a hill. When I turned around, I was overcome with a very intense feeling. Despite the overcast day, the trail was completely illuminated by sunlight and a thought came to me with perfect clarity as if spoken aloud: "Stay on the path, and you will be all right."

I was an agnostic at the time, and I took this experience to mean that I had been given some kind of reassurance by some unknown force. Oddly, I felt no need to define it or investigate further, but I took comfort in the message I'd been given. I spent the next decade convincing myself that I was on the path, while knowing on some level I was not. I told myself I was doing great, when in reality I was fighting my way through the muck and the thorns of life.

I led a willful, selfish existence. I was the center of the universe. I wanted to be in control, but then my life became uncontrollable. My ex-husband sued me for custody of our son while I was pregnant with my third child. I had to go to trial just days before my due date. Thirteen days after the trial, my daughter was born. Sixteen days after that, my ex-husband died a tragic, horrible death, and I was left utterly overwhelmed with a severely traumatized 16 year old, a two year old, and a newborn.

I began to lean on the bottle to help me cope, and my alcohol consumption took a scary turn. As soon as I tried to find comfort in drink, it sunk its claws into me and took over. Before long I had no control and no choice. I was so far off the path I didn't know if I could ever get back. Unless something changed for me, I had only bad consequences ahead. But I couldn't stop drinking.

One morning after a night of particularly bad behavior, I woke up to the absolute certainty that I was an alcoholic. A tremendous wave of relief washed over me. This resolved my horrible internal conflict, and I hit my knees and asked a God that I wasn't sure about and didn't entirely believe in to help me. He did. That terrible compulsion to drink was lifted and has yet to return.

In the days that followed, I remember wondering what would become of me. Somehow, my feet found their way to the pavement. Running calmed the storm inside me. From the start, it was a form of communication. My first attempts were clumsy, somewhat incoherent (probably profane) conversations with myself. I knew I had to be done playing God; I wasn't good at it. I embraced recovery and through it found a true connection with God. Prayer and meditation became part of my daily discipline, and I found it easiest to do this while running.

The repetition of foot hitting pavement (breath in, breath out, repeat) quiets and clears my mind. As I run, I pray. I ask my Lord to move into my heart, direct my thinking, and run my life. I ask Him to mold me and shape me into the person He would have me be. I am at peace, because I have faith He will do these things. I no longer have to carry the burden. As my body has become stronger, my will has bent to Him. Each step has deepened my surrender. I am able to run, because He allows it.

God returned me to the path. He took my hand in His and ran with me. For years, He lovingly nudged me this way or that while I learned my lessons (sometimes gently, sometimes not so gently). When the day comes that I'm no longer able to run, it will be a sad day indeed, but God will be there. He will help me find other ways to connect to Him. For I am His now, and there is nothing better to be.

Linda Holloway – Jamestown, OH

get in the word

Psalm 23

The Lord is my shepherd;

I shall not want.

2 He makes me to lie down in green pastures;

He leads me beside the still waters.

3 He restores my soul;

He leads me in the paths of righteousness

For His name's sake.

4 Yea, though I walk through the valley of the shadow of death,

I will fear no evil;

For You are with me;

Your rod and Your staff, they comfort me.

5 You prepare a table before me in the presence of my enemies;

You anoint my head with oil;

My cup runs over.

6 Surely goodness and mercy shall follow me

All the days of my life;

And I will dwell in the house of the Lord

Forever.

Psalm 30

I will extol You, O Lord, for You have lifted me up,

And have not let my foes rejoice over me.

2 O Lord my God, I cried out to You,

And You healed me.

3 O Lord, You brought my soul up from the grave;
You have kept me alive, that I should not go down to the pit.[a]
4 Sing praise to the Lord, you saints of His,
And give thanks at the remembrance of His holy name.[b]
5 For His anger is but for a moment,
His favor is for life;
Weeping may endure for a night,
But joy comes in the morning.
6 Now in my prosperity I said,
"I shall never be moved."
7 Lord, by Your favor You have made my mountain stand strong;
You hid Your face, and I was troubled.
8 I cried out to You, O Lord;
And to the Lord I made supplication:
9 "What profit is there in my blood,
When I go down to the pit?
Will the dust praise You?
Will it declare Your truth?
10 Hear, O Lord, and have mercy on me;
Lord, be my helper!"
11 You have turned for me my mourning into dancing;
You have put off my sackcloth and clothed me with gladness,
12 To the end that my glory may sing praise to You and not be silent.
O Lord my God, I will give thanks to You forever.

Psalm 46:10
Be still, and know that I am God;
I will be exalted among the nations,
I will be exalted in the earth!

scripture memorization

Write out the scripture(s) in the space below and recite them ten times.

_____

_____

_____

_____

_____

_____

_____

_____

_____

_____

_____

_____

_____

_____

_____

something to ponder

HOW DOES running connect you with God?

_____

_____

_____

_____

DO YOU trust that God is in total control of your life?

_____

_____

_____

_____

DO YOU ever feel as if the only one who can take control of your life is you? Why?

_____

_____

_____

_____

running observations
by dean

Logging the Miles

WHEN A SCIENTIST IS PERFORMING EXPERIMENTS he keeps meticulous notes on everything he does. The reason he takes such good notes is to be able to replicate his successful effort. In addition, and sometimes more importantly, he wants to be able to remember what not to do. Thomas Edison discovered hundreds of ways not to make a light bulb. If he had not documented what he had done, how would he have remembered what he had already tried?

Likewise, we should document our training so that we can replicate our successes and avoid making the same mistakes over and over. If you're like me, I have a hard time remembering what I did last week. There is no way I am going to remember the details of what I did a year or two ago. With a training log, I can look back and see what I did to prepare for the same race a year ago. Depending how you log your runs and how much information you keep track of, you can spot trends, commonalities, issues related to weather, how well training went in a particular type of shoe, or any number of other concerns or revelations.

Sometimes you can go back and discover things you never would have realized otherwise. I remember looking back at my training for a marathon and comparing it to the same race the year before. I thought I had prepared for them the same, but I really crashed the second year. It didn't make any sense. Looking back, I discovered I had one extra down week about six weeks prior to race day the first year and my hard workouts were actually much faster the second year. Now I know that at least one of those two things had a negative impact on my training the second year. As old as I am, I'm still learning about what is best for my body.

Another benefit of logging your miles is motivation. When you know that you are going to record what you do, it has an impact on what you do. You don't want to write down zeros on days when you intend to run. You don't want to have an 18-mile week when you have been running 30. You have a tendency to hold yourself accountable when you write it down. You can also see the accomplishments come to life right in front of your eyes. Being able go back a year or two (or longer) and see those positive achievements can keep you going when you get down about your training.

Sometimes when I am studying my Bible, I will write down notes. I do this because it helps me to remember things I read. I also try to have good documentation for my group Bible studies so that I can always go back and teach the same class at some point in the future. Again, it helps me to remember what I am studying and reminds me of the details so that I can answer questions from the group. When I pick up the same study a couple of years later, it tends to go better the second time around because I've already been there. Whether you are keeping track of your running miles or your Bible study, taking notes helps make you better focused and more refined.

> • *Logging your miles reminds you of successes and misses and helps you replicate or avoid duplicating previous training.*

> • *Logging your miles provides motivation to keep you going when it gets tough.*

• *Writing down thoughts, ideas, or things you learn helps you to retain those things.*

sticky notes

_____

_____

_____

_____

_____

_____

_____

_____

_____

_____

_____

_____

my running prayers

WHAT IS A PERFECT PRAYER? DURING my early years in Catholic School, my dear teachers would not teach us how to pray, but rather told us to pray. As an eight-year-old girl, how was I supposed to know how to pray? I could not even begin to understand the power that prayers have.

My parents were cradle Catholics, but never accepted Jesus as their Savior. However, I was baptized and received First Communion and Confirmation, because it was the socially correct thing to do. At the time, I did not grasp the gravity of receiving those sacraments, yet something inside of me was craving for the love of God ever so fervently. My parents always remained cold, quiet, and closed to the idea of me loving God, almost as if loving God was lessening my parents' power over me.

As the years went by, so did the lack of religious education in my life. My parents or teachers never talked about God. It was somewhat taboo. I vividly remember my mother asking me to recite twenty Hail Marys in the car on our way to school. I used to ask her, "Why?" She would answer sternly, "Just because I told you so!" Is this a perfect prayer? Is this a prayer coming from a place of love for God? I did not think so, but reluctantly I started reciting the Hail Mary aloud with her. Looking back at that moment, I feel an ache in my heart as I imagine God watching me lovingly, in pain for me.

Year after year, I reflected on what my perfect prayers could be. I thought about the fact that God created each one of us uniquely in His image. Because of that He would address us in many different ways, a lot like a parent should adapt to his child's needs. Alleluia! I then realized that my praying to God could be my very own, a bond that He and I would share in a very special way. I started praying in the shower and while I was flying or driving, in hope to hear Him talk back to me.

Four years ago when my life was at one of its lowest moments, I began to pray while I was running, and I soon felt my Lord's wonderful excitement over me. I felt close to Him. I know He was pleased, because He would show me His joy in miraculous ways. One day it was in the form of a rainbow in the middle of a hot summer day with no rain clouds in sight. Another time, a bird gently swirled back and forth leading me through the path of my run. I felt the most amazing testimony of His happiness and joy through the enormous strength I would always have when running, as if He did not want me to stop. Running was like breathing. It came to me effortlessly. I was unstoppable. The more I ran, the more God seemed delighted. Running was healing, grieving, praising, and praying. I had finally found my perfect prayer, my way of communicating with God as if during those times we were one. He lives in me, and I am in Him.

So wherever we are, whatever we are doing, let's pray without ceasing. God will bless us beyond our wildest dream. Along the way, let us discover our very own intrinsic relationship with God. Amid being still and quiet, we will actually hear Him. As I run, I breathe, and with each breath I know that Jesus is right there pushing and listening to me.

I strayed very far from the socially correct Catholic ways my family had me following. I now feel intimately close to God and have an overflowing amount of love for Jesus Christ, our Savior. Today, I understand what prayer is about—giving yourself, all of yourself, back to God without any reservations. For me, these are my running prayers.

Claire Hilton – *Temecula, CA*

get in the word

Psalm 32:7

You are my hiding place;
You shall preserve me from trouble;
You shall surround me with songs of deliverance.

1 John 3:24

Now he who keeps His commandments abides in Him, and He in
him. And by this we know that He abides in us, by the Spirit whom
He has given us.

John 15:7

If you abide in Me, and My words abide in you, you will ask what
you desire, and it shall be done for you.

scripture memorization

Write out the scripture(s) in the space below and recite them ten times.

_____

_____

_____

_____

_____

_____

_____

_____

_____

_____

_____

_____

_____

_____

_____

something to ponder

BLIND FAITH or blindly faithful: which one would you choose?

_____

_____

_____

_____

WHERE DOES God take you spiritually on your runs?

_____

_____

_____

_____

DO YOU think God rejoices and smiles down upon us when we offer our runs to Him?

_____

_____

_____

_____

running observations by dean

Warming Up and Cooling Down

DO YOU REALLY NEED TO WARM up before a race? The answer is yes, no matter what your ability may be. Even if your goal is to simply finish the race, it is still important to warm up. If you plan to run hard and your finish time is important to you, warming up is imperative. So what does it mean to warm up, and what does it look like?

First, let me say that warming up is only part of race preparation. By the time you begin your warm up, you should have already run the race several times in your mind. You should have prepared yourself mentally for the task at hand. If you have done that, you will use those thoughts to help you with your warm up. Once again, if your goal is to finish the race, you should have envisioned yourself doing just that in your mind prior to race day. Your mind is a powerful thing. Make sure you make use of it.

Second, decide when to begin your warm up. You should time your warm up so that your heart rate is up before the race begins. I see a lot of runners begin their warm up too early and then stand around for twenty minutes prior to the race. Although that is better than not warming up, it is certainly not as effective as good timing. Your warm up time should be appropriate for your race distance. The shorter the race, the longer and more intense the warm up should be.

Third, if you plan to run hard, begin your warm up by jogging to get your legs loosened up. The idea is to get loose enough to get to the next stage, which is to spend some time stretching. Make sure you stretch all muscle groups. I see a lot of half-hearted stretching, only performing those that feel comfortable. If you plan to run a little more slowly, begin by walking and then stretching. Feeling loose at race time is important to being faster.

Finally, I like to make sure that I spend at least part of my time warming up by myself so that I can recount the thoughts I had in preparation for the race. At this point, I am getting my game face on. The race is going to hurt, and I want to prepare my mind for it. Once I have embraced that fact, I am ready to go.

Once the race is over, it is a good idea to cool down. Cooling down means low intensity jogging or walking that will allow your legs to work out some of the soreness you are going to have the next day. A good cool down will last ten to twenty minutes and will help to prevent injury in the days to follow. Once again, I see a lot of people finish races and get in the car within ten minutes of crossing the line. Take the time to do some preventative work and cool down.

A good friend of mine talks a lot about getting ready for church. He regularly reminds us to spend time in prayer before worship to ask God to make us receptive to His urging. In addition, praying that His will be done through teachers and messengers reveals to Him that we have a yearning to see Him move in powerful ways. We could say the same about our daily walk with Christ. We can warm up for handling conflict, bad traffic, disappointments, and job successes by spending time dwelling on who Christ is and who we are in Him. It's preaching the gospel to ourselves daily, like the old preachers have said. That's like warming up before a race.

• *A good warm-up is most effective when you have spent time thinking about the race before race day.*

• *A cool down will ensure a lower level of soreness. It won't eliminate it completely, but it will be better.*

• *Spending time in preparation for worship will ensure the deepest possible experience from God.*

sticky notes

_____

_____

_____

_____

_____

_____

_____

_____

_____

being obedient when your mind says 'no' but your heart says 'yes'

I LOVE RUNNING AND JESUS. I love helping others, but I don't like to teach.

When an opportunity to teach came to me, my heart said, "Go for it," but my mind said, "No, you can't do this." I eventually gave in. I knew that once I committed, God would lead my steps, but I feared I would fail every week when it came time for the study. Every time, God showed up and gave me just the right words to say.

There were days when I felt I just could not do it. Just as in running, I have good days and bad days in teaching. I learned to keep my eyes on Jesus instead of what I could or could not do. I learned to focus on the things around me, such as the beauty that God created.

I'm not sure where God will lead me from here, but I know the study made a difference in the spiritual walk of my team. They are more confident about themselves in Christ, and they have to work on building active, healthy habits. Some day we will all hear our Savior say, "Well done, my good and faithful servants." Obedience is what it's all about. When God leads, He provides.

Sylvia Miller – *Lubbock, TX*

get in the word

Acts 20:19–24

Serving the Lord with all humility, with many tears and trials which happened to me by the plotting of the Jews; how I kept back nothing that was helpful, but proclaimed it to you, and taught you publicly and from house to house, testifying to Jews, and also to Greeks, repentance toward God and faith toward our Lord Jesus Christ. And see, now I go bound in the spirit to Jerusalem, not knowing the things that will happen to me there, except that the Holy Spirit testifies in every city, saying that chains and tribulations await me. But none of these things move me; nor do I count my life dear to myself, so that I may finish my race with joy, and the ministry which I received from the Lord Jesus, to testify to the gospel of the grace of God.

Philippians 3:12–14

Not that I have already attained, or am already perfected; but I press on, that I may lay hold of that for which Christ Jesus has also laid hold of me. Brethren, I do not count myself to have apprehended; but one thing I do, forgetting those things which are behind and reaching forward to those things which are ahead, I press toward the goal for the prize of the upward call of God in Christ Jesus.

2 Timothy 4:7

I have fought the good fight, I have finished the race, I have kept the faith.

scripture memorization

Write out the scripture(s) in the space below and recite them ten times.

_____

_____

_____

_____

_____

_____

_____

_____

_____

_____

_____

_____

something to ponder

WHAT IS God calling you to do?

_____

_____

_____

_____

ARE YOU feeding your soul with things of God or things of this world?

_____

_____

_____

_____

ARE YOU using your passions to glorify our Lord?

_____

_____

_____

_____

running observations
by dean

Thoughts on Boston 2014

HAVING THE OPPORTUNITY TO PARTICIPATE IN the Boston Marathon one year after the bombings was a God-given blessing. I've written down some of my favorite observations:

Google glasses—Very early in the race I passed a guy wearing Google glasses. I had never seen them before. I wonder what he was doing with them. Maybe reading the Wall Street Journal.

The gray-haired lady—I was running along at about the fourth mile and noticed a short, gray-haired lady coming up on my right. I was surprised to see what looked like a fifty-something lady running at a 6:12 pace. When I pulled up next to her, I realized it was Joan Benoit Samuelson, winner of the first ever women's Olympic Marathon in 1984! I ran beside her for about half mile just to say I did. Wow.

Team Hoyt—I passed Team Hoyt at about the six-mile mark. Thinking about what Dick Hoyt has done for his son Rick was an inspirational boost early in the race. Knowing that this was their 32nd and final Boston Marathon was even more special.

Ten-mile boost—My wife Debbie was going to get on the train from near the start and ride to Natick and cheer for me there. We had agreed where she was going to be standing so I was looking for her as soon as I entered Natick. The crowds were so thick that I was convinced I would never see her, especially since she is not a loud person and the crowds were very loud. But I heard my name and looked to see her in the front row. It was such a great boost!

Bombing survivors—I passed a number of participants who were on crutches and/or prosthetics, most of them missing one or both legs. I had heard that there were a number of survivors of the bombing who would be running, and I'm sure some of those participants were the ones I saw on crutches. My wife told me about one of them who was handing out high fives like cups at a water station and taking selfies with the crowd in the background while he was coming through Natick wearing one of the biggest smiles you've ever seen. What a celebration!

Welcome to our town—Every time we entered another town along the route someone was yelling welcome to (insert town name). They were so proud, and they came out in huge numbers. They expected one million participants. I felt them all.

Race plan changed by God—I had some physical problems before the race and prayed for the Lord's help. Pressing on, I decided I would run a certain pace for as long as I could and just hang on. I did it for the first half and could have kept it up for a while longer, but I felt God's urging to slow down. Once I slowed down about 25 seconds per mile, I was able to maintain that pace to the finish. God answered my earlier prayer, and I was able to finish strong enough to really enjoy the second half.

Kids with drinks and food—I love seeing the children that line the course and hand out drinks, orange slices, and bananas. If you can't draw some energy from those children lining the Newton hills, you can't be energized.

Run for God—Wearing the Run for God logo means getting a lot of cheers for

God! Of course, since I was in Boston, many of those cheers were said with a thick Boston accent sounding like "Run fa' Gad!" It sounded sweet no matter what the accent was, especially over the final 10K!

Citgo sign—I had run Boston once before and never even saw the Citgo sign at 25 miles because I was hurting so badly. This time I was able to savor it.

The Finish Line—I remember, as I approached the finish line, I looked to my left to see the location of the bombing and said a short prayer for everyone whose life was changed that day. I felt like time slowed down for a few seconds and the pain of the race left me as I remembered the pictures of that day.

After the Finish Line—I remember being so thankful for the thousands of volunteers who make this event possible and wanting to thank everyone I saw as I walked through the finish area. And then I heard a man sitting in a high chair tell everyone that Meb Keflezighi had won. The day was already special, but that just made it more special to know an American had won the Boston Marathon for the first time since 1983.

I found Debbie at the family meeting area, and we began to look for a place to eat. I remember how many non-runners congratulated me as I walked down the street. It was amazing. Businessmen, who had every reason to be frustrated with the crowds infringing on their turf, graciously shared their city with us. It was one of the most touching things I remember.

It doesn't happen often enough, but people with differences can rally around a good cause. For a time, we drop our pettiness, look past the things that do not matter, and focus on what is good. The Boston Marathon is one of those things, especially in 2014. As believers, we have an even better reason to come together— the redeeming blood of our Lord and Savior, Jesus Christ. If we can drop our biases and judgmental attitudes for a race into downtown Boston, shouldn't we be able to do it for His sake?

Ephesians 4:1–3 talks about "bearing with one another in love, endeavoring to keep the unity of the Spirit…" The word endeavoring means giving diligence. The Boston Marathon is a great example of diligent unity for a cause. Imagine what we could do if we were all in unity for Christ. Of course, reading the Scripture closely reveals that we have to do it with humility, gentleness and longsuffering. Those are not naturally occurring traits for many of us. It just drives the point home that we have to be purposeful to have an impact.

sticky notes

_____

_____

_____

_____

_____

_____

_____

_____

Week

when God told me to run

IT HAD BEEN OVER A YEAR since I'd been in the hospital, and I needed to tell God the truth. After a grueling year of trying to heal from two intestinal surgeries, I was better—to a fault. I felt so much better that I stopped caring about healthy eating and exercise altogether, but I knew He didn't want that for me. "God," I prayed, "my give-a-care is busted." I told Him that on a walk to pick up my kids from school.

I'm not sure what I expected, but a little while later when we returned home, a voice message was waiting for me. It was Team In Training, the endurance sports fundraiser organization for The Leukemia & Lymphoma Society. They wanted to let me know that their information meeting for that season would be held the next day. Wow. Okay, God, I'll go.

It was terrifying and exhilarating. Should I, a stay-at-home mom, train for the 2014 San Diego marathon and raise almost $3000 in four months? I committed. I believed God had called me to the task and that He would be supply what I needed. Of course, He was faithful.

One day, I was gearing up to do hill work, and God gave me the encouragement I needed in Habakkuk 3:19, "He will make me walk on my high hills." Another time when I was hoping to back out of a super early morning run, He gave me Psalm 139:12, "Indeed, the darkness shall not hide from You, but the night shines as the day; the darkness and the light are both alike to You." He provided faithfully for the fundraising part of my task, which truly strengthened my faith, but all of that hardly compares to another reason He asked me to run.

Very early in my training, I received a note from a friend in a different state who was going through a seemingly impossible trial. She was depressed and struggling to maintain hope. God has orchestrated this all along. Not only did my friend agree to run the marathon with me, but she also trained so well that she lost fifty pounds before the race. I could hardly believe her dedication. God had her best in mind and her healing when He asked me to run. What a compassionate God we serve!

Jennifer McCarthy – *Tempe, AZ*

get in the word

Ephesians 2:10
For we are His workmanship, created in Christ Jesus for good works, which God prepared beforehand that we should walk in them.

Habakkuk 3:19
The Lord God is my strength;
He will make my feet like deer's feet,
And He will make me walk on my high hills.

Psalm 139:12

Indeed, the darkness shall not hide from You,
But the night shines as the day;
The darkness and the light are both alike to You.

scripture memorization

Write out the scripture(s) in the space below and recite them ten times.

_____

_____

_____

_____

_____

_____

_____

_____

_____

_____

something to ponder

DO YOU believe that God can accomplish Kingdom-size tasks through your running?

_____

_____

_____

_____

DO YOU believe that God is wholly on your team and ready to encourage you when the going gets tough?

_____

_____

_____

_____

WILL YOU prayerfully offer your body to God as a living sacrifice, asking Him to work through you and the world as you run?

_____

_____

_____

_____

running observations
by dean

Muscular Balance

I'VE BEEN RUNNING A LONG TIME and have discovered many different ways to hurt myself while running. I have had a stress fracture, strains, sprains, aches, pains, more tendonitis than I like to think about, and many, many days of soreness. Sometimes experience is a good thing, but other times it hurts. I have noticed, through many visits to doctors, that I see a recurring theme in many of these injuries. The problem often lies in muscular imbalance. I spend a lot of time strengthening the muscles around the area of the injury or discomfort.

I try to be cognizant of muscle soreness. As I get older, injuries are much tougher to overcome, so it is more important than ever to detect problems as early as possible. When I have persistent soreness, I focus on the muscles that are opposite and around the sore area. For example, if my quads are persistently sore, it could be because my hamstrings are weak and the quads are taking too much of the load. Even if that is not the cause of the problem, it doesn't hurt to work my hamstrings to see if it will help my quads. Often, it works to strengthen the opposite muscle group.

Another common example for me is knee soreness. When I feel knee soreness, I have found that tight quads often cause it. I will spend extra time stretching and loosening my quads, and the knee pain goes away. The key is to notice it early when you can still do something about it.

We talk so much these days about core strength and how important it is to injury prevention. As a runner, I love to run, so I usually don't spend a lot of time on activities that work non-running muscles. By neglecting my other muscle groups, I create the imbalance that leads to injury. For that reason, it is important for me to make myself build those core muscle groups.

In the summer, it is much easier because we spend time outdoors on yard work or activities at picnics or other gatherings. We take vacations and spend time on other events and happenings. We busy ourselves with physical activities when the weather is nice. In addition, muscles stay looser in the warm weather, lessening the possibility for injury. Wintertime is a different story. When the weather is cold, it is best to supplement our running with core strengthening workouts. There are hundreds of exercises we can use to help in the effort. If we can find just a few to form into habits, it will improve our running health.

Balance in our spiritual life is also sometimes difficult to maintain. We are so busy with everything else that we tend to focus on the easiest things to do. Those things tend to be different for each of us. Some of us are prayer warriors and spend a lot of time praying for others and for God's will to be done. Some of us love to spend time in God's Word trying to understand all we can about His plan for our lives and those around us. Still others are focused on calling and visiting people in nursing homes and hospitals. Those are all good. We just have to be careful that we don't spend all of our available energy in one area to the neglect of other important endeavors.

- *Muscle imbalance can lead to a number of painful injuries, so it is important to have good muscular balance.*

- *The less active winter season is prime time for allowing yourself to get to a point of muscular imbalance.*

• *God wants us to be all in for Him. He provides us with many ways to draw closer to Him, and we should be careful not to spend all our energy on the things that come easy to us.*

sticky notes

_____

_____

_____

_____

_____

_____

_____

_____

_____

_____

_____

my journey

AS I WAITED TO TURN LEFT onto the highway, I heard click, click, click.

"What is that sound?" I asked myself.

It was the turning signal. I didn't even know it made a sound.

You see, I was leaving my audiologist's office, wearing my new hearing aids. The next few days were full of new sounds, the rustle of the wind in the trees, the splash of water on the beach, and the one that brought tears to my eyes, the sound of my granddaughter singing to me over the phone. Another pleasant addition to my life was the decline in my need to ask, "What did you say?"

I could tell this was going to be an amazing journey. For most of my life I had not even noticed a problem with my hearing. There were times I had to have people repeat things or I had to turn up the television, but I was able to function without struggles. In my 20's, I began having difficulty in crowds hearing what people were saying. It wasn't a big deal so I just played it off as listening to rock music too much in high school. By the time I reached 40, I started to notice a significant difference in my hearing. I felt like I was in a rain barrel, everyone sounded far away! Again I pushed it aside.

Not long ago, I became a single mother with four children. I did not have time to worry about my ears. I had enrolled in a nursing program in hopes of fulfilling my dream and providing a better life for my children. After two semesters I had to drop out, because I was having a hard time with the classes. I had never had trouble with school before, so my family and I decided it was time to seek the advice of a hearing specialist.

The audiologist connected a long wire from a computer to my ear canal. She played an array of sounds, and I lifted my hand each time I heard one. Then she put a huge set of earphones over my ears, and again I lifted my hand with each sound. She examined my ears with an otoscope, then held a tuning fork up to them and asked me what I heard.

"Pam, you have a significant hearing loss." I was astonished. I thought maybe she would just clean them out or she could just give me something to fix it. "No. Your particular condition is congenital. It affects the nerves in your ears. It is not reversible or fixable with surgery, and it will get progressively worse."

Immediately the faces of my children passed in front of me. How is this going to affect them? Will I still be able to become a nurse? My life passed before my eyes. I thought it was over. The doctor told me to come back the next week, and we'd talk about my options for hearing aids. Hearing aids at 43!

After a few days of feeling sorry for myself and walking around with a chip on my shoulder, the Lord began speaking to me. He said, "I am with you always, even to the end of the age" (Matthew 28:20). I was embarrassed. The Lord had brought me through so much, and yet I doubted that He could help me through this. Even though my physical ears did not hear well, my spiritual ones heard loud and clear. I decided my life needed to take a new turn.

I began reading the Bible and watching Christian television. The following verse seemed to stick in my head. "Therefore, if anyone is in Christ, he is a new creation; old things have passed away; behold, all things have become new"

(*2 Corinthians 5:17*). I wanted to be a new creation. I decided to look into going back to nursing school. I found the perfect college in the mountains, and was accepted. I went back to my audiologist and was fitted with hearing aids.

On January 2, 2012, I packed my car and headed to Tennessee. In two days, I found a place to live (child-care in exchange for a basement apartment). In three days, I found a job (the library on campus hired me on the spot). God opened the doors wide, and for the first time in my life I listened to what He wanted and not to what I wanted.

I was baptized on April 21, 2012, and was accepted into the nursing program at Southern Adventist University January 2013. I have faced many challenges related to my hearing loss, but with each challenge came a lesson learned and a battle won. I have to admit there have been times when I wanted to give up, times when the doors seemed to be slammed shut, and times when my strength was weak, but in those moments God always sent someone to encourage, someone to take my hand, someone to say, "You can do it."

So here I sit with one more year of nursing school to complete, a dream that I thought would never come true. I may have to work a little harder, I may have to find ways to overcome challenges, I may get doors slammed in my face, but I will not give up. "I can do all things through Christ who strengthens me" (*Philippians 4:13*).

Pamela Fox – *Collegedale, TN*

get in the word

Matthew 28:20

*"...teaching them to observe all things that I have commanded you;
and lo, I am with you always, even to the end of the age." Amen.*

2 Corinthians 5:17

*Therefore, if anyone is in Christ, he is a new creation; old things
have passed away; behold, all things have become new.*

Philippians 4:12–13

*I know how to be abased, and I know how to abound. Everywhere
and in all things I have learned both to be full and to be hungry, both
to abound and to suffer need. I can do all things through Christ who
strengthens me.*

scripture memorization

Write out the scripture(s) in the space below and recite them ten times.

_____

_____

_____

_____

_____

_____

_____

_____

_____

_____

_____

_____

_____

_____

something to ponder

WHEN DO you feel the Lord's presence the most? When do you feel it the least?

_____

_____

_____

_____

WHAT DOES Scripture say about God's involvement in our daily lives?

_____

_____

_____

_____

CONSIDERING PHILIPPIANS 4:12–13, how does the Lord strengthen you and what does He strengthen you for?

_____

_____

_____

_____

running observations
by dean

I'm Growing Up, But Not Older

JIMMY BUFFET SINGS A SONG ENTITLED, "I'm Growing Older, But Not Up." It's a great sentiment. I love the idea of not letting age turn us into boring old people. It's applicable to running too, because there are improved methods and equipment turning up all the time. If we don't evolve with the trends, we aren't able to take advantage of advancements.

For example, when I was younger, conventional wisdom said there was no better fabric than cotton. Today, we know that polyester is the fabric of choice because of the wicking properties built into the construction.

It's easy to think about what has worked in the past and stick to it, because it is safe. We like safety, and the older we get the more comfortable we tend to be with being conservative. However, we have to keep an open mind to what's possible.

If we modify the song title a bit, we could say, "I'm growing up, but not older." This statement may be even more applicable to running. It says, "I'm getting wiser, and I'm not letting age catch up to me." It's important that we learn from our trials and tribulations and modify our training accordingly. There are many training plans available. The differences from one to another are tremendous. So which one is the best? They all have potential to be great, for the right person, and what is right for one person is not necessarily right for the next.

We have to be wise enough to make changes incrementally and note what works and what doesn't. There are times when it makes sense to stick to what we know. For me, shoes are a great example. There are hundreds of advertisements for new styles and trends in shoes pulling at us constantly but, as a rule, when I find a shoe that feels great and works, I stick to it. I have bought the same style 15 times in a row because it works.

The best attribute that usually comes with age is patience. I am so much more patient now than I was when I was younger. Making small changes and waiting to see if they work is a standard now. Twenty years ago, I would change three different things at once and then wonder why the changes didn't work. Of course, my body was more resilient then too.

There are parts of our faith that never change, but as we grow in Christ, our understanding or the application of what we understand does change. That means being open to discovering new things from the Word or hearing new things in our daily conversations with God. We all have a tendency to stay comfortable and do the things we like to do. If we remain infants in Christ and never feed ourselves from the Word, if we never change our prayers, and if we never develop Christian love in our relationships, we will not grow. He wants to see us look more like Christ in order to become the most effective witness we can be.

- *We have to be open to changes in training methods, gear, and gadgets related to running.*

- *Changes to our training should be made with caution.*

- *Patience is a virtue when it comes to being an older runner.*

- *We have to be open to new things that God is trying to show us.*

sticky notes

_____

_____

_____

_____

_____

_____

_____

_____

_____

_____

_____

_____

_____

watch your step

WATCHING YOUR STEP IS ALWAYS A part of a safe run, but it becomes an even greater priority on a very rainy day. As I try to avoid puddles and mud on my run today, I consider this metaphor. Even when I misjudge and step in a mess, my path doesn't change and my run certainly doesn't end. I may be a little dirty or have a wet sock for the rest of the journey, but my route and my destination remain the same.

A few times this morning, I am discouraged when I make a wrong step, particularly since I am working the entire time to make the right step. For example, when I become distracted by my armband slipping off, I land in a puddle I could've easily avoided by paying attention. How silly would it be to stop in a muddy puddle and give up on my run? It wouldn't do any good. In fact, it would be worse for me to stand there and scold myself or shake my fist up at God for leading me into a mess.

"There is therefore now no condemnation to those who are in Christ Jesus... (Romans 8:1). "...for the accuser of our brethren, who accused them before our God day and night, has been cast down. And they overcame him by the blood of the Lamb and by the word of their testimony" (*Revelation 12:10b–11a*).

As we run in Christ, we will make mistakes. In fact, we may make a mess of things even when we do everything right (as far as we and our friends can tell). But Christ Jesus has saved us completely and made us righteous in Him. We are not condemned. We are conquerors.

Amanda Reed – *Tacoma, WA*

get in the word

Romans 8:1

*There is therefore now no condemnation to those who are in Christ
Jesus, who do not walk according to the flesh, but according to
the Spirit.*

Revelation 12:10–11

*Then I heard a loud voice saying in heaven, "Now salvation, and
strength, and the kingdom of our God, and the power of His Christ
have come, for the accuser of our brethren, who accused them before
our God day and night, has been cast down. And they overcame him
by the blood of the Lamb and by the word of their testimony, and
they did not love their lives to the death."*

scripture memorization

e out the scripture(s) in the space below and recite them ten times.

_____

_____

something to ponder

CAN YOU THINK OF TIMES YOU'VE sinned and been tempted to condemn yourself and dwell on your shame instead of immediately remembering and receiving the grace of God? What kind of self-talk have you used in those times?

_____

_____

_____

_____

HAVE YOU SEEN THE ENEMY BE the accuser of anyone close to you?

_____

_____

_____

_____

SPEND SOME TIME IN HONEST PRAYER right now about some messes you may still be splashing in. What do you hear the Spirit telling you about your standing in Christ? If condemning words come to mind, I have to wonder if they are from our Father or from our accuser.

_____

_____

_____

_____

running observations
by dean

I Have Never Regretted Going for a Run

I HAVE NEVER RETURNED FROM A run and said, "Wow, I sure wish I had stayed home and watched TV instead." I find that the solitude of running is good for my soul. The time I spend running takes me as close to God as I can get without my Bible in hand. Idleness is not one of my strengths, so running is a great way for me to listen to God because I'm moving, but my mind is calm. I believe this is the reason I feel so peaceful after a run.

Still, I find I have to make plans to ensure I get my run in every day. There are days when I know I will not have time to get out after work, so I plan to get up early to run in the dark, which is my least favorite time to run. Then there are times when unexpected things come up, and before I know it, it's 9:30 p.m. and I still need to run. Going out the door when it's close to bedtime is tough, but I do it anyway and never regret it. Don't get me wrong; there are plenty of things that are more important than running. I can think of a lot of reasons to prioritize something ahead of a run, but no good reason to skip a run.

So the next time you find yourself dreading to go out the door to run, remember it will feel good when you are done and you have overcome that urge to take the easy path. Our challenges with motivation should pass by more easily than they often do. They will when we focus on positive rather than negative thoughts. We know the author of those negative thoughts, and we should resist them.

I have never finished reading or studying my Bible and thought, "Wow, I should have watched my favorite TV show instead." Like running, it's sometimes hard to get started and make a habit out of it, but once you do, it's hard to find a reason not to do it. Once again, getting Satan out of the way will motivate you, because you will never regret any time that you spend with our Lord. Whether happy, sad, upset, joyful, tired, disappointed, mournful, or thankful, any time is a good time for a run or Bible study.

- *In order to get the most out of running, you have to be intentional about getting it done.*

- *There are many things in our lives that are more important than running, but that doesn't mean we have to short-change running.*

- *It's okay to feel the difficulty in finding time to run or read God's Word, as long as we don't use it as an excuse to not do it. You will never regret it.*

sticky notes

_____
_____
_____
_____
_____
_____
_____
_____
_____
_____
_____
_____
_____
_____
_____
_____

26.2 miles to freedom

IN THE SUMMER OF 2010, I was involved with a study called The Wounded Heart by Dan Allender. This book is for childhood victims of sex abuse. I decided to join because I had some situations as a pre-teen and teenager that would probably not be considered sexual abuse by public standards, but they affected me and frustrated the intimacy in my marriage. According to The Wounded Heart, there are different levels of abuse, and what had happened to me qualified as abuse.

About this same time, two of my friends, Jenny and Sheila, challenged me to start training to run or walk a full marathon. My first thoughts were, "Are you kidding me? I can't do that. It's too hard." During that year, I had already run two half marathons, and those were challenging enough. Could I run a full marathon? No way.

Well, my God is bigger than I am and His ways are always better than mine. Isaiah 55:8 reminds us: "'For My thoughts are not your thoughts, nor are your ways My ways,' says the Lord." He showed me how participating in this marathon would be symbolic of my healing journey and that the race would lead me straight into His loving arms and His saving grace. The 26.2 miles would represent the freedom from 26+ years of bondage to memories of the pain and the sins that followed. Soon after, I shared my decision with my Wounded Heart mentor, Kaye.

The Lord kept telling me, "Michelle, your life is not your own." I didn't know what that meant. One day I decided to Google the words to see if they came up in the Bible somewhere. The first verse I came across was 1 Corinthians 6:19–20, which says, "Or do you not know that your body is the temple of the Holy Spirit who is in you, whom you have from God, and you are not your own? For you were bought at a price; therefore glorify God in your body and in your spirit, which are God's." There it was plain as day.

The context of these verses is sexual immorality among the church of Corinth. In The Message translation, 6:14–15 say, "God honored the Master's body by raising it from the grave. He'll treat yours with the same resurrection power. Until that time, remember that your bodies are created with the same dignity as the Master's body. You wouldn't take the Master's body off to a whorehouse, would you? I should hope not." That is a strong statement, and one I'd liked to have heard growing up.

Growing up, what I heard about the purpose of sex came from the media and my oldest sister (older by almost four years). They didn't tell me immorality would make me feel used up or cause intimacy issues in my marriage later on; that I would feel like a whore. They didn't tell me I would have issues with insecurity and addiction or that I would attempt to meet my own needs, even though they had already been met in Christ.

God desired to do something new in me through this marathon. It was to represent everything He wanted me to experience so that I could give my life over to Him completely to be used for His glory. As race day approached, a conflict arose that would prevent me from running that day, so I had to change my plan. One of our 23-mile training runs was scheduled for New Year's Day 2011. I told Jenny I was going to finish off an additional 3.2 miles. I needed this run to be complete so I could finish my spiritual and physical goal. My teammates were not going to let me do this alone, so together we ran a course I designed in beautiful Stuart, Florida.

Our awesome journey began at the church. Before we left, we read Isaiah 40:28–31. We carried the verse with us on a small piece of paper during the race and read it out loud at least two other times when we wanted to quit. During the 26.2 grueling miles, I think I experienced every human emotion possible: laughter, joy, pain, sadness, defeat, and sweet victory, but most of all, I experienced my Heavenly Father's presence in all of it.

At mile 17, I hit a wall and felt nauseous. A few minutes later, Kaye started running alongside us on the other side of the road. My tears started flowing as I felt her encouragement and support, not through words only, but through her act of running beside us like a friend coming to my side in my greatest time of need.

Nine miles later, as we closed in on the finish line, I was filled with even more emotion and deeper pain. I pushed through and crossed the line. The journey was complete. A few minutes later, I rolled into a fetal position and sobbed into the ground. I wasn't really sure why. After a few minutes of crying, I looked up to see Kaye standing beside me, teary-eyed. At that moment, I remembered why I had run this distance. I had not thought about it all day. Again, I broke down and let it all out, while deep inside I was thinking about my newfound freedom. Now I could choose freedom, a new place my Lord had planned for me all along. No longer was I broken, used, or messed up. I was whole. I was free. I was paid for. I had been bought. I was not my own. I was His completely.

Michelle Howe – *Stuart, FL*

get in the word

Isaiah 55:8

"For My thoughts are not your thoughts, nor are your ways My ways," says the Lord.

1 Corinthians 6:12–20

All things are lawful for me, but all things are not helpful. All things are lawful for me, but I will not be brought under the power of any. Foods for the stomach and the stomach for foods, but God will destroy both it and them. Now the body is not for sexual immorality but for the Lord, and the Lord for the body. And God both raised up the Lord and will also raise us up by His power.

Do you not know that your bodies are members of Christ? Shall I then take the members of Christ and make them members of a harlot? Certainly not! Or do you not know that he who is joined to a harlot is one body with her? For "the two," He says, "shall become one flesh." But he who is joined to the Lord is one spirit with Him.

Flee sexual immorality. Every sin that a man does is outside the body, but he who commits sexual immorality sins against his own body. Or do you not know that your body is the temple of the Holy Spirit who is in you, whom you have from God, and you are not your own? For you were bought at a price; therefore glorify God in your body and in your spirit, which are God's.

Isaiah 40:28–31

Have you not known?

Have you not heard?

The everlasting God, the Lord,

The Creator of the ends of the earth,

Neither faints nor is weary.

His understanding is unsearchable.

He gives power to the weak,

And to those who have no might He increases strength.

Even the youths shall faint and be weary,

And the young men shall utterly fall,

But those who wait on the Lord

Shall renew their strength;

They shall mount up with wings like eagles,

They shall run and not be weary,

They shall walk and not faint.

scripture memorization

Write out the scripture(s) in the space below and recite them ten times.

_____

_____

_____

_____

something to ponder

DO OLD WOUNDS CONTINUE TO SURFACE in your mind or emotions?

_____

_____

_____

_____

WHERE CAN YOU GO TO FIND healing and restoration?

_____

_____

_____

_____

HOW CAN YOU USE YOUR NEXT race's finish line to overcome your past and move forward into God's purpose for your life?

_____

_____

_____

_____

running observations
by dean

I Don't Even Drive That Far

PEOPLE, IN GENERAL, DO NOT UNDERSTAND why we run. I wish I had a dollar for every time someone has said to me, "I hate to run." Somehow, this is an acceptable thing to say to a runner. If I started a conversation with someone who loves to play guitar by saying, "I hate the sound of a guitar," I don't think the conversation would last very long. But as runners, we don't mind the contempt for our sport. As a matter of fact, we wear it like a badge.

We take pride in our toughness, and we like it when a social contact says, "You ran 50 miles last week? I don't even drive that far." It makes no difference that we have heard that comment 50 times. What we hear is, "You're an endurance machine." And then there's this one: "When I played football, we had to run as a punishment. I swore I would never run again." What we hear is, "You're tougher than a football player."

Then there are the clichés that have the potential to become annoying. "Run, Forrest, run!" For most people, meaning non-runners, being compared to Forrest Gump would not be positive. But even this is okay, because in the back of our mind we're thinking, "That dude ran across the United States. Yeah, I can run like Forrest." And how about, "I only run if something is chasing me"? Sounds negative, right? But when you think about it, if there really is something chasing a group of people, the runners have a better chance of survival.

Finally we hear a few race-specific phrases over and over. "Pick it up" is usually reserved for a coach or someone with a vested interest in your performance. When I hear it, I think, "Why didn't I think of that?" How about, "Lookin' good"? Usually when someone tells you how good you look, you don't look so good, but we love to hear it anyway. The most used phrase in all of racing is, "You're almost there." This is a great phrase to hear, if you're almost there. Sometimes you're not really almost there, but we know that those who come out to cheer us on only have our best interest at heart. After all, there is no heckling in running. That makes the shout-outs okay, even desirable.

In our spiritual walk, we have to understand that God knows what's best for us. Like the lady two miles from the finish line yelling, "You're almost there," God always has our best interest in mind. The difference is that He actually knows what's best for us. We just have to take out the headphones to hear Him.

- *If a running phrase gets under your skin, find a way to turn it into a positive.*

- *When someone tells you how good you look while you're running, take his or her word for it, put it in high gear, and cruise to the finish line.*

- *God knows how incredible you are, and you will too, if you will let Him show you.*

sticky notes

the power of a running shirt

IT WAS MY THIRD SEASON WITH the Run For God program at Riverland Hills Baptist Church in Irmo, South Carolina, and I was about to discover that the "Couch to 5K" program was much more than running. I signed up for the first 12-week program at my wife's encouragement. I thought everything about it was strange and spent most of the 12-weeks walking the parking lot course and trying to handle the constant pain in my body, especially my knees. The second time through the program I began to jog and found myself actually enjoying the three-a-week practice sessions, especially the Sunday Bible studies.

During the practice sessions, a young lady in her early 20s named Zia would often go up to other runners and encourage them. She always had a glowing personality and radiated with God's Word. I found myself wishing I had a little of her confidence in me. For my third Run For God season, I set a personal goal of losing weight, running faster, and becoming a stronger Christian. By now I had acquired three different colors of "Run For God" shirts, and I would often wear them during the weekly practices at the church. Often my wife, son, and I would get dinner after practice, and people often commented on my shirt.

One Sunday I got dressed to run early and drove to the local grocery store to buy the weekly groceries. I got out of my car and headed toward the store entrance when a teenager ran up to me. He held up his iPhone and asked if I would pose with him for a selfie. He quickly snapped the picture and ran off. A bit startled by this event, I headed into the store and tried to remember what was on my grocery list. As I went up and down the aisles of the store, I seemed to be getting an unusual number of stares from people, so I reexamined my clothing, thinking something must be out of place.

In the last aisle, I noticed a jam of people at the other end. I waited patiently, while an elderly African-American woman, grasping her grocery buggy, stared at me from the crowd. As I was about to pass by, she politely stopped me, pointed at my bright yellow, "Run For God" shirt, and said she had prayed for me. I was stunned. She explained that she had been battling cancer for some time and had depleted her savings. Now she found herself caring for three grandchildren with little money. She said she had placed her faith in God to help and prayed for assistance before going to the grocery store. I summoned the Confident Zia within me and prayed with her before paying for her small basket of groceries.

Today I learned that the Run For God program is much more than just learning to run. It is about putting your trust in God for daily living. "Putting hay in the barn" now had a greater significance. I discovered the importance of putting both physical and spiritual hay in the barn so you are ready for God's calling.

Scott Farrand – *Irmo, SC*

get in the word

Romans 1:12

That is, that I may be encouraged together with you by the mutual faith both of you and me.

1 Peter 3:15

But sanctify the Lord God in your hearts, and always be ready to give a defense to everyone who asks you a reason for the hope that is in you, with meekness and fear.

Matthew 5:14–15

"You are the light of the world. A city that is set on a hill cannot be hidden. Nor do they light a lamp and put it under a basket, but on a lampstand, and it gives light to all who are in the house."

scripture memorization

Write out the scripture(s) in the space below and recite them ten times.

_____

_____

something to ponder

CAN PEOPLE SEE THE CHRISTIAN LIGHT coming from you?

_____

_____

_____

_____

ARE YOU PUTTING SPIRITUAL HAY IN the barn so you will be ready someday to answer God's calling?

_____

_____

_____

_____

DO YOU WEAR YOUR "RUN FOR God" shirt in public or leave it in the closet for no one to see? My challenge to you is to put on your shirt, pray to God to seek His will, and see what happens.

_____

_____

_____

running observations
by dean

I've Been Doing LSD for Years

WHEN A RUNNER BEGINS TALKING ABOUT LSD, he's not referring to the drug lysergic acid diethylamide. Long Slow Distance is the backbone of our training. It forms the base of nearly all successful training programs. I can get by without any other portion of training, but these runs are critical.

Like anything else, running long is relative. If you are running 20 miles a week, your long run may be six to eight miles. If you're running 70 miles a week, your long run may be 20–24 miles. Many studies show you don't have to run long to be successful. Perhaps it's true for some, but for me, running for at least two hours builds strength that I cannot replace with any other form of training. I have tried training without the long run with little success, but I have friends who never run for two hours that are successful marathoners.

If you are like me and need to run long to make yourself the best you can be, here are some things to keep in mind. First, you can't run long every week and expect to remain healthy. I try to follow a pattern of three weeks of long runs, often increasing mileage each of those weeks, and then a recovery week where I refrain from intense training. In other words, about every fourth week I decrease mileage by ten to twenty percent and run easy to moderately paced runs for seven days. I don't take days off unless absolutely necessary, but I do have days when I run so easy that it feels like I took the day off. After an easy week, it's back to regular training.

Pacing on the long run is not as important as it is on most other runs. A wealth of studies show how running slower than your normal pace will provide big benefits, just like the faster paced long run. However, like anything else, I believe this is individualized. I know guys who run effective marathons and they take their long runs at what I would describe as a snail's pace. I know others who don't know what the word slow means. For me, I am most effective when I run my long runs at a pace that is around average for any other moderate effort run.

Just as running long builds the foundation of a good training program, attentive Bible study is critical to our Christian walk and forms the foundation of our relationship to Him. Long runs, combined with other training methods, will help you to become the best runner you can be. It is through Bible study that we learn how to worship and how to pray. For example, when we know the trials Israel faced, it provides us an example of how to pray for our nation's leaders. Bible study, combined with prayer and worship, will help you to become what God wants you to be.

- *Long Slow Distance (LSD) is the backbone of training.*

- *The length of your long runs depends on you. Some do well without them while others need them.*

- *Don't worry about pace in the long run. As long as you're not running too fast, it is hard to run too slow.*

- *Bible study is a foundation builder to our faith. Understanding God's will is critical for us to bear spiritual fruit.*

sticky notes

running with abe

ATTACHED TO ONE OF MY RUNNING shoes is a tiny pouch. Inside the pouch is my ID, a love note from my wife, and a shiny penny dated 2011 to celebrate the year I turned 60. Engraved on that penny is the likeness of Abraham Lincoln, sixteenth president of the United States. Just above the picture of Abe are the words, "In God We Trust."

I began running at a doctor's recommendation as therapy for depression. The prescription worked. Now over twenty-five years later, I'm still running—sometimes not as far and sometimes not as fast, but I'm moving forward. For my efforts I earned a stack of medals, a pile of t-shirts, and some bragging rights. I met some great people, and most importantly, my faith grew as the miles added up.

At one of my first races, I saw a runner wearing a shirt with a picture of an eagle and the words of Isaiah 40:31, "But those who wait on the Lord shall renew their strength; they shall mount up with wings like eagles, they shall run and not be weary, they shall walk and not faint." When I ran a marathon I decided to wear a shirt with that same verse. Then I came up with an idea to make my adventure even more fun.

I started asking family and friends to sign my race shirt. With a permanent laundry marker, people happily signed their names and added their favorite Bible verses or affirmations. Here's some of what I got:

Right foot, left foot, a whole bunch of times.

With determination comes success!

"I can do all things through Christ who strengthens me" (Philippians 4:13).

"Run like you stole something."

"Winners get up, losers give up."

"Be in the light."

"I can + I will = I did!"

"See you at the finish line."

One friend drew a picture of some feet and beside it wrote, "The thrill of victory and the agony of de feet." Another friend had been a prisoner of war in Vietnam. Another had spent her life in a wheelchair. I had names of people with alcohol and drug problems, victims of abuse, and parents of delinquent teenagers. As I ran my marathon, I prayed for the folks on my shirt and the marathons in their life. At mile 22, my legs were aching, and several little voices in my head were competing for my attention. One of those voices wanted me to quit. Another said to keep going. And yet another said I was crazy to be doing this in the first place. Then I heard a voice that didn't belong to me. I looked at the man running beside me. He smiled and said, "Can you believe we're paying to do this?" We both laughed. And from there to the finish line the only voice I heard was the one telling me to keep going.

Proverbs 17:22 reminds us that "a merry heart does good, like medicine."

Remember that Lincoln penny attached to my shoe? He reminds me of this great statement, "In the end, it's not the years in your life that count. It's the life in your years." And Jesus said, "I have come that they may have life, and that they may have it more abundantly" (John 10:10).

Jerry Snider – *Lancaster, OH*

get in the word

Isaiah 40:31
But those who wait on the Lord
Shall renew their strength;
They shall mount up with wings like eagles,
They shall run and not be weary,
They shall walk and not faint.

1 Chronicles 16:10–11
Glory in His holy name;
Let the hearts of those rejoice who seek the Lord!
Seek the Lord and His strength;
Seek His face evermore!

John 10:10
The thief does not come except to steal, and to kill, and to destroy.
I have come that they may have life, and that they may have it
more abundantly.

scripture memorization

Write out the scripture(s) in the space below and recite them ten times.

_____

_____

_____

_____

_____

_____

_____

_____

_____

_____

_____

_____

_____

_____

_____

something to ponder

HOW CAN YOU MAKE YOUR RUN with God more fun?

_____

_____

_____

_____

IN WHAT WAYS HAS THE DISCIPLINE of running helped you grow as a Christian?

_____

_____

_____

_____

IF YOU HAD A CHANCE TO write something on my running shirt, what would it be?

_____

_____

_____

running observations
by dean

Flash, Pause, Flash

AN INTERVAL IS AN INTERVENING PERIOD of time or a pause. In running, it can be defined by many single words: Painful, torturous, and masochistic, to name a few. But the real definition of running intervals is when you run fast, take some time to rest (usually jogging), and then run fast again. In running, interval training is a great way to get faster. There are many permutations of interval training, each with a specific purpose. To me, this is the most effective form of speed work.

It has been said that in order to run faster, you have to run faster. It sounds silly, but it is so true. It doesn't matter if you are training for a 5K or a marathon, or if you just want to finish the race or set a personal record. Interval training will help your body adapt to the demands of running faster and easier. In addition, it provides variety in your running that motivates you to get out the door each day. Interval training is not something you do every day, but once a week will make a big difference.

I believe the three most important elements of a training program designed to make you run your fastest are the long run, tempo runs, and interval training. As long as I have these three tools in my plan, I can get the most out of my schedule.

How do you work interval training into your plan? I prepare for a racing season by running longer reps with short rest periods. As the season approaches, I gradually add more rest during the interval and increase the intensity of my runs. Getting ready for a 10K, I may begin with eight 800s with a 400 jog between and work my way down to eight 400s with a 400 jog between, focusing on running fast. For a marathon, it may be five times two miles, working towards ten times 800. There are ladders and more intricate interval workouts, which add more variety, but I think basic repeats are very effective if run properly. I'm a simple guy, so basic repeats of varying lengths work just fine for me.

Today's GPS watches make it easy to run intervals almost anywhere. Just a few years ago, you almost had to have a track to ensure you were running the right pace. Now we only need a line of sight to a satellite to enable us to run intervals. We're so spoiled.

Repetition in Bible study makes us stronger too. It never ceases to amaze me how I can read the same passage I have read many times before only to have God reveal something I've never seen. For example, after finding myself unemployed, I read Jeremiah 29:11 a little differently. I always thought this passage was telling me that God knows what my life will be. In other words, He knows all. But there is so much more there. He has plans for a great future for me. Just as interval training makes us better runners, regular Bible study, along with time to reflect on it, brings us closer to God.

- *You have to run faster to get faster.*

- *Interval training adds variety to your running and keeps you motivated.*

- *Repetition in running, weight lifting, or Bible study is a key to getting stronger.*

sticky notes

_____

_____

_____

_____

_____

_____

_____

_____

_____

_____

_____

_____

_____

_____

_____

overcoming lies

GOD STARTED A WORK IN ME by telling me to run. As an overweight, non-athletic girl who had never run, I was scared. I started training anyway. About ten months later, I had entered my second 5K. My goal was to run the entire thing. (I couldn't run the first one. I kept taking walking breaks). I was determined to run all 3.1 miles, even though I had never run more than two miles at one time.

It was a local "for fun" color run. There was no pressure to finish first. I was excited. I started a little too strong. As I approached mile one, I was feeling discouraged and losing energy. People were just flying by me. I kept praying, "God, help me do this." When I got close to mile two, I was moving so slowly that walkers began passing me. I sobbed as I ran. And that certainly doesn't help anything! My head started filling up with things like, "Just walk, no one cares," and, "It really doesn't matter, just quit," but then I heard God's booming voice, saying, "I care! I told you to run, and I will help you!"

He started giving me Scripture, reminding me that He began this work in me and He would make sure it was completed. Also I would have an amazing story of His faithfulness to tell someday. I dried my face with my shirt and pushed through. It wasn't easy. I kept whispering Jesus' name every time it became too hard to breathe; every time the pain became too much. And He helped me through.

It was a beautiful moment crossing that finish line. I spent the entire day just thanking my Lord, thanking Him that His voice booms louder than any lie Satan wants to tell me. God is bigger. He used that day to build my faith, and I've been able to share with other women who are scared to try running. I have encouraged others who are struggling. God took all of my fear and pain and turned it into something beautiful, which I share with other women who are going through the same thing I did.

I still struggle to run 3 miles. It's still hard, but one day it won't be. I am getting better with practice and discipline. He helps me every day. Remind yourself of the truth, so you can overcome the lies.

Randi Whaley – *Marlow, OK*

get in the word

Hebrews 12:11
Now no chastening seems to be joyful for the present, but painful; nevertheless, afterward it yields the peaceable fruit of righteousness to those who have been trained by it.

1 Peter 5:8
Be sober, be vigilant; because your adversary the devil walks about like a roaring lion, seeking whom he may devour.

Philippians 1:6
Being confident of this very thing, that He who has begun a good work in you will complete it until the day of Jesus Christ.

scripture memorization

Write out the scripture(s) in the space below and recite them ten times.

something to ponder

WHAT LIES are you believing that are keeping your from doing what the Lord asks?

_____

_____

_____

_____

HOW CAN you overcome those lies?

_____

_____

_____

_____

CAN YOU set down the negativity and trist God?

_____

_____

_____

_____

running observations by dean

Running Improves My Memory

I KNOW IT SOUNDS CRAZY, BUT having a basic understanding of running times and being able to recall race times improves my memory. "How?" you ask. Here's a great example. My grandmother has been gone for more than a decade, but I still remember her address. The reason I remember her address is because the number for her street address was 1532, which is equal to a five minute pace finishing time for a five-kilometer race. Without that frame of reference, I don't think I would still remember. There are a number of other things that I remember based on running times, such as PIN numbers, codes for alarms, and even phone numbers. I try to look at any number I need to remember in a way that relates to running.

Prices are easy too. I think it's because there's a decimal point that makes it feel more like a time. Of course, you have the problem of numbers above a five because times are recorded in numbers below six. So I have to be creative and think in terms of tenths or hundredths of a second. If that doesn't work, sometimes using military time works. And then there are times when the numbers just don't fit anything, and I can't remember it any better than anything else. But it doesn't make my memory worse. I just have to live with the same inadequate memory I have when trying to remember names of things.

Running also helps me to remember spacing. For example, if I want to determine the distance between two buildings, I can relate it to how long it takes for me to run that distance. If I can run to it and time myself, I can tell you how far it is. I can eyeball the distance too. I know, from running races, how far two tenths of a mile is by seeing how far the six-mile mark is from the finish line in a 10K. If you have ever run that last two tenths, you know that distance well yourself.

When I'm on vacation, running helps me to understand the lay of the land. When you're a runner, you notice landmarks that others may not acknowledge. Going for a run helps to recall where everything is located. I suppose it's because you travel by the scene much more slowly when you're running than when you're driving.

Bible verses are also easier to remember. Chapters and verses are numbers that can often look like an interval time. It comes in handy when you want to recall a verse for a conversation with someone you are trying to comfort or share your witness. We all know someone who is able to comfort us no matter what the circumstances. In many cases, they have a Scripture reference that goes with any situation. If you are one of those people who feel that Scripture memory is difficult, try thinking about running analogies or anything else that may help you remember. If you're still worried about memorization, think about this: It is not necessary to always remember word for word. With the many translations of the Bible today, just being able to recall the idea and the location are adequate for many applications. Don't put too much pressure on yourself.

- *Racing paces and workout times help me to remember some of the details in life that would otherwise be difficult to recall.*

- *Running connects you to your environment better, enabling you to remember the lay of the land.*

• *Memorizing Bible verses may be difficult for you, but relating them to other things can help us to remember. In addition, the realization that we don't have to remember every word every time takes some pressure off.*

sticky notes

_____

_____

_____

_____

_____

_____

_____

_____

_____

pride and priorities: a lesson after the finish line

I ARRIVED HOME AFTER THE RUN for God: Run at the Mill both exhausted and riding the high from the entire experience of the morning. However, I was not too exhausted to keep from carefully laying out my shirt, medal, bib, and other items collected during the course of the previous 13 weeks. I was a proud person. I had finished, even though there were times when I seriously doubted that I would. I stood admiring the items I had laid out in such a neat manner on the table. Gosh! I was proud. I even thought about getting a shadow box and putting it all inside and mounting it on my wall. Yes, I thought, that would be really nice. My family and friends and even strangers could see it when they came to my home.

Funny, isn't it, how we swell up with pride at even the smallest of milestones. I could already see myself leading my age group in the Boston, New York, and Atlanta marathons. I admired these trophies so much that I just had to take a picture, not just one, but several. I just had to capture this moment and preserve it forever. Then it hit me, much as other thoughts had during the course of my training. These items are only trophies. They are not the reason I joined the class. These items are not the items of significance that I really brought home.

These items will shortly fade, but there are lessons learned: the quiet time in running that only you and the Father share; the struggles of my training and how that related to a closer relationship with God; learning that in my moments of greatest weakness, His strength was always available to help me carry on; and a thousand more lessons are the real trophies of this journey. Unlike the items that lay so neatly out on the table, no lens of any camera can capture the meaning of the trophies of this experience. It is only through the eyes of others that the significance of these lessons can be seen, and I sincerely hope that when others look at me, they see those truths. If not, my journey has been in vain and the important finish line is not in sight.

Dan Strange – *Dalton, GA*

get in the word

Matthew 6:19–21

Do not lay up for yourselves treasures on earth, where moth and rust destroy and where thieves break in and steal; but lay up for yourselves treasures in heaven, where neither moth nor rust destroys and where thieves do not break in and steal. For where your treasure is, there your heart will be also.

Matthew 6:33

But seek first the kingdom of God and His righteousness, and all these things shall be added to you.

Philippians 4:19

And my God shall supply all your need according to His riches in glory by Christ Jesus.

scripture memorization

Write out the scripture(s) in the space below and recite them ten times.

something to ponder

WHAT TREASURES ARE WE WILLING TO share with the world after we cross the finish line?

_____

_____

_____

_____

WHAT ARE THE ITEMS THAT WE treasure during a RFG class?

_____

_____

_____

_____

DOES GOD'S GOODNESS AND FAITHFULNESS MOTIVATE us to put Him first in our lives?

_____

_____

_____

_____

running observations by dean

Feeding the Furnace

ONE OF MY FAVORITE RUNNING BOOKS is John L. Parker's Once a Runner. The detailed accounts of the main character, Quentin Cassidy, make you feel his struggles and triumphs. If you're a recreational runner who's wondered what it's like to be in the mind of an elite runner, read this book and you will get a sense of just that. At one point in the book, Quentin is thinking deeply about what it means to be who he is and is refuting those who worried about anything other than focusing on running and training. He thinks about those who worry about what they eat and muses, "If the furnace is hot enough, anything will burn, even Big Macs."

People often ask me about my diet and its role in performance. Those conversations lead everywhere from Krystal hamburgers to vegetarianism. I have internalized those conversations, shook them around my head along with all the nutritional advice I read about in books, magazines, and online, and I think the ultimate truth is that reasonable nutrition is unique to the individual. I think Quentin Cassidy was correct, in a way.

I remember reading a piece on chocolate milk being a good recovery drink and then reading the comments at the bottom of the article. Some of them remarked that it was irresponsible for the writer to tell people that chocolate milk was good for them, completely missing the point. It was not that it was good for us, but that under the proper circumstances, it could have a positive effect. I doubt that drinking two glasses of chocolate milk per week would land anyone in the local emergency room, unless he has a dairy allergy, of course. When we look at food as either compliant or non-compliant, I think we take the fun out of eating. And if we are paying attention, we will realize that we feel better when we eat better, so we should make good eating habits. We just don't need to be so hard on ourselves that we make eating a job complete with rules and regulations.

When I tell people what I eat and where I eat, they're surprised. Most conversations about nutrition begin with someone trying to find out what kind of magic food I eat to make me run fast. The truth is I eat a lot of fast food, but when I do, I am selective. For example, if I order a Whopper, I leave the mayonnaise off and eat it with a side salad with a light dressing, not the Ranch dressing. When you look at the nutritional info, you find that this is better, in many cases, than a loaded salad at another restaurant. Also, I eat healthy snacks. (I love broccoli.) The bottom line is that you just need to be sensible, and here's where Quentin was right: The more you run, the less you have to worry about it.

If Jesus had spent His time focusing on rules and regulations, He wouldn't have defended the adulterer as she was about to be stoned. The Pharisees, who focused on rules, were the problem, because they failed to see the big picture of loving each other as we love ourselves. Jesus reminded them of their own sin and their equal need for the saving grace of the Father. They wanted to set themselves up as judges, both of the women and Jesus, but God is the One who judges. We don't need to help Him out.

It is great to focus on eating well, but it doesn't need to be our main focus. We run by our Lord's grace, and in His grace we have great freedom.

• *Eating well is essential to healthy running.*

• *Don't be too hard on yourself when you aren't perfect in your eating habits.*

• *Instead of focusing on select dietary rules, focus on meaningful changes to your eating habits.*

• *In our efforts to love others, remember the freedom found in God's grace.*

sticky notes

_____

_____

_____

_____

_____

_____

_____

_____

the finish line

WHEN I SAY I WAS NOT a runner before this journey began, it is not an understatement. I had never run a mile in my entire life. I was blessed with an eye condition that kept me from playing most sports in junior high and high school. I believed the lie that I was not an athlete and settled for what I thought was the best I could do. When a Bible study called "Run for God" was brought to my attention, I was intrigued. I really felt that God was calling me to teach this study. But that was craziness, since I had never run a mile. There was no way I could run three miles, and besides that, I was the last person in the world to teach other people about fitness. That is where a life-changing journey with my Savior began.

I went through the study in its entirety to make sure I could do it before I asked anyone else to join me. After several 5K races and a half marathon, God has taught me so many lessons through my running journey. Here are a few:

I learned that I am more than I once thought I was. Romans 8:37 says that we are "more than conquerors" through Christ who gives us strength. I had believed the lies about my fitness and my faith. My God is able to deliver me and desires a real relationship with me. When I rely on His strength, He will make me more than I seem for His glory.

I can worship anywhere. Worship is about focusing on Jesus and giving Him the glory. I can do that while cooking dinner, teaching school, driving down the road, or running. I have worshipped Jesus many times on the road alone, just Him and me (*1 Corinthians 10:31 and Deuteronomy 6:6–9*).

If I don't constantly fill my mind with truth, I will inevitably believe lies. I must remain in His Word daily. Regardless of how many miles I have run, I still doubt myself. I doubt my ability to complete the run. I can fight these lies because I have done it many times. When Satan tries to fill my mind with lies about my worth, I can fight him with truth. I know that my identity lies in the fact that I am a child of the King. I have experienced His faithfulness and can rest assured He never changes (*John 8:32*).

I must run my race. My race plaque bears this phrase. I have learned that God created me intentionally. He has created me with purpose. My purpose is to glorify Him in everything I do. God has given me talents and spheres of influence, intending me to run my race to the best of my ability. He doesn't want me wasting energy on bitterness, envy, condemnation, or apathy. He needs me to train for and run my race to bring glory to Him. My weakness demonstrates His strength.

I can never teach this class without knowing that blessings come from stepping outside my comfort zone.

The most important lesson I have learned is the importance of a finish line. It is the most important part of a race, the reason for our joy as runners. The finish line represents victory. No runner has ever been upset to see the finish line. We welcome it. We strain to see it. We run harder when we can catch a vision of it. It motivates, inspires, and demands our best. Whether running a 5K or marathon, the finish line represents the completion of a goal. We fix our eyes on it, knowing that it is the reason for all our training, all our sweat, tears, pain, and sacrifice. As you cross that finish line, it all seems worth it. With people cheering you on, the finish line brings forth indescribable pride and emotion.

So how does this apply to our faith? In 2 Timothy 4:7–8, Paul says it best. "I have fought the good fight, I have finished the race, I have kept the faith. Finally, there is laid up for me the crown of righteousness, which the Lord, the righteous Judge, will give to me on that Day, and not to me only but also to all who have loved His appearing." Paul knew that the finish line was Jesus! He knew that nothing mattered apart from an eternity with his Savior.

Eternity with our Savior is clearly our finish line. This should motivate and inspire us. It should demand our best. It should influence our every decision. It requires training in the Word. It requires time and sacrifice. When we are able to stand face to face with the God who loved us enough to send His one and only Son to die for us it will be worth all the training, sweat, tears, pain, and sacrifice. It will all be worth it.

Focus on the finish line. Nothing else matters.

Jennifer Gonzalez – *Silverton, TX*

get in the word

1 Corinthians 10:31
Therefore, whether you eat or drink, or whatever you do, do all to the glory of God.

Deuteronomy 6:6–9
And these words which I command you today shall be in your heart. You shall teach them diligently to your children, and shall talk

of them when you sit in your house, when you walk by the way, when you lie down, and when you rise up. You shall bind them as a sign on your hand, and they shall be as frontlets between your eyes. You shall write them on the doorposts of your house and on your gates.

2 Timothy 4:7
I have fought the good fight, I have finished the race, I have kept the faith.

scripture memorization

Write out the scripture(s) in the space below and recite them ten times.

_____

_____

_____

_____

_____

_____

_____

_____

something to ponder

THERE IS ALWAYS A STARTING LINE. In our faith, our starting line is when God calls us into a relationship with Him. You cannot cross the finish line if you never start the race. Describe your starting line. Where does your testimony begin?

_____

_____

_____

_____

OUR RACE OF FAITH REQUIRES TRAINING. Pray about the following areas of spiritual discipline. How does your training need to improve so that you can run your race in the manner God intended?

_____

_____

_____

_____

Daily time in the Word

Prayer

Fellowship

Evangelism

Service

DESCRIBE THE WAY YOU FELT THE last time you crossed a finish line. If you were to die tonight and cross the ultimate finish line of this life into eternity, would you be able to say like Paul, "I have fought the good fight, I have finished the race, I have kept the faith"?

_____

_____

_____

_____

running observations by dean

Doing Your Best

"**IN THE DUST OF DEFEAT AS** well as the laurels of victory there is a glory to be found if one has done his best." — _Eric Liddell_

Eric Liddell of Chariots of Fire fame was right. There is nothing quite like the feeling of giving everything you have and knowing that you didn't have anything left at the finish. You have run the race according to the plan, and when your body screamed at you to slow down, you overcame the urge and kept your plan together.

You felt like collapsing as you crossed the line because you couldn't have taken another step. You found it difficult to remain standing as the race volunteers kept you moving through the chute. You did it. You laid it all on the line and couldn't have done any more. You did your best.

Two definitions for best: 1) of the highest quality, excellence, or standing; 2) most advantageous, suitable, or desirable. Sounds about right. We just have to remember that doing our best doesn't rely on other people. The goals are not set by other people. Your best is yours and only yours. No one really knows when you have done your best, except you. It doesn't mean you are the fastest or better than someone else. It may not even be a personal record. It isn't part of the awards ceremony and won't get printed in the paper. It's better than that. It means you left it all on the course or the track, and you have nothing to regret. You won't say, "I wish I would have pushed a little harder at mile three," because you know you couldn't have done any more.

Part of doing your best is knowing what to do and how to do it. I don't think you can do your best without having a plan and executing the plan. If I go into a race with no plan, it doesn't matter how hard I run, I could have done better. It may not even matter if the race unfolded in a way that I executed the plan perfectly. The plan is part of doing your best.

God expects our best. After all, He gave his best for us. We fall short every day, but we should still plan to do our best for Him and give it all we have. I would say that I am only actually able to reach deep enough to do my absolute best three or four times a year. After many other races, I have those questions about what I could have done differently. It's the same with God. I have intentions of giving Him my best, but my human nature will get in the way and cause me to fall short.

It feels so good when I am able to give Him my best and I know that He is smiling at what I have accomplished in His name. The amazing reality is Jesus already finished our race for us and offers all of His strength to us for our running by faith. While we strive to give our best to Him, He has already accepted our lives and declared them the best because of Jesus' blood.

- *Giving it your best means not being able to look back and think about what you could have done to perform better.*

- *Part of doing your best involves good planning and execution of the plan.*

- *God expects our best, which we can offer through Christ, who lived a perfect life in order to make us perfect in faith.*

sticky notes

our 5K turned into a marathon!

WHEN RUN FOR GOD WAS MENTIONED at our church, I was intrigued and decided to sign up. I had never run before or run a race, but I wanted to show my Grandkids that you are never too old to try something new. Soon after I signed up, my husband, Doug, followed me, and we were both in training for our church's first **Run for God** race!

We had about 40 people from all backgrounds, including those who had once run and individuals who had begun a new journey. The leaders in our group helped us at every step, from the physical aches and pains to the triumph of actually running for 3 minutes straight. We enjoyed the Bible studies, comparing our race to our walk with Christ, each person needing training and discipline, each person receiving the eternal prize. Everyone mattered in our group—everyone. Ecclesiastes 4:9–10 came to mind: "Two are better than one, because they have a good reward for their labor. For if they fall, one will lift up his companion. But woe to him who is alone when he falls, for he has no one to help him up." I later learned the true meaning of this verse.

At first, the training wasn't too bad, and as it got harder, my husband and I stuck it out. About a month before the race, we decided to take a two-week trip south to see family and friends. We did our best to keep up the training, but it was difficult. Once we returned, refreshed and ready to go again, I received a phone call from my mother's assisted living home, telling me she was sick and needed to go to the emergency room. The doctors did all they could for her, but the Lord called her home. My heart grieved yet rejoiced that her pain was gone. The funeral was three days before our 5K race, and we were faced with the question of what to do. We decided to join our group in this race.

On the morning of April 28th, 2012, we gathered to recite Hebrews 12:1–3 and pray before our 5K race. My husband and I were at the starting line together, but that was the last time I saw him until near the finish line. I found a walking partner, and we were on our way. I enjoyed it all, listening to my music and even singing along the way. As I approached our final destination, I noticed a couple of leaders running toward me as an ambulance whizzed by me. I asked why the ambulance and they replied, "It's for Doug." They each grabbed one of my arms, and off we ran.

About the time I arrived, they were preparing him for the ambulance. He had a cardiac arrest. When I joined him in the ambulance, I was in total shock, but I remember our pastor, who was also running in the race, giving me a card with Hebrews 12:1–3. God had prepared the way for Doug. He had each step covered: the friend that recognized that something was wrong, the two nurses running right behind him who were able to start CPR immediately, the police officer who had a defibrillator in his car, and our whole group who instantly went to the throne room of God in prayer. God did not leave us or forsake us.

As soon as we arrived at the hospital, they were able to do a heart cath. and found a 95% blockage in his main artery, which the doctors referred to as the "widow maker." Thank God they were able to put a stint in and his heart was not damaged. Two of our Run for God class leaders came to the ICU and presented us with our race medals and right away, Doug wore his.

A few days later Doug returned home from the hospital. We decided to go back to the finish line several weeks later and actually walk across it, take pictures and cheer for each other. Silly, but a great feeling! Shortly after that day, Doug went back to the hospital with pneumonia and fluid on the outside of his lung. The doctors were concerned he could lose a lung. We saw improvement after many tense weeks, and he was home once again.

Then our race began to turn into a marathon. We were home for about a week before Doug began feeling abdominal pains. Once again we were back in the ER where he was diagnosed with C-Diff and spent our 41st anniversary there. Even though we did not understand the Lord's plan, He was still there by our side, never leaving us. After many prayers, words of encouragement and support, God took us through the finish line, healed and praising Him for His grace and mercy. The doctors have since looked at his heart and stint and have given him a clean bill of health. God's timing and steadfastness in the lives of His children are immeasurable. "Being confident of this, that He who began good work in you will carry it on to completion until the day of Christ Jesus" (Philippians 1:6).

In this season, we definitely learned to trust God's plan for each of us. Though we don't understand it, we will follow Him. Run for God has made an impact on our lives forever. God knew we needed to be in that race that morning and provided everything we needed for our journey. My husband's life depended on God's faithfulness that day. We are forever thankful for God's promise in Deuteronomy 31:6. "Be strong and of good courage, do not fear nor be afraid of them; for the Lord your God, He is the One who goes with you. He will not leave you nor forsake you."

Linda Vile – *Sterling Heights, MI*

get in the word

Hebrews 12:1–3

Therefore we also, since we are surrounded by so great a cloud of witnesses, let us lay aside every weight, and the sin which so easily ensnares us, and let us run with endurance the race that is set before us, looking unto Jesus, the author and finisher of our faith, who for the joy that was set before Him endured the cross, despising the shame, and has sat down at the right hand of the throne of God. For consider Him who endured such hostility from sinners against Himself, lest you become weary and discouraged in your souls.

Ecclesiastes 4:9–10

Two are better than one,
Because they have a good reward for their labor.
For if they fall, one will lift up his companion.
But woe to him who is alone when he falls,
For he has no one to help him up.

Deuteronomy 31:6

Be strong and of good courage, do not fear nor be afraid of them; for the Lord your God, He is the One who goes with you. He will not leave you nor forsake you.

scripture memorization

Write out the scripture(s) in the space below and recite them ten times.

_____

_____

_____

_____

_____

_____

_____

_____

_____

_____

_____

_____

_____

something to ponder

HOW CAN WE BE OBEDIENT TO what God is calling us to do even when the future is not clear?

_____

_____

_____

_____

IT IS EASY TO TRUST GOD when our path is clear and our road is easy. How can we trust Him when we are facing insurmountable challenges?

_____

_____

_____

_____

GOD USED MANY PEOPLE FOR HIS purpose in our story. How are you being used for God's purpose in someone else's story?

_____

_____

running observations
by dean

If You're Not Happy, Make a Change

I REMEMBER READING A QUOTE ONE time, "If you're not happy, make a change." It goes hand in hand with another quote, "You can't change the results by doing the same thing you did the first time." We all know these things, right? So why is it so hard to change what we're doing? Is it habit? Is it because we don't want to leave our comfort zone? Is it because it's too hard? The truth is that they are all excuses that we use to keep ourselves from moving forward. How do we break the cycle, or more to the point, how do we motivate ourselves to the point where we want to do what it takes to change more than we want to be comfortable in doing what we have always done?

First, you have to prepare to make changes. It sounds simple, but many people skip this step because they feel it's obvious what needs to be changed. But there is more to it than that. We have to sit down and think through the change and define what our goal is and how we plan to negotiate the course on the way. Do you want to run faster? How fast? Do you want to run farther? How far? Do you want to lose weight? How much?

If your plan is good enough, execution is all it takes. But be careful with the plan and think about these things:

Give yourself time for the changes to occur. You will need to have patience along the way and understand that these changes cannot happen with two weeks of hard work. It's going to take longer.

Understand that you will need persistence to follow through. Those old habits are going to try to come back. Be prepared for that before the time comes. It's easier to say no when you have already decided against it. If you fall back to an old habit once, don't panic. Get back to work and be stronger next time.

Realize that it will take perseverance to overcome obstacles. What are you going to do when you have a scheduling conflict? What happens when you are sore and want to take the day off? Again, answer these questions before they come up. Convince yourself that you are willing to do whatever it takes to reach your goals.

Once you have the plan and begin to execute it, make changes to your lifestyle to support your plan. For example, I am never without my running clothes. If things go crazy and I need to fit in a run at a crazy time, I do it. In conjunction with that, I have learned to live with the fact that I will have to run, take a sink bath, throw on some deodorant, and go back to work, church, or wherever I have to go next. Being prepared is a lifestyle change. Another lifestyle change would be to make sure you always have the right food available so you are not tempted to eat something you will regret later. There are many other things to do to make it easy on yourself.

Finally, never forget the results you are going to achieve. Keep reminders around to motivate you to keep going. Share with others what you are doing and they will support you and you will feel obligated to follow through with what you have committed to. Be creative with photos, mantras, and quotes, whatever it takes. Prepare to have a big celebration when you get there. Sometimes that is motivation enough.

When our lives are not what we want them to be, it is easy to give up and fall into an unfulfilling routine. The Bible says nothing is impossible with God's strength. Being born again means having Him for your strength. If you are not born again, you can have this amazing gift that God tells us is awaiting all who believe. If you are born again, remember that the Lord doesn't want you to live unfulfilled. All you have to do is lean on Him for the strength. Go ahead, He's plenty strong enough.

- *In order to change, begin by planning where you want to go and designing a plan to get there. Make sure you plan for the impending negatives that will try to throw you off-track.*

- *Plan lifestyle changes around your goals to make reaching them easier. It will take extra effort, but it will be worth it.*

- *Understand that God wants us to live fulfilled lives that, not only satisfy our needs, but also glorify Him.*

sticky notes

_____

_____

_____

_____

workouts

RUN FOR GOD – BEGINNER 5K TRAINING PLAN

WEEK	MON	TUES	WED	THURS	FRI	SAT	SUN
1	WARM UP-5MIN WALK Alternate 60sec Jog /90sec Walk for 20min Then 5min Walk	Off	WARM UP-5MIN WALK Alternate 60sec Jog /90sec Walk for 20min Then 5min Walk	Off	WARM UP-5MIN WALK Alternate 60sec Jog /90sec Walk for 20min Then 5min Walk	Off	Off
2	WARM UP-5MIN WALK Alternate 90sec Jog / 2min Walk for 20min Then 5min Walk	Off	WARM UP-5MIN WALK Alternate 90sec Jog / 2min Walk for 20min Then 5min Walk	Off	WARM UP-5MIN WALK Alternate 90sec Jog / 2min Walk for 20min Then 5min Walk	Off	Off
3	WARM UP-5MIN WALK Alternate 90sec Jog / 2min Walk for 20min Then 5min Walk	Off	WARM UP-5MIN WALK Alternate 90sec Jog / 2min Walk for 20min Then 5min Walk	Off	WARM UP-5MIN WALK Alternate 90sec Jog / 2min Walk for 20min Then 5min Walk	Off	Off
4	WARM UP-5MIN WALK Repeat 2 times (90sec Jog /90sec Walk, 3min Jog/3min Walk) Then 5min Walk	Off	WARM UP-5MIN WALK Repeat 2 times (90sec Jog /90sec Walk, 3min Jog/3min Walk) Then 5min Walk	Off	WARM UP-5MIN WALK Repeat 2 times (90sec Jog /90sec Walk, 3min Jog/3min Walk) Then 5min Walk	Off	Off
5	WARM UP-5MIN WALK Repeat 2 times (Jog 3min, Walk 90sec, Jog 5min, Walk 2min) Then 5min Walk	Off	WARM UP-5MIN WALK Repeat 2 times (Jog 3min, Walk 90sec, Jog 5min, Walk 2min) Then 5min Walk	Off	WARM UP-5MIN WALK Repeat 2 times (Jog 3min, Walk 90sec, Jog 5min, Walk 2min) Then 5min Walk	Off	Off
6	WARM UP-5MIN WALK Repeat 2 times (Jog 3min, Walk 90sec, Jog 5min, Walk 2min)Then 5min Walk	Off	WARM UP-5MIN WALK Repeat 2 times (Jog 3min, Walk 90sec, Jog 5min, Walk 2min) Then 5min Walk	Off	WARM UP-5MIN WALK Repeat 2 times (Jog 3min, Walk 90sec, Jog 5min, Walk 2min) Then 5min Walk	Off	Off
7	WARM UP-5MIN WALK Jog 5min, Walk 3min, Jog 5min, Walk 3min, Jog 5min Then 5min Walk	Off	WARM UP-5MIN WALK Jog 5min, Walk 3min, Jog 5min, Walk 3min, Jog 5min Then 5min Walk	Off	WARM UP-5MIN WALK Jog 5min, Walk 3min, Jog 5min, Walk 3min, Jog 5min Then 5min Walk	Off	Off
8	WARM UP-5MIN WALK Jog 20min 5min Walk	Off	WARM UP-5MIN WALK Jog 20min 5min Walk	Off	WARM UP-5MIN WALK Jog 20min 5min Walk	Off	Off
9	WARM UP-5MIN WALK Jog 23min 5min Walk	Off	WARM UP-5MIN WALK Jog 23min 5min Walk	Off	WARM UP-5MIN WALK Jog 23min 5min Walk	Off	Off
10	WARM UP-5MIN WALK Jog 27min 5min Walk	Off	WARM UP-5MIN WALK Jog 27min 5min Walk	Off	WARM UP-5MIN WALK Jog 27min 5min Walk	Off	Off
11	WARM UP-5MIN WALK Jog 30min 5min Walk	Off	WARM UP-5MIN WALK Jog 30min 5min Walk	Off	WARM UP-5MIN WALK Jog 30min 5min Walk	Off	Off
12	WARM UP-5MIN WALK Jog 3 Miles 5min Walk	Off	WARM UP-5MIN WALK Jog 2 Miles 5min Walk	Off	20min Walk	Race	Off

RUN FOR GOD – BEGINNER 10K TRAINING PLAN

WEEK	MON	TUES	WED	THURS	FRI	SAT	SUN
1	Off	1.5M Tempo	2M ESR	2M FGR	Off	3M LSD	Off
2	Off	1.5M Tempo	2M ESR	2M FGR	Off	3.5M LSD	Off
3	Off	2M Tempo	2M ESR	2M FGR	Off	4M LSD	Off
4 Recovery	Off	2M ESR	2M ESR	2M FGR	Off	3M LSD	Off
5	Off	2M Tempo	3M ESR	3M FGR	Off	4M LSD	Off
6	Off	800m wu/cd 4x400m w/ 400 recovery	3M ESR	3M FGR	Off	4.5M LSD	Off
7	Off	2.5M Tempo	4M ESR	3M FGR	Off	5M LSD	Off
8 Recovery	Off	2M ESR	3M ESR	3M FGR	Off	4M LSD	Off
9	Off	3M Tempo	4M ESR	4M FGR	Off	5.5M LSD	Off
10	Off	800m wu/cd 4x800m w/ 400 recovery	5M ESR	4M FGR	Off	6M LSD	Off
11	Off	3M Tempo	4M ESR	4M FGR	Off	5M LSD	Off
12	Off	3M Tempo	3M ESR	3M FGR	Off	Race	Off

TEMPO Run at or just above race pace.
ESR Easy slow run. Take it easy.
FGR Feel good run. Just run based on how you feel.
LSD Long slow distance. Keep your pace steady and breathing in check.
RECOVERY Backing the intensity down these weeks. Get rested!
INTERVALS 800m wu/cd 4x800m w/ 400 recovery
800-meter warm up and cool down. Run ½ mile (800m) fast 4 times with a slow ¼ mile (400m) in between each fast effort.

RUN FOR GOD – HALF MARATHON TRAINING PLAN

WEEK	MON	TUES	WED	THURS	FRI	SAT	SUN
1	Off	4M Tempo	2M ESR	3M FGR	Off	5M LSD	Off
2	Off	4M Tempo	2M ESR	3M FGR	Off	6M LSD	Off
3	Off	4.5M Tempo	2M ESR	3M FGR	Off	7M LSD	Off
4 Recovery	Off	5M ESR	3M ESR	3M FGR	Off	5M LSD	Off
5	Off	6M Tempo	3M ESR	3M FGR	Off	8M LSD	Off
6	Off	800m wu/cd 4x800m w/ 400 recovery	4M ESR	5M FGR	Off	9M LSD	Off
7	Off	6M Tempo	3M ESR	5M FGR	Off	10M LSD	Off
8 Recovery	Off	7M ESR	3M ESR	4M FGR	Off	8M LSD	Off
9	Off	7M Tempo	4M ESR	6M FGR	Off	11M LSD	Off
10	Off	800m wu/cd 4x1600m w/ 400 recovery	5M ESR	7M FGR	Off	12M LSD	Off
11	Off	8M Tempo	5M ESR	8M FGR	Off	8M LSD	Off
12	Off	7M Tempo	5M ESR	8M FGR	Off	Race	Off

TEMPO Run at or just above race pace.

ESR Easy slow run. Take it easy.

FGR Feel good run. Just run based on how you feel.

LSD Long slow distance. Keep your pace steady and breathing in check.

RECOVERY Backing the intensity down these weeks. Get rested!

INTERVALS 800m wu/cd 4x800m w/ 400 recovery

800-meter warm up and cool down. Run ½ mile (800m) fast 4 times with a slow

¼ mile (400m) in between each fast effort.

RUN FOR GOD – MARATHON TRAINING PLAN

WEEK	MON	TUES	WED	THURS	FRI	SAT	SUN
1	Off	6M Tempo	4M ESR	3M FGR	Off	10M LSD	Off
2	Off	6M Tempo	4M ESR	3M FGR	Off	12M LSD	Off
3	Off	7M Tempo	4M ESR	3M FGR	Off	14M LSD	Off
4 Recovery	Off	6M ESR	6M ESR	3M FGR	Off	10M LSD	Off
5	Off	8M Tempo	6M ESR	3M FGR	Off	16M LSD	Off
6	Off	800m wu/cd 4x1600m w/ 400 recovery	8M ESR	5M FGR	Off	18M LSD	Off
7	Off	9M Tempo	6M ESR	5M FGR	Off	20M LSD	Off
8 Recovery	Off	7M ESR	6M ESR	4M FGR	Off	16M LSD	Off
9	Off	10M Tempo	8M ESR	6M FGR	Off	22M LSD	Off
10	Off	800m wu/cd 6x1600m w/ 400 recovery	10M ESR	7M FGR	Off	24M LSD	Off
11	Off	12M Tempo	10M ESR	8M FGR	Off	16M LSD	Off
12	Off	8M Tempo	8M ESR	8M FGR	Off	Race	Off

TEMPO Run at or just above race pace.
ESR Easy slow run. Take it easy.
FGR Feel good run. Just run based on how you feel.
LSD Long slow distance. Keep your pace steady and breathing in check.
RECOVERY Backing the intensity down these weeks. Get rested!
INTERVALS 800m wu/cd 4x1600m 4x1600m w/ 400 recovery
800-meter warm up and cool down.
Run 1 mile (1600m) fast 4 times with a slow ¼ mile (400m) in between each fast effort.

sticky notes

_____

_____

_____

_____

_____

_____

_____

_____

_____

_____

_____

_____

_____

_____

_____

STEPS TO PEACE WITH GOD

Where are you?

PEOPLE (sinful)

CHRIST

GOD (holy)

1
GOD'S PURPOSE:
Peace and Life

God loves you and wants you to experience peace and life— abundant and eternal

 "We have peace with God through our Lord Jesus Christ."
—Romans 5:1 (NKJV)

"For God so loved the world that He gave His only begotten Son, that whoever believes in Him should not perish but have everlasting life." —John 3:16 (NKJV)

"I have come that they may have life, and that they may have it more abundantly." —John 10:10 (NKJV)

Since God planned for us to have peace and abundant life right now, are most people having this experience?

Our choice results in seperation from God

PEOPLE (sinful)

GOD (holy)

4
OUR RESPONSE:
Receive Christ

We must trust Jesus Christ as Lord and Savior and receive Him by personal invitation...

 "Behold, I stand at the door and knock. If anyone hears My voice and opens the door, I will come in to him and dine with him and he with me." —Revelation 3:20 (NKJV)

"But as many as received Him, to them He gave the right to become children of God, to those who believe in His name." —John 1:12 (NKJV)

"If you confess with your mouth the Lord Jesus and believe in your heart that God has raised Him from the dead, you will be saved." —Romans 10:9 (NKJV)

RUN FOR GOD.®

2
OUR PROBLEM:
Seperation from God

God created us in His own image to have an abundant life. He did not make us as robots to automatically love and obey Him, but gave us a will and a freedom of choice.

We chose to disobey God and go our own wilful way. We still make this choice today: This results in separation from God.

 "I have come that they may have life, and that they may have it more abundantly." —John 10:10 (NIV)

"For the wages of sin is death, but the gift of God is eternal life in Christ Jesus our Lord." —Romans 6:23 (NIV)

OUR ATTEMPTS TO REACH GOD

Through the ages, individuals have tried in many ways to bridge this gap between themselves and God...without success.

"There is a way that seems right to a man, but in the end it leads to death." —Proverbs 14:12 (NIV)

"But your iniquities have separated you from your God; and your sins have hidden His face from you, so that He will not hear." —Isaiah 59:2 (NKJV)

3
GOD'S REMEDY:
The Cross

Jesus Christ is the only answer to this problem. He died on the cross and rose from the grave, paying the penalty for our sin and bridging the gap between God and people

 "For there is one God and one mediator between God and men, the man Christ Jesus." —1 Timothy 2:5 (NIV)

"For Christ also suffered once for sins, the just for the unjust, that He might bring us to God." —1 Peter 3:18 (NKJV)

"But God demonstrates his own love for us in this: While we were still sinners, Christ died for us." —Romans 5:8 (NIV)

PEOPLE (sinful)

CHRIST

GOD (holy)

NO BRIDGE REACHES GOD... EXCEPT ONE

PEOPLE (sinful)

GOD (holy)

**Good Works?
Religion?
Philosophy?
Morality?**